GLOBAL TRENDS
in
STATE FORMATION

An Enquiry into the Origin, Survival and
Demise of States

Godknows Boladei Igali, Ph.D.

Order this book online at www.trafford.com
or email orders@trafford.com

Most Trafford titles are also available at major online book retailers.

Printed in the United States of America.

ISBN: 978-1-4907-2081-4 (sc)
ISBN: 978-1-4907-2080-7 (hc)
ISBN: 978-1-4907-2082-1 (e)

Library of Congress Control Number: 2013957007

Trafford rev. 05/21/2014

 www.trafford.com

North America & international
toll-free: 1 888 232 4444 (USA & Canada)
fax: 812 355 4082

Praises for Global Trends in State Formation

"Ambassador (Dr.) Godknows Igali's new book is a thoughtful and expansive work of great erudition in which he surveys broadly trends in nation-state formation across the world with emphasis on the Western experience. It is a good example of the work of an African scholar who mastered western philosophy, theology and social sciences thoroughly and applies it with ease in his study. This is a must read for all those who wish to be educated and re-educated in the complexities of nation-state formation in ancient and modern times. Enter this book and you will emerge the richer for it. I fully recommend this book to all seekers of knowledge."

Justice Chukwudifu Oputa, LLD,
Retired Justice,
Supreme Court of Nigeria

"This is a rare intellectual compendium of profound philosophical insight aimed at establishing critical global imperatives as validated by emerging historical and diplomatic trends."

Dr. Jide Ojo,
Former Head,
Department of Philosophy,
Lagos State University,
Nigeria.

"When the Council of the Historical Society of Nigeria decided, recently, to induct Dr. Igali as a Fellow, it was in appreciation of his erudition as a scholar whose contribution to knowledge remains towering. His interdisciplinary approach to historical enquiry and narrative is of a peculiar genre. To understand, more profoundly contemporary global political evolution, this work is a must read."

Professor Olayemi Akinwumi, AvHF, FHSN,
National President,
Historical Society of Nigeria (the premier Academic Society)

Dedication

To Newton Aaron Igali (1926 – 2012) and
Fanny Igali both of whom started it all.

Acknowledgements

T he raising of a child, as often said, involves a whole village. Therefore, showing special appreciation and acknowledging the contributions of people to a work of this nature is truly extending it to the entire chain of men and women whom I passed through.

Of special note are my academic mentors during my years at the University of Port Harcourt and University of Lagos, both in Nigeria and Central University of Venezuela, Caracas. They are too numerous to mention individually as could be seen from the way their works are acknowledged in several places in this book.

A number of my aides and associates also contributed immensely to the work, especially in typing and proofreading. In particular, I wish to mention my Personal Assistants, Tajudeen Abdul-Azeez and Benjamin Nenge and my friends, Dr. Jide Ojo and Prof. Ehiedu Iweriebor.

Beyond that point, what all seem to agree with, is our continued expression of gratitude to God for strength, knowledge and wisdom.

Contents

Part III: Anecdotes for the Legacy of Crisis

Preface

The search for knowledge is one of God's greatest gifts to mankind. In all respects, creative imbuement with an appetite for knowledge is the vortex of the how, why, and when of events of human activities. With a background on the study of history and law, the hunger for answers for such an enquiry will not be out of place. The combination of the tools of a historian with political philosophy and internationalist was used to search for the truth on some of the issues pertaining to the most difficult topics of our time: why the state exists, what leads to their birth, what keeps them strong and fledgling? The other issue is regrettably about what leads to their ultimate demise—this does not apply in all cases.

The linear nature of the peripheral metropole route in the search for knowledge by African scholars is known and predictable. African scholars, researchers, and students were therefore more likely to move rather incestuously from second-generation or even third-generation high-performing universities like University of Port Harcourt, Nigeria, where the likes of Robin Horton, Joe Alagoa, Claude Ake, Nnoli Okwudiba, and others have held sway in discourses of sociopolitical, political economy, and political history, to first-generation universities such as University of Ibadan, Obafemi Awolowo University, Ile-Ife, University of Legon, University of Nairobi, and others. At best, the more privileged moved to the centres of Europe, Paris, London, or to the new-found centres of scholarship like the United States.

In my case, my movement, which appeared as a special act of faith, like many of our forbearers, was across the Atlantic to the shores of Latin America. The significance of my presence particularly at the University of Venezuela, Caracas, which has been one of the centres of knowledge, founded in 1721, was that I was offered unique opportunities for discourse on the issue of political community. After nearly two hundred years of attainment of independence from imperial rule, most of South America was basking in the euphoria of celebration of fifty years of uninterrupted democracy. But then suddenly a threat lurked ominously in the form of an erstwhile colleague and *accomajen,* El Commandate, Hugo Chavez, who attempted twice unsuccessfully to overthrow the government of President Carlos Andres Perez. The rest of this is history as Chavez eventually attained political success and fame. The faculty of political science had assembled some of the best brains in the Spanish world, Latin America, the Caribbean, and the United States. The likes of Castro Leiva, Oxford research professor, Garcia Pelayo, University of Madrid, and Carlos Romero were the masters of the day of this discourse as to what went on year after year. It was my exposure to this discourse that eventually whetted my appetite to open up this topic for a more global enquiry.

This work is primarily a philosophical enquiry and partially a historical survey into the origins of the various political formations such as nations, nation-states, states, societies, and so on from the perspective of Western political and religious thought. It was partly inspired by the state of the world in the late twentieth century as it moved towards the twenty-first century. On the one hand, by the end of the twentieth century, it would seem that Western societies had attained such enviable political and social stability, technological advancement, and material affluence that their scholars and intelligentsia spoke of their world as being 'post-modern'. At the same time, much of this world was experiencing serious ethno-national claims of cultural autonomy, self-government, and the upsurge of a variety of social, gender, and identity political groups. This range of serious social and political disruptions raised questions about the assumed stability of these societies.

In other parts of the world which did not claim to be post-modern, political, economic, and social challenges including incomplete political integration, inter-ethnic conflicts, climate change, environmental degradation, human trafficking, economic decline, austerity, rising poverty, persistent underdevelopment, religious extremism, and terrorism were also on the upsurge and threatening the stability of various nations, especially the new nation-states. In short, it seemed as the last century was drawing to an end, much of the world was thrown into a situation in which all established assumptions about the political and social stability of societies could not be taken for granted in both old and new nations and nation-states.

It was the complex and challenging context that partly stimulated the interest of the author to undertake a philosophical-historical enquiry into the various perspectives of Western political philosophy on the emergence, types, growth, and consolidation of state systems in the context of Western thoughts.

The historical survey outlined aspects of the processes of the emergence and formation of nation-states including the processes of political integration and state consolidation, especially in the Western experience with primary focus on the countries of Switzerland, Canada, and Israel. A discussion of nation-state formation in India examines how these processes have been undertaken in other societies outside the Western world.

As was noted, this era has seen the emergence of two powerful contradictory trends in the global political order. The first is the thrust towards external integration which is better known as globalisation. It is a product of the combination of the emergence of a powerful and truly global communications system that has bound all parts of the world socially, economically, commercially, and practically into an integrated social circuit. Its flip side is the ascent of global financial and economic transactions that seems to be creating a new world order that appears to diminish the place of nation-states.

On the other hand, there is a trend towards weakening and, in some cases, the disintegration of nation-states that previously seemed so stable and solid. The most dramatic expression of state disintegration in the twentieth century was the collapse of the Soviet Union and its reconstitution into fifteen new nation-states. For a state that seemed so powerful and cohesive, its collapse was a shocking development that seemed to forebode a new era of the disintegration of nation-states.

These thrusts towards globalisation and state disintegration and movement towards new forms of state and societal organisation underscore the significance of this work as an enquiry into the processes of the birth, growth, and demise of state systems. Such knowledge should help prepare people and societies to address the challenges that threaten societal stability. If this work helps to understand and appreciate the philosophical underpinnings and historical processes of state formation from the perspective of Western political philosophy, it would have served its purpose.

Godknows Boladei Igali
Abuja, March 2014

Introduction

Over time, man developed elaborate political structures to manage his social environment. One thing that increasingly happens when one attempts to define the ethical foundation of society is the rather debilitating realisation that extant knowledge and scholarship seem to raise more questions than answers. The only solace lies in that the starting point of wisdom is the asking of questions. This is the reason the attempts at explaining society by contractualists, theologians, and even traditionalists have left a lot of grey areas and raised new questions, despite the fact that they have also gone a long way to present very pertinent explanations that offer wide panoramic perspectives to understand the course of political and social change. The imperfection of each approach does not only provoke the need for more study but also calls attention to the fact that no line of thought standing on its own would avail all the desired answers.

A more worthwhile process of investigation as to why human society exists may therefore lie in a concerted multidimensional venture. But in all, what seems obvious is that man has always tried to model the state after the dual nature of himself as a social being and in the image of the angels—a kind of celestial utopianism. As an intelligent social being, man recognises the contradictions embedded in the need to preserve individual identity and yet ensure the perpetuity of his social existence. His limitations in achieving this are obvious, but then he does not rest on his oars and daily strives for an ideal. The actual truth is that his craving for heavenly patterns may not be far short of his creative attribute, which according to the Bible came about when God said, 'Let us create man in our image and after our likeness.' For conservative Christian and Islamic scholars, the state is simply a gift of God where underpinning divine laws exist.

Although radical political thought prefers to underplay the relevance of mystical unity between man's political actions and his creative personality, it is interesting to note that in its etymological composition even Marxist-Leninist thoughts elevate the state to replace the intangible God!

In such cases, the state has been ascribed with certain anthropomorphic attributes and made to exercise the most direct influence over man and his environment.

Of all the various ways of ordering civil society, in the course of time, the duo, federalism and republicanism, have emerged in modern society as some of mankind's most celebrated political ideals. This is easy to appreciate due to the fact that the republic seemed to have offered a more participatory platform in the process of governance for everybody while federalism further afforded another opportunity to share in the national course, but at the level of the various constituent units.

That means republicanism in its classical usage gave the individual an opportunity for civic activism while federalism gave each of the ethnic or sectarian groups, regions, or states the fair chance of having a say in how things function for the common benefit. These have special attraction for multi-ethnic societies such as those in Africa.

The political history of Europe like other parts of the world has been marked by a monumental process of dynamism—the rise and fall of kingdoms and states. For a long time, however, diplomacy remained the preoccupation of princes and the Roman Catholic Church. In fact, almost all of Europe formed different parts of the Holy Roman Empire, as the various princes drew political power and authority from the Church. In the midst of European political horse trading and diplomacy, a series of wars took place, including the Thirty Years' War which ended in the

Treaty of Westphalia of 1648. The significance of that truce lay not in the relative peace that it brought to Europe but in the gradual attenuation of papal power which followed. In allowing a measure of religious freedom and liberty of personal devotion, there was a great shift in power from the Church to individual rulers. The treaty also went as far as to delineate land territories between several countries and gave them sovereign rights to enter into treaties among themselves.

With the fervour for nationalism that ensued, by 1800 most European states had evolved into clear 'nation-states'. Since most of the new states were ruled by people of their own nationality, the quest for national independence was quite seldom. So while Europe's political history did not start with the rise of the Holy Roman Empire, it is pertinent to note that the latter's gradual collapse in a major way orchestrated the process of transformation of old empires into sovereign states. This is not to feign ignorance of other factors, mostly internal, which were at play in these countries. For instance, there was the rise of 'Enlightenment'—the rebirth of knowledge and social enquiry, the emergence of a new social group, and the acquisition of power by secular state officials. The balance of power which had always oscillated among Church, feudal nobility, and monarchy began to include a new social class drawn from those entrepreneurially inclined. In several cases, such new elites were not of aristocratic extraction, as would have been the case in the past. Change, which began hypothetically from a renascent Italy of Machiavelli, quickly spread like a wild wind into England, France, the Americas, and, as the Scriptures say, to the 'uttermost parts of the world'.

In other parts of the world, states began to emerge as acts of national consciousness. However, in most cases, the eventual fine-tuning of the political culture into what it seems today involved decades and in some cases even centuries of deep internal crisis, wars, adjustments, and re-adjustments of diverse forms. Often the processes ended up in bringing about a stronger centre even if aspects of authority had to be shared with the units. In England, jurists such as Hume and Lord Acton advocated for a strong central government that would unite it not just to Ireland, Wales, and Scotland but also the many possessions abroad into a single Commonwealth, with the monarchy as an illustrative head.

Furthermore, many countries eventually had to settle for completely republican systems, even though a common feature which many other countries went for was a mixture of tradition and modernity—a constitutional monarchy. These include among many others: Japan, Thailand, Jordan, Lesotho, Morocco, Britain, the Lower Countries, and Scandinavia. The truth is that besides the nominal and ceremonial existence of the monarchy, the rest of the political system was democratic if not republican. If we were to follow the classical definition of republicanism as explained by Ancient Rome, such a prudent blend of the three traditional forms of government could qualify to be so categorised.

Even more fascinating is the fact that a lot of republics where the monarchy was never established or faded away, such as Germany, Israel, and India, have still replicated this yearning for a kind of father figure at the national level by having a *de jure* President and a *de facto* Prime Minister who carries out the actual functions of governance. The Canadian, Australian, and several Caribbean 'dependency' examples are even more overwhelming in that despite the non-monarchical political mix, they have opted to keep themselves under the banner of the House of Windsor as some form of national symbol.

It would, therefore, appear that the actual significance of political liberalism does not lie in the appellation which people give to its system but the elements that actually constitute it. But in all, the modern state has emerged under the banner of political liberalism, political pluralism, and political unity from constituent units. But how have they achieved these?

Before proceeding to consider how these political doctrines have impacted the modern states, it is paramount to see how the present state system came about and how these ideas helped states in other places to grow and remain integrated or disintegrated. Indeed, why do states exist?

Similarly, man always aspires for liberty to compete, take initiatives in all spheres of human endeavour, and be so rewarded. Sadly, the Soviet system denied all of these, so it started to breed internal seeds of discord and eventually imploded bringing about great changes in world affairs.

It is stated in Africa that when a big tree falls, several things happens. It not only renders the nesting birds homeless but also affects the entire surrounding environment. In this case, it paved the way not only for the plethora of dependent states to realise their nationalistic goals around it but also brought about fundamental changes in international politics.

In the rest of Europe and around the world, the states emerged out of normal cause of fusion and diffusion of peoples and nations, no less out of the broad interplay between faith and secular thought. But till date, none have claimed to attain the ideal, although it remains fraught with the struggle for survival.

The cases of Asia, especially China and India as well as the Middle East—with such case studies as Israel and the Arab world, are *sui generis*. The same can be said of, say, Latin America and Africa, which for some deliberate reason we have towed rather perfunctorily in this work. The complexities of the African experience are dealt with in another work.

Part I (chapters one to three) of this work deals with conceptual issues and various trends of philosophical reasoning on the state. Part II (chapters four to eleven) attempts to take us through some case studies, giving an insight into few states. Part III (chapters twelve to sixteen) of the work is rather reflective, prescriptive, and audaciously suggestive of the routes, and if taken, it would allow peace and stability in our countries.

These thoughts, reflections, and ideals in no way derogate the universality of knowledge about states. It raises on the overall a flag to summon more intellectual investment and conscription into the arena of research and prioritisation on such matter.

Part I

Philosophy of State Formation

Chapter One

States and Nations: Few Conceptual Issues

hether in international politics or national affairs, the 'state' has for some time emerged as the most dominant influence on human life. Since the signing of the Treaty of Westphalia in 1648, when the modern political system as we know it today began to take its shape, the state has grown to become a kind of 'god on the earth', controlling man's life from the time he is born, gets married, dies to the time he is buried. But like many other concepts in the social sciences, there is much divergence among thinkers over the exact meaning of what a state is and in what ways this is different from other concepts, such as 'nation' and 'society'. It is not the intention in this book to rehash in any detailed form the merits of various angles of this controversy, but it will be enough for the purpose of better understanding to draw a line on some general properties of these related concepts.

The writers of the first edition of the *Encyclopaedia Britannica* in 1763 simply defined the state as 'extent of country under the same government'. The emphasis to them is the possession of a marked or definitive territorial mass and the existence of an appropriate political authority that exercises control. But this definition seems much unsheathed from philosophical attack, especially in view of the complex forms of political establishments that have since emerged in the modern world.

There have been colonial states, protected and trusted territories, and the like. In some of them, there has effectively been more than one form of political administration at the same time. For instance, with the handover of Hong Kong by Britain to China, on July 1, 1997, it has been operated by a complex governmental system called 'one country, two systems'. Under a special agreement, the territory has maintained its Western system and has a pseudo-independent administration, but technically it is regarded as part of China. There were also occupied territories such as West and East Germany. Yet they were regarded as full-fledged states entering into treaties with other states. In retrospect, at the end of World War II, the allied forces occupied Germany. This meant that the entirety of Germany was divided into different parts among the United States, Britain, France, and former Soviet Union. This had a lot of legal implications and continued until 1995.

It is as a result of these more complex political structures that Hugh Seton-Watson adds to the earlier definition in a modernised detail: 'A legal and political organization, with the power to require obedience and loyalty from its citizens.'[1] Here the issues are the legality of the political system, the loyalty of the ruled towards it, and its ability to ensure effective control.

But again, we may run into problems if this definition is left on its own. For instance, who determines the legality of political sovereignty? Let us take the example of Taiwan or Israel. Seen from the narrow points of view of China and the less moderate Arab countries, respectively, these two countries are not recognised.

From the point of view of international law, one of the best accepted definitions of the state has been derived. This is in Article 1 of the Montevideo Convention of 1933 on the Rights and Duties of States, which require the following:

> *The state as a person of international law should possess the following qualification: a permanent population; a*

---

[1] Hugh Seton-Watson, *Nations and States: An Inquiry Into the Origins of Nations and Politics of Nationalism.* London: Methuen, 1977.

defined territory; a government and a capacity to enter into relations with other states.[2]

The requirements appear self-explanatory, but a brief explanation would still be necessary. Although international law is replete with persuasive views suggestive of the fact that the existence of a clearly defined territory is a *sine qua non* for a state, it has been accepted as crystallised law that lack of precise boundaries does not fetter the existence of the state. It was on this account that Israel could be admitted into the United Nations in 1949.

The idea of the eminent authors of the Montevideo Convention was not to take the permanence of the human numbers as static, which by natural processes is impossible, but to avoid the confusion that could come if nomadic and pastoral states could be allowed. Furthermore, the requirement of a capacity to enter into conventions is a relative one, depending on with whom the convention is being made. Even China, which has not recognised the sovereign existence of Taiwan, is known to have concluded a number of commercial accords with that island under wording and phraseology that are mutually accepted. Similarly, despite the near universal acceptability of the Montevideo Convention definition, opinions also exist that the absence of a government on the territory, as was

---

[2] Starke, *General Principles of International Law.* New York: Butterworth, 1967.

the case with Norway and other countries during the Nazi occupation between 1939 and 1945, did not call into question their existence at the time.

The Nation

These thoughts on the state contrast in the main with the concept of 'nation'. The 'nation' is more of a community of people whose members are bonded in one by a sense of communal solidarity, cultural traditions, and feeling of a common identity. Indeed, the difference between the phraseologies 'state' and 'nation' would seem to lie in the fact that the former is more of a legal and geographically determined entity, often evolving historically, but several times artificially created by a decree of men, as was the case with Africa and Asia. But with the concept of 'nation', there is a more ethereal and emotional appeal among its members as it is a factor of nature—i.e. a people. We can take as example the gypsies of Europe or Fulanis (Fulbe) in West Africa who recognise their distinct cultural and national identity but are found in several states due to their historically itinerant nature.

British Diplomat and Former Prime Minister, Arthur Balfour, Addressing the First Meeting of the Council of the League of Nations in Geneva, November 15, 1920

This realisation should not, however, becloud us from the fact that in reality both phenomena are coterminous, just like two broad and overlapping circles with a large common area. That is why apart from a few examples such as Somalia, in the case of Africa, most states comprise several nationalities.

Similarly, in many instances, especially on the African continent, whole nations are dispersed across many countries. The Hausa nation in West Africa is found in not less than six countries across the sub-region, the German or French nations are spread out in almost all the countries of Central Europe, and the gypsy nation found in nearly all parts of the world.

It is for this reason that President Woodrow Wilson and others, who authored the world order which emerged in the post-World War I era, called it the 'League of Nations', and the generation that succeeded after World War II led by President Theodore Roosevelt also adopted the name 'United Nations' to categorise what they created. The two international organisations, which emerged on both occasions and succeeded each other, were a collection of states as represented by their governments. But interestingly, in view of the obvious account of the overlying relationship between these two conceptions, in both instances, the designers of the systems believed that the various people who made up the different member states would one day be fused into a globalised world. This easily lends the modern state system its name of 'nation-state', and in strict contemporary usage, the words are employed interchangeably.

Woodrow Wilson, Former American President

On Ethnicity

Still on this, United States Senator Daniel Moynihan, a leading expert on ethnicity, further extends the definition of nation by contrasting it with the word 'ethnicism'. According to him, ethnicism is primarily concerned with the basic identification of 'one with his own kind'—a kind of 'we' against 'them' or 'them' against 'us'. The word 'ethnic' itself has its origin in the Greek usage *ethnos* or *ethnic* meaning 'people, tribe or nation'.

So to Moynihan, the nation and the attendant display of nationalism are the highest forms of ethnic group, denoting a subjective set of mind, as regards ancestry, but also, almost having an objective claim to some form of territorial autonomy ranging from regional assembly to full-blown independence. He asserts that nations seldom go to war against each other, but ethnic groups fight all the time.

The related and interchangeable word—'tribe'—pertains to the same distinct subgroup identification of common ancestry and shared values, albeit as we saw earlier producing a more pejorative connotation. Nigerian expert on ethnicism, Professor Okwudiba Nnoli believes that the two terms are the same, only that the colonial governments that ruled Africa simply preferred to use the less appealing one as it related to the various African people. Simply put, the words 'ethnic' and 'tribe' whether in a national framework or in global sociological application simply mean 'a people' as different from other peoples.[3]

One common defining manifestation which ethnic groups, tribes, or nations display is nationalism. Perhaps it may be useful to mention, even if tersely, that nationalism, as a political creed, has existed in society from the beginning of social and political organisation.[4] Its prominence in recent history arises out of the emergence of the nation-state system, as it legitimises and claims authority and supreme loyalty of a people to a leadership of the same ethnic complexion. The *Oxford Advanced Learners Dictionary* simply terms it as 'favouring political independence in a country that is controlled or part of another'. Nationalism has been crucial in the formation of the nation-state and is in many instances increasingly becoming the main challenge to its eternity.

The Society

For the purpose of a better clarification, it would be important to make a contrast between state and another common usage—'society', which has been defined by some writers as a collection of:

---

[3]   Ruth Lapidoth, *Autonomy: Flexible Solutions to Ethnic Conflicts.* Washington: United States Institute for Peace, 1996, p. 20.

[4]   *Encyclopaedia of Social Sciences*, vols. xi-xii, 2000, pp. 63-67.

persons united for their mutual assistance, security and interest . . . The social principle in man is such an expansive *nature that it cannot be confined within the circuit of a family, of friends, of neighbourhood: it spreads into wider systems, and draws men into larger communities and commonwealth; since it is in these only, that the more sublime powers of our nature attain the highest improvement and perfection*[5]

A society is more of any informal gathering of men in a social organisation. Most philosophers also agree that the human society arose out of the need to establish a political and social order, which over time evolved into states and nations.[6] The ultimate process of growth of bare human societies into states and nations has a far antiquity—going down to the very dawn of human pre-history.

Having known that men live together in such overlying subdivisions, the critical question could be raised further as to why the early men did not contend themselves with living in hoards and loose groups, but instead erected the rather cumbersome and meddlesome societies and states or encouraged the evolution of ethnic and national groups.

The answer to this question is a pointed one as every intelligent being would have a distinct point of view on this,

---

[5]   *Encyclopaedia Britannica*, 1768, p. 614.

[6]   Charles Van Doren, *A History of Knowledge*. New York: Ballantine Books, 1991.

including on how the political edifice could be managed. This forms the very nerve centre of political enquiry, knowing that a normal rational being would want to perpetuate its self-survival. Aristotle tried to draw a common line by answering that 'the state originated in the bare need of a good life'.[7]

Beyond this authoritative assertion, there is no single universally acceptable postulation as to why the state exists. In attempting to answer this question, a plethora of points of view exist. For now, let us consider the thoughts of two leading philosophers from the main branches of thought which have emerged on this—social contract and theology. In each case, we have tried to trace the background and sociopolitical setting in which the philosophers and thinkers operated, in order to have a better appreciation of the ideas illustrated.

---

[7]   Aristotle, *The Republic* (reprinted), University of Chicago, 1991.

Chapter Two

Why Do States Exist: (Raison d'être)

The most held notion in political studies is that the state exists as a social contract between it and the people therein. Another variant posits that the state is a contrast between individuals in one sense and between the individual and the state on the other. Let us examine further with the ideas of some of the philosophers along this line of thought.

Social Contract Philosophy

In trying to explain the 'reason for the state', the most popular voices come from the social contract philosophers. As many as they are, so are the variants and abstractions of their ideas. Let us examine Kantianism side by side with other social contract philosophers.

Kantianism

Prussian Enlightenment thinker and metaphysician, Immanuel Kant (1724-1804) has emerged over time to be one of the most profound influences on modern philosophy. In general, his methodical contribution to the discussion on knowledge, morality, and aesthetics has advanced to the discipline much of its empiricism and idealism.

His approach to the study of philosophy was to deviate from what was considered as disconcertion of many of his intellectual ancestors, such as French philosopher Rene Descartes (1596-1650). Many of the latter generation defined the subject as an understanding of the nature of the world, from the point of view of reason. At this time of study, which Kant considered rather imperious, they first traversed the contingencies and bounds of reason before actually getting into the search for knowledge. Kant called this technique as 'transcendental'. His own approach entailed a more penetrating insight, intended at elevating philosophy to the scientific level of, for example, mathematics or physics.

Renes Descartes, French Philosopher

Kant's attitude was completely antipathetic to the dogmatism, speculative naturalism, and irrationalism that pervaded the discipline of his day. His concern was for empirical knowledge and such things as the relationship between experience and the human mind and the circumstances or 'structure', to use his term that relates man's knowledge to his moral action.[8] Kant considered experience to have little bearing on this structure, which in reality existed theoretically, and rather traced the existence of *a ding an sich*—the description of the sum of human reasoning that could be brought to bear in attempting to understand the world in which we exist, i.e. to understand or attempt to understand 'things in themselves'.

Though in many writings, not elevated to the same level as this, for example, the masters of social contract philosophy such as Englishman Thomas Hobbes (1588-1679), John Locke (1632-1704), or Swiss thinker Jean-Jacques Rousseau (1712-1778) in discussions on 'The Social Contract' and its relevance to the existence of the state, Kant made some of the most impressive and systematically lucid postulations on this branch of political philosophy.[9] It is worth noting that these Enlightenment philosophers all operated during the same period, oscillating between Paris and London.

---

[8] J. L. Mackie, *Ethics.* London: Puffin Books, 1977, p. 27.

[9] Robert Wolff, *Understanding Rawls.* Princeton: Princeton University Press, 1990, p. 112.

Thomas Hobbes, English Philosopher and Political Theorist

Jean-Jacques Rousseau, French Political Philosopher

Without getting immersed in all the details, social contract philosophy puts forward the hypothetical existence of a kind of social covenant between the society and individuals and between the ruled and their rulers, particularising the limits placed on each and the rights and obligations so generated. It is assumed that some time in historical antiquity, man roamed about in an anarchic and tiny system such as now known with the animal world. Then by a deliberate exercise of natural reason, he formed a society and appointed a government over it.[10]

It could easily be argued that among the Greek Sophists and other strands of philosophical ancestry such lines of thought could be instilled. However, what seems to have drawn attention to the latter-day social contract premise was the insistence of a rational consent at the level of the individual. It is unnecessary here to go into the wide differences that exist on every minute issue among social contract philosophers, whether old or new, nor in the eventual results that they intended and actually produced in different European states where they emerged or were eventually imbibed. What is important to note as Professor Scheltens points out is that in different ways, all the exponents of this school of thought agree:

> *Considered the liberal state (which social contract produced) the ideal that unite all human beings with each other in liberty and equality, and even fraternity. They deemed it obvious that this liberal freedom state would evoke in all subjects an attachment for their country, because they would really recognize it now as 'their' country, the country in which they would feel fully at home because it would be governed by their common will.*[11]

---

[10] D. F. Scheltens, 'The Social Contract Philosophers', in *Journal of the History of Ideas*, 1977, p. 321.

[11] Scheltens, *ibid.*, p. 318.

Of course, with such idealistic simplification of the actual course of social relations and the trans-historical altruism associated with such pattern of thought, it offers at first instance the best explanation for the principle of law.

Kant's contributions to social contract philosophy or what he calls the 'Political Commonwealth', 'Ethical Commonwealth', or 'Highest Good' are stretched across his different works. Like his other peers in this camp, he begins his thesis with the insistence about the fictitious existence of a pre-juridical realm at the dawn of time. Considering the absence of a juridical norm at that stage, it is presumed that natural law is the only order that existed. The intuition one receives from reading Kant is that during that phase there existed only a handful of people with equal claims on liberty and equality. In his *Science of Rights*, Kant writes that all in the commonwealth have this right to liberty, insofar as the latter (being human) has a nature that is capable of having rights.

Liberty is assumed to be intrinsic to man even though the supposed equality co-exists with some absurd inequalities in socioeconomic terms. In this respect, he points out:

> *The general equality of the people in a state, as its subjects, can however, very well coexist with the greatest inequality of the masses and the extent of which they own goods, whether the latter consist of physical or mental superiority over others, or of gifts of fortune, or of*

any kinds of rights over others. Thus one person's welfare will depend to a great extent on the will of another; or one must obey while the other commands; or one will hire himself out, while the other pays him; and so on. But before the law, as subject they were all equals.[12]

Stages of the Contract

Kant alludes to the unavailability of these built-in disproportions such as imbued upon by nature; for example, physical prowess, mental acumen, gender, age, and economic asymmetries which veer in favour of some over time. Despite this apparent socioeconomic imbalance that could have existed among man's autochthon precursors, he maintains the existence of juridical equality of all under natural law.

Natural law itself, which is moral and positive in essence, exists irrespective of the origin and end of juridical provinces. So natural law creates liberty and equality without necessarily affecting the socioeconomic status. The reality of such socioeconomic differences does help endorse the possibility of human mobility on the social ladder.

It would be important to comment that, either due to a deliberate design for the convenience of his hypothesis or inadvertently, Kant conveniently forgot the fact that such a system could place very far-reaching strictures on vertical

---

[12]   Scheltens, *ibid.*, p. 320.

mobility, and in the thoughts of those of anarchist tradition, such as Robert Nozick, he failed to see people's abilities and talents as resources for each other.[13]

Another truth that arises from this position is that the mere existence of the least form of inequality *ab initio* creates the basis for the 'appalling amount of injustice' in the state of latter days. It means that natural law is not as equitable as it would be portrayed in the textbooks and justifies the inequality and exploitation in society.

Now let us go to the next stage of social union. The social contract philosophers generally believe that having seen the need for some form of coming together, members of the group then agreed on a set juridical system that would best meet their aspirations. Again, the impression one gets that could be distilled here is that an informal 'constituent assembly' was at some time in the past convened, maybe by a charismatic leader, even though Kant makes things a bit clearer by showing that the contract is actually a 'mere idea of reason'. It only lays down a norm which lawmakers have to conform to.

As already pointed out, natural law by itself cannot bring about a juridical order, yet the first duty it imposes on all is to abandon the juridical state and move towards a union. After all, as the English philosopher Thomas Hobbes (1588-1649) puts it, the 'first and fundamental duty of law

---

[13] Robert Nozick, *Anarchy, State, and Utopia*. New Jersey: Basic Books, 1977, p. 228.

of nature is to seek peace and follow it'.[14] Again by way of critique, by limiting suffrage to only citizens having full legal right or capacity, Kant had already adverted to the subsisting dominance of society by only the rich, so the basis of all having an equal say becomes doubtful.

At the third stage, men enter into a kind of universal agreement, binding one to another and all into one. In the process, a fictional 'united will of all' is formed and the citizens become 'limbs of a common being'. Kant sees the eventual social setup, or more formally called the 'commonwealth' or 'state', as a simple juridical community and a *Zweck an sich*—an end in itself. In so doing and by asserting that the civic association should not be based on law but on freedom of the subjects, Kant slightly deviates from the points of emphasis of, say, the English enlightenment thinker and father of classical liberalism, John Locke (1632-1704), and Hobbes, but comes closer to the French philosophical maestro, Jean-Jacques Rousseau (1712-1778), in his thought.[15] We shall see some of these in detail in later chapters, but unlike the former two, both Kant and Rousseau insist that the legislative power of the state can only reside in the 'common will of the people'. What this means is that power relations in the commonwealth must be in such a manner that it does not promote the distribution of injustice.

---

[14] Thomas Hobbes, *Leviathan*, part 1, chapter 14 (reprinted), University of Chicago, 1991.

[15] See Norman Daniels, *Reading Rawls*. Stanford: Stanford University Press, 1989.

John Locke, English Philosopher

With regards to the dispensation of social justice, Kant proposes that when one decides for himself there is no possibility of injustice; however, inequity is apt where the subject is another person. So the best juridical foundation would be to ensure that only the common will of all as expressed in the social pact prevails. This is a kind of aggregate collection of the minds of all the people.

In a general sense, Kantian thoughts amidst others in the social contract camp have considerably contributed to political evolution of the modern nation-state. By the time the founding fathers of American democracy began to put together their thoughts, it was not surprising that both— the first paragraph of the 1775 *Declaration of Independence* and the rest of the ideas of Alexander Hamilton (1755-1804) and James Madison (1751-1836)—were loaded with social contract philosophy.[16]

The indirect impulse of social contract to the development of an abstract ethical doctrine of utilitarianism helped considerably in the evolution of normative decorum in the liberal society. Later, English political economist and bureaucrat John Stuart Mill (1806-1873) argued that utilitarianism coincides with natural sentiments that originate from humans' social nature. Therefore if society were to embrace utilitarianism as an ethic, people would naturally internalise these standards as morally binding. He also argued that happiness is the sole basis of morality and that people never desire anything but happiness. Mill thought to support this claim by showing that all the other objects of people's desire are either means to happiness or included in the definition of happiness. To him, the sentiment of justice is actually based on utility and that rights exist only because they are necessary for human happiness.17

---

[16] *American State Paper and the Federalist* (reprinted), University of Chicago, 1991.

[17] Brian Phillips, Jeremy Zorn & Julie Blattberg, SparkNotes Study Guide, New York: SparkNotes Publishing, 2002.

However, in an in-depth analysis, Kantian thought offers a good guide and explanation to society and political existence. As Hobbes himself alluded, the historical authenticity of the process outlined is actually doubtful. With regards to some of the objections, principally the juridical norm or general which will eventually be set in place would require the personal interpretation and bias of individuals in political authority. So for the purpose of pursuit of selfish political intentions, a falsity over claims of pursuit of supposed communitarian ideals has been advanced. Such perversions of the social contract philosophy have led to the most absurd consequences, especially in the twentieth and twenty-first century political history.

The Hegelian Addition

It is on account of this that fellow German philosopher and ideologist Hans Hegel (1770-1831) submits that the state 'is the divine idea as it exists on the earth'. He asserts further that 'the march of God in the world that is what the state is.'[18] So man always seems to be trying to order his political environment in the image of an unknown ideal, which in a strict social sense as already alluded to is a farce.

---

[18]   Hans Hegel, *The Philosophy of History* (reprinted), University of Chicago Press, 1991. Also see Manuel Garcia-Pelayo, *Idea de La Politica*. Caracas: Colecion Cuademos, 1967.

From the above detailed statement emerges two broad points of conclusion: One gives the signal that men's political associations came about as a result of a natural instinctive urge to live together. Though he is in no way comparable to other social animals, such as termites and bees, he shares an inborn gregarious attribute with them. Therefore, the disciples of this school of thought, including most theologians, see social defiance as an aberration from man's natural make-up.

On the contrary, there exists the other point of view which holds that man is a thoughtful and conscious animal and his actions are often self-willed and voluntary. His existence in a civic form is a conscious decision, based on either shared values according to Aristotle or on the reasoning of Thomas Hobbes dictated by nature for the purpose of self-preservation and maximisation of peaceful attainment of his needs. These two thinkers are, however, quick to distinguish man from the bees, insisting that human political associations are founded on the basis of shared values while the communes of such social animals grow out of completely insentient and involuntary actions.

On this point, Hegel has again tried to qualify that the state so formed, even if self-willed, is not based on a social contract, in the manner of, say, a marriage or a business deal, i.e. a kind of 'capricious' will of the individual, but on the contrary, the individual cannot separate himself from it as it is his rational end. From the initiation of his earthly permanence, man is born into a state, and thereafter he cannot enter or leave it without consent. The truism of this is seen clearly when it is considered that man needs his state to issue him travelling document in order to move.

What Ends Do States Stand For?

Socrates, Classical Greek Philosopher

The next set of conclusions takes us back to the fundamental question that remains to be asked: What ends do these states and their governments serve to protect? In one of his writings, Socrates argued that the object of the state is 'not the disproportionate happiness of any one class, but the greatest happiness of the whole'.[19] Similarly, Aristotle held that the state was supreme and existed for 'the sake of the good life', but unlike Socrates, he concedes that some would out of necessity enjoy that good life more than others.

On his part, Kant explains that a 'state is a union of men under judicial law . . . in which there is no distributive justice.'[20] So the end of the state in this case is its own welfare—*salus republicae*. To this extent, Kantian thought seems to place a locus on the welfare of the generality as a means towards the well-being of the individual. Locke disagrees with this position since to him the state is a social contract freely arrived at, so its ultimate goal should always be *salus populi*—the good of the citizens. Still on this, others like Adam Smith maintain that the state 'in reality is instituted for the defence of the rich against the poor, or those who have some property against those who have none at all'. These ideas of Smith aptly captured the thoughts of Rousseau, but also provided ingredients of thought for later-day Marxist philosophy.

It is for this reason that twentieth-century socialism was based on the premise of the inevitability of the dissolution of inequalities within society by strengthening the authority of the state and, by extrapolation, constituting the ruling class to something of a leviathan or monster. But as history

---

[19]   Socrates, *The Republic* (reprinted), University of Chicago, 1991.

[20]   Immanuel Kant, *Postulate on Public Rights* (reprinted), University of Chicago, 1991.

showed us, what it succeeded in doing was in the manner portrayed by George Orwell: 'making some pigs more equal than others'.[21] So although the aim of the state is unselfish, according to Hegel it becomes perverted towards the 'attainment of selfish ends' obviously of a particular class. He, however, warned that if not all is well then, if their subjective aims are not satisfied, if they do not find that the state as such is the means to their satisfaction, then the footing of the state is insecure.

Unfortunately, the Communist leaders of the Soviet Union did not seem to have heeded this counsel and a system that had taken them seventy years to construct and appeared impregnable shattered just *mit ein augenblick*! The critical question still remains—how ought states to be organised?

Both totalitarianism and communism are the most xenophobic political ideologies which seem to have paraded their extremist standpoints in recent history on the defence of the common will. This has helped to reinforce the contention of the anarchist school that in its search for a community the modern state lacks the ability to transform itself into a true 'human community'.[22]

---

[21] In that classic novel *Animal Farm,* George Orwell tried to provide what the then nascent communist regimes in Russia would turn out to be. True to his prophesy, communism turned out to be exactly what the novel presented.

[22] Aldo Tassi, *Journal of the History of Ideas,* 1976, p. 274.

Rather, what it has done, given in the words of Nobel Laureate and economic theorist, James Buchanan (1919-2013), is to form a government that:

> takes on independent life of its own, when Leviathan lives and breathes, a whole set of additional control issues come into being.

He calls this 'ordered anarchy' and concludes that 'neither the state nor the savage is noble, and this reality must be squarely faced'.[23]

Hence in times past, not just contemporary anarchists like Robert Wolff but others like American libertarian and political philosopher Robert Nozick (1938-2002) have joined in the argument that man's metaphysical freedom is incompatible with political authority as presently constituted. Things would have been different if an actual transformation in the thought pattern took place in the minds of all individuals as Wolff suggests:

> The entry into civil society by means of the social contract works a moral transformation of the original contractors. Not merely the substance but the form, of men's moral reasoning is changed by the contract. Prior to agreement, each individual has what Rousseau calls

---

[23] James Buchanan, *The Limits of Liberty: Between Anarchy and Leviathan*. Chicago: University of Chicago Press, 1975.

a 'private will'. But upon entering the compact, each individual acquires the opportunity for the first to have or exercise a general will. The transformation is moral, not psychological.[24]

Robert Nozick, American Political Philosopher

Unfortunately, this has been seen to be only good in a purely hypothetical sense. This is why critics of this school contend that the failure of the liberal state to usher in the promised ideals of social order is not a historical accident. On the contrary, it arises from the ingrained recidivism of the social contract philosophy, Kant not being an exception.

These critics like Nozick ask the question: 'If the state did not exist, would it be necessary to invent it?' Yes, but for the

---

[24] Wolff, *ibid.*, p. 14.

purpose of placing strictures on individual liberty. He calls for an 'ultra-minimal state'.[25]

But what do Christian and Islamic theologies which easily ascribe to themselves the superiority of understanding the mind of the author of society say?

---

[25] Nozick, *Anarchy, State, and Utopia*, 1974., p. 26.

Chapter Three

Balancing Faith, Revelation, and the Reason for the State

The other main school of thought which has greatly influenced modern political philosophy on the subject of the state is theology, of which the ideas of the Church and Islam stand out. Bred in a common socio-historical setting, Christian thought has formed the foundation on how Western society is ordered. Similarly, Islamic faith, which has emerged globally as a renowned force, dictates its norms for the existence of the state. The others are thoughts from more traditional societies in Africa.

Theology of St Thomas Aquinas

Dominican Friar and a key Christian Theologian St Thomas of Aquinas (1225-1274) stands out on the issue of thought on the state. Raised in early thirteenth-century Europe, a time when the impact of the much eventful reign of Frederick II of Swabia (1090-1147) was at its very peak, St Thomas of Aquinas had bequeathed to the study of political philosophy and theology some of its most invaluable intellectual treasures.

His personal synthesis on the metaphysics of human identity, creation, and life has continued to form the foundation of traditional Christian thought and theology, as well as modern jurisprudence and social theory.

In a general sense, the development of philosophy during the medieval period marked an important watershed between Graeco-Romanic scholarship and the rebirth of knowledge in the fifteenth century.[26] With the celeritous expansion of Christian faith in the period just before the fall of the Roman Empire, the tilt of philosophical speculation had begun as a hub, using neo-Platonism to rationalise conversion to the faith. Early Christian Platonists such as St Augustine had strongly argued that beyond the world of the senses existed a world of reality.

---

[26] Van Doren, *A Hisory of Knowledge*. Random House, 1991, pp. 86-124.

Having identified the world of truth as centred on the Christian God, Aquinas pinpointed an inner recourse to the human mind as the route towards arriving at the desired truth. Religion and philosophy came to be seen as intrinsically webbed together and the explanation of one found more in the other. For instance, reason was seen as the only means of making a rational explanation of faith plausible while religious creed on its part became the principal inspirational substance for deeper reflection by Christian thinkers.

St. Thomas Aquinas, 13th Century Italian
Theologian and Philosopher

Although this great interlock of reason and faith began to wane with much later thinkers such as English jurist and empiricist Francis Bacon (1561-1626), the impact had become fundamental, in particular offering useful religious insight into the nagging preoccupation on the principle of law in civil society. This became particularly important with the later upsurge of scholars, such as thirteenth-century theologian of Bavarian descent, Albertus Magnus (1193-1206), and the immense admiration for Aristotelianism as against the more circumspect Christian traditionalist who preferred Platonism. This marked the rise of what some call the age of the 'schoolmen' or scholastics, which included the Dominican Friar Aquinas.

Like other 'schoolmen', Aquinas dug deep not only into ancient Greek philosophy but laterally into contemporary Arabic and Jewish thoughts to enrich his Christian conviction. His central argument, as contained in the masterpieces *Summa Theologica* and *Summa Contra Gentiles,* is that faith and reason are intertwined and are not mutually contradictory, since they both derive their source from the same well spring; within the confines of faith lies philosophy without necessarily losing its own distinct identity and laws.

According to him, the mystery of God is made manifest to human cognition and could be reduced into rationally appreciable components in the light and guidance of faith. In a purely Aristotelian sense, theology could be appreciated as a kind of 'science', the only difference being that while faith's enquiry focuses on God as revealed in the sacred

Scriptures philosophy searches for the first cause of things through human intellect. Man starts this search by first using the data available to the five sensory mechanisms.

With regard to the social community, Aquinas married Aristotelian and Christian faith in arguing about the existence of a primary immutable reality, but unlike Aristotle, he identified the God of Christianity and Judaism as that ordinate reality. To him, God is pure and has made his creatures participate in material existence to as much extent as their humanity permits. However, Creation is continuous also to the extent that the creature, by depending on the creative wisdom of the Creator, can impose the orderliness of Creation in the created realm. Although God reigns sovereign over all of Creation, by His divine consultation He has endowed each human creation with a will that enables him to conform to His creative purpose. The existence of this 'will' conjures man's innate autonomy and self-willed existence. In order words, man is born a free rational being that can only fulfil his divine purpose by staying linked up with the creative essence.

St. Augustine of Hippo, one of the Great
Fathers of Early Christian Church

Overriding the Augustine Legacy of 'Two Cities'

It should be explained that before Aquinas, philosophy
and theology was intrigued with how to reduce if not
eliminate the gap between the much known empirical and
the less known spiritual setting. In particular, with respect

to the teaching of St Augustine of Hippo (354-430), which had become accepted more or less for nearly one thousand years with orthodoxical reverence by theologians of the day, a wide discrepancy existed between them—philosophy and theology. As a matter of fact, Paris where Aquinas was based was a major centre of intellectual activity and polemics of the day, as it was preoccupied with this subject and several other points of philosophical discord, especially between the 'universalists' and the 'nominalists'.

For instance, another subject of primary interest which also has a bearing on this dichotomy was the diatribe between those who held a 'normalist' attitude towards nature and others who were more 'realist' in approach. For the normalists, reality and name, for instance 'green', could only be limited in its reference to a particular object. They accepted that objects could be similar but rejected the generalisations associated to them. On the other hand, Augustine and other nominalists argued on the real existence of universals, so all of nature was only a shadow of a spiritual reality.

In explaining the social comportment of man, Augustine established that 'two cities' had always contended for dominance and would continue to do for eternity.[27] He called one such city—'Pax Romana', in which he lived and was well familiar to him and everyone, i.e. the shadowy 'City of Man'—replete with human imperfections and sin.

---

[27]   Van Doren, *ibid.*, p. 93.

But then it provided man with a foretaste, i.e. a platform to prepare for promotion into the eternal glory of the second and more important 'City of God'.

St Augustine identified the constitution of that heavenly city as founded on the 'Sermon on the Mount' in chapter 5 of Mathew's Gospel, a place where the poor, humble, peacemakers, and oppressed would be blessed among other oppressed. For a man to make it to this celestial bliss, his best preoccupation was to be mortified as it were his human passions in this phase (City of Man) to try to live the life depicted on the 'Sermon on the Mount' and aspire for the amaranthine glory (City of God).

Aristotle, Greek Philosopher

Augustine argued that just like Caesar, man had tried for countless generations to replicate the 'City of God' on the earth by way of various juridical systems, through his strength and imperfect disposition, but this has proved abortive. This, he suggests, was why Christ told Peter to give to Caesar what was Caesar's. The conversion to that perfect city could only be achieved by an undaunted submission to his *magister interiore,* the inward ministering by the risen Christ. The centre stage is the human heart.

Let us realise that Aristotle, who had come before Augustine, tried to combine the age-old dichotomy between the universals and the realists by pointing to the fact that all things in the world have two elements: form and matter. However, his thoughts seriously overlooked the basic disparity between the soul and the body and left a lot of unanswered questions on the relations among the form, soul, and spirit. This is what made it unattractive to early Christian theologians, including Augustine.

This was exactly the terrain that Aquinas took courage to tread on. Although broad and open in his outlook to life relative to the Church establishment, he never forsook his clerical calling; hence, he argued that philosophy and theology were not at irredeemably antipodal ends of a rope, but rather two concentric circles with a very large common area. He argued that philosophy on its part needed theology because:

> it *was necessary for man's salvation that there*
> *should be a knowledge revealed by God, besides the*
> *philosophical sciences built by human reason.*[28]

So Why the State?

It was against this backdrop that Aquinas had to describe his ideas on how man's social existence could be explained. He made two points that are worthy of attention. Human beings were deliberately made with the power of conceptual thought and a will and were placed on the earth by a loving God.

While stressing on the underlying introduction of faith, he argued that it was not too likely that God's intentions were that men should turn themselves into merely dormant creatures or some kind of programmed androids with no appetite to exercise their conceptual faculties and capacity to appreciate their physical surroundings. He pointed forcefully that nature itself or matter created by God's own Divine Providence offered so much that outright mortification of the flesh would neither help appreciate Eternal Glory as depicted in the corporeal nor advance properly the reality of social existence. Perhaps it would be important to mention here that this pattern of argument was the same as used by the early Church to justify the inclusion of icons in its

---

[28] Thomas Aquinas, *Summa Theologica,* part 1, q 1.

worship. It has been reasoned that if God did want man to only set his eyes on the paradise to come without any concern as to how he existed in this physical realm, He would not have 'manifested in the flesh' as Christ did. It was tenable to portray the Scriptures in colourful and imposing works of arts to help increase the reverence of worship and the conundrum of the life to come—'the Heavenly City'.

In his books *Summa Theologica* and *De Regime Principum*, Aquinas argues that rather than see human existence on the earth as that caught in a web of 'two truths', man was actually at the confluence of the two 'universes'. Deep in man's heart laid not just the separating line between spirit and nature but the unity of both.

Rather than reject the 'City of Man' as chaotic and irredeemable and contend one's self as a pilgrim to the promise of the 'Heavenly City', Aquinas, with much criticism from the Church hierarchy of the day, attempted to bring also to bear his stint or rather attraction for Aristotelian thought to draw an integrating constitution for both cities. This is a kind of synthesis that would enable man fulfil his highest social hopes in society and at the same time remain a candidate for the ultimate 'City of God'.

It is on this premise that Aquinas begins his ideas on society with the personality of God, if it may be permissible to say that. He sees God as the author of all Creation both physical and incorporeal, for 'every being that is in any way is from God'.[29] But then rather than see the material world as having gone through a pre-state period with confusion and atavistic anarchy, he sees God as depositing his infinite perfection into the created world. He states:

> *The perfection of all things is in God. Hence He is spoken of as universally perfect, because he does not lack any excellence which may be found in genus . . . Since therefore God is the first effecting cause of things, the perfection of all things must pre-exist in God in a more eminent way.*[30]

This may be why the Garden of Eden was such a blissful place. It is with this reasoning that he proceeds to suggest that the existence of imperfection be it somatic, convivial, or otherwise does not in any way attenuate the perfection that this is God. He argues that the 'wisdom of God is the cause of the distinction of things, so the same wisdom is the cause of their inequality'.[31]

These inequalities and distinctions in the physical attributes of matter have been deliberately placed there by God for the purpose of perfecting the universe. This may be why at the mid-point of comfort and ethical purity in the Garden of Eden, God still permitted Satan to

---

[29] Aquinas, *Summa Theologica*, part 1, q. 44.

[30] Aquinas, *Summa Theologica*, part 1, q. 4.

[31] Aquinas, *Summa Theologica*, part 1, q. 83.

wield a corrupting influence over man. But in the midst of what seems to be a 'diachrony', to borrow the words of contemporary Venezuelan political theorist Graciela Garcia-Pelayo, Aquinas sees a perfect harmony perhaps like the rainbow. But then, God has given both the ability to appreciate and differentiate what is right from wrong and also the 'will' and the 'intellect' to choose to be a normal man.[32] In this circumstance, as the modern-day evangelicals would say, the choice to do what is right is a perfecting process towards the attainment of the 'City of God'. At the time of Creation, man was perfect in his social and moral comportment, but by the exercise of the embedded power of cognition of good and evil, man chose to fall out of His Grace.

By doing so, he allowed the forces of corruption, which exist alongside good as already mentioned, to predominate in his civil society, which in the beginning had been ordered in line with the perfection of God. With regards to civic government and law, rather than see civil society as that constituted and administered by humans, as put forward by many other philosophers, Aquinas saw God as the Supreme Monarch of the entire universe. In this respect, he states:

> God the Ruler of things for the same reason as He is their cause, because the same being gives perfection, and this belongs to government. Now God is the cause not

---

[32] Aquinas, *Summa Theologica*, part 1, q. 103.

only on some particular being, but of the whole universal
being . . . Therefore as there can be nothing which is not
created by God, so there can be nothing which is not
subject to His Government.[33]

Aquinas further tenders the point that particular
things can indeed be done in the exercise of human will
and intellect that resist and contradict the perfection in the
Divine Government. The great theologian states that if God
wills, he can immediately annihilate all human political and
social arrangements and impose his divine perfection, but by
His own course. He has preserved these civic structures to
enable man to have the opportunity to develop virtue. It is
on this premise that Aquinas explains that the main purpose
of law in society is to give the state 'a measure of acts' by
which a man ought to perform an act or desist from it. But
to be effective, the law must be made by him who cares for
the community and must be directed by the common good.

Since the end of human life in the plan of Creation is
happiness, the emphasis for the lawmaker has to be guided
by Divine Reason, which is the eternal source of Divine
Providence. The human lawgiver also has to be guided by
the basic laws of nature. This is because 'eternal law is the
plan of government in the Chief Governor, all plans of
governments in the inferior governors, must be derived from
the eternal law'.

---

[33] Aquinas, *Summa Theologica*, part 2, q. 91.

St Aquinas yet contends that human laws would be insufficient for the correction of all of man's wrongdoing, so some form of superior ethical axiom (Divine Law) which operates at the level of the conscience would still be required to shepherd human social relations.

There is no doubt that in the thoughts of Aquinas one finds a desperate effort to marry the former antagonistic row between the dogmatic world of faith and the rationalistic world of reason into a single ethical organised system. However, as it turned out to be, the frantic rationalisation of Aquinas only bred further controversy in the centuries that followed as thinkers in both ways continued prodding for the incompatibility of the two seeming truths.

Apart from this, in thirteenth-century Europe when the Church was virtually the 'hand of Esau' behind the civil government, the treatise was very useful, though not in the way desired by his ecclesiastical authority in the same period in further justifying the status quo of clerical political activism. Some other queries which have been raised against the theological explanations for the reason of the state relate to the implied tone of the necessity of conversion.

Although ingeniously analytical of all philosophical studies before him, the thoughts of Aquinas are strongly Bible based. This creates some problems. For instance, for the lawgiver in civil society to be able to receive the inspiration for the right intuition necessary for Divine Reason, it is not clear if he would need conversion or accept some form of doctrinal cognition. If not, can an atheist, agnostic, or, better still, a proselyte of another form of metaphysical rationality be deemed capable to receive the divine signals needed to complement natural and human law?

Islamic Dictate and the State

Pre-Islam political thought in the Arabian Peninsula was a goulash and mixture of different strands of civilisations and influences. The eclectic spread of Hellenistic thought of near Eastern world views amalgamated with indigenous thinking to give the people of the area a type of neo-Platonic orientation. The existence of major early centres of learning in Damascus, Baghdad, and Alexandra in Egypt, among others, created ample ambience for the growth and nurture of all forms of classical studies from pre-Socratic and post-Aristotelian learning. Indeed, it is of interest that a good part of works from some of the patriarchs of Western classic scholarship was originally translated and retained in Arabic writings before their retrieval. In this context, the works of such Nestorians as Hunayn Ibn Ishaq (830-910) are easy reminders of the generation of such writings, especially from the second century AD.

The views of such writers which saw reason and logic as the basis of thought and therefore definitions of the foundations of the state were seen by many in founding days of Islam as rather antithetical to faith or revelation. Early days Islamic writers saw that the reason for the state and the cause and effect of societies was to find explanation only in its relevance to the 'revealed truth' as stated by the Holy Prophet Mohammed (570-632) and other canonical precepts. Arising from this, early scholars in the founding days of Islam questioned whether what was regarded by some as 'Islamic philosophy' existed since the legal basis of society could only be found in theology.

In retrospect, after the flight of Prophet Mohammed from Mecca to Medina in AD 622, the setting of political community in Medina was founded on strong theocratic basis. This became a primary centre, where thoughts on the basis of the faith of the people found in the Koran, Hadith, teachings of the Prophet and the righteous caliph (his immediate successor and associate) became crystallised and took a conservative outlook. The *'Suna'* containing the practices of the community and the system of *'Fiqh'*— Islamic law had ample provision on how Muslims were expected to live in the society. It is argued that the Koran and other religious literature dictate not only to Muslims but also places before all of mankind who are able to understand everything pertaining to life and societal existence. Without explicitly keeping away reason, it suggests the finality of the revealed matter forming the basis for logic which as we know is the cardinal ingredient of philosophy.

Al Ghazali, Muslim Cleric and Philosopher

Theologian and jurist of Persian stock, Al-Ghazali (1058-1111), similar to the towering influence of Augustine's dogmatic conservatism in holding tenaciously to this approach, refuted neo-Platonic influence on Islamic thought. He was orthodox in view. Unabashedly, he espoused in his works *Revivification of Religious Sciences* and *Incoherence of Philosophers* a clear rejection of Socrates, Aristotle, and Plato, deflating the emerging group of 'talasifa'—the so-called Islamic philosophers. He was obviously adverse to logic, mathematics, and the sciences and advocated a strict return to the religious science—Islamic jurisprudence and spiritual purity. In promoting Sufism, he advocated for the return to religious dogma, including the introversion of living associated with it. The foundation of the state was therefore God-based as revealed.

The gradual spread of Islamic rule, political power, and the religion that came with it eastward to such centres of scholarship as Damascus and Cordova in Spain accorded to the faith and this philosophical system a more cosmopolitan outlook. This was further enhanced by the rise of such Islamic scholars as Al-Kindi (801-873), who did not see Islamic thought and philosophy as being circumscribed in two compartments but rather saw the synergy. Also known as 'the philosopher of the Arabs', scholar Al Kindi, using Baghdad as a base, argued that the thoughts of Plato and Aristotle were not hiatus to the explanation of society from the prism of faith, but rather were a tool for a better understanding of the truth provided by Islam.

Philosophical insight into Islamic thought about human society was argued more forcefully by his later heirs— Ibn Rushd of Cordova (Averroes) (1126-1198), Ibn Sina (Avicenna) (980-1037), and Ibn Al-Haytham (965-1045), the master of centralised logic into Islamic scholarship. In his main decisive treaties, Ibn Rushd insisted that philosophy and the logic that came with it were critical ingredients for arriving at the right conclusions in most religious questions. Hence, his assertion was that banning philosophy, as was easily canvassed by those who were antagonistic in his time, was 'a wrong to the best set of people and to the best set of existing things'. His thoughts were also to set free many Muslims of the time whose philosophical outlook had become much influenced by the teachings of Al-Ghazali, which had loomed large one hundred years.

In trying to set aside the teachings of Al-Ghazali, philosophers such as Ibn Rushd, as was done by Aquinas in the West, argued that 'philosophy, religion and truth do not contradict themselves'. To him, philosophy provided an intellectual insight into the appreciation of esoteric aspects of dimension of faith. It is part of the unending search for '*hikma*' or wisdom in the path already set by the Islamic world-view covering life ethics and the society. In other words, such philosophical thoughts are basically prophetic and help bring about a better illumination of what is divinely revealed in the Koran and Sunna. Hence he concluded that philosophy sees the reasons to be not transitory in nature but a critical thread tying man to one and supreme God through knowledge that has been revealed.

Ibn Rushd, Muslim Cleric and Philosopher

The aim of this philosophical debate by Al Rushd and company, which had its apogee the 'Islamic golden age' between the eighth and twelfth century, is not just the theoretical knowledge of substance and accident of the universe. It was also the experience of their time and some kind of instantiation in such a way to enable the soul to free itself from the confines of the universe. The universes (in this case) are experienced not as something external but rather as a succession of stages along a path on which one is travelling.

Al-Rushd and others of his tradition posit that it could be that Islamic philosophy was hinged on the fact that God expects human beings to use their reason to seek to understand the nature of reality as guided by the teachings and tenets of Islam.

The period from the Middle Ages, especially in the twelfth and thirteenth and subsequent centuries, saw the rise of many Islamic scholars to occasion, that is, to explain the coterminous link between their faith and philosophy (although, in the course of time, it solely became the basis of the revival of anti-Western philosophical elucidations in some of the centres of learning). Working closely with many Christian and Jewish scholars, they became seized with translations into diverse languages of much of their classical predecessors, especially of Latin and Greek origin, preserved almost exclusively in Arabic. This was in contradistinction to the situation in Europe which was at the time regarded to be in 'Dark Ages'.

In the early sixteenth century, many Arabic scholars became heroes of Islamic philosophical renaissance. Indeed, by 1584, an Arabic press was set up in Rome, and teaching of this philosophy became of interest in several contemporaneous European centres of learning.

The eventual unfettering of Iberian Peninsula (Portugal and Spain) from Islamic control created a level of detachment of Islamic thought from the continued stream of influence from the West. Even where it existed, Islamic philosophy itself started to divide into Eastern and Western compartments. However, some measure or levels of study continued as scholarship was developed by Othmans Mamluks, Abbassids, and Safavid Dynasty of Persia. It was in this period of the Middle Ages that Tunisian-born Ibn Khaldum (1332-1406) propounded his 'Theories of Social Cohesion and Social Conflict'. This tradition of seeing philosophy as compatible with Cannon law in general sense continued, even though it was not as robust as in the preceding generation. Islamic scholars through diverse languages and centres, especially in Urdu, Persian, Hindu, and in Timbuktu, became effusive with ideas. The search however continues by contemporary scholars to find rational principles to put in place a separately Islamic philosophical thought which could be in tune with science and technology of modern life.

The Recline to Conservative Thought

However, it must be noted that a branch of Islamic scholars and religious leaders throughout the course of history had always regarded the eclectic combination of Koranic revelations and Judaeo-Christian teachings of explaining the existence of the state as rather syncretic. They preferred a return to a purer form of traditional Islamic dogma. This led to the revival in the Islamic world of the teaching of some radical scholars. Of particular importance was the influence of the Iranian Cultural Renaissance by Mulla-Sadar (1571-1690), who developed an Islamic fundamentalist approach to philosophy. To him, Western philosophy and scholarship have been regarded in true form as a type of imperialism with a value system that is at variance with Islamic thoughts.

It should be noted in retrospect that even if scholars such as Al-Rushd, as seen earlier, therefore were advocates of centralising Western philosophy into Islam the political setting did not remove the covering of suspicion against secular scholarship. Even the great Al-Rushd himself at the height of attacks stated rather that such a venture into philosophical understanding of religion of Islamic faith should not be at the disposal of uneducated and should be taught with care.

The revival of fundamentalist, doctrinaire Islam got more life in the eighteenth and nineteenth century particularly. This became all the more defiant as Western civilisation tried to bare its fangs in a pax human fashion in the twentieth century. The classical hypothesis of the great 'Clash of Civilisation' espoused so prophetically by Samuel Huttington therefore began to hang ominously or adumberate itself as well thought through.

African Thought and the State

Africa is unarguably the cradle of humanity and the cradle of human civilisation. Archaeology and anthropology have revealed that the first species of homo-sapiens lived in the Olduvial Valley in Kenya, while the land of Egypt, even in pre-dynastic times had a right repertoire of philosophical tradition. Recorded history from hieroglyphics also showed rich philosophical works in the times of the pharaohs of Egypt, which had strong influence on Greek Judeo-Christian and Islamic thoughts.

With the advent of Christianity, some of the most profound scholars such as Augustine of Hypo (AD 354-430) from Algeria made great elucidation of Christian theology. His teachings on what he considered as divine grace, further expounding 'the Pauline Doctrine' in the place of grace and salvation, brought immense contributions to early Christian thought. With the rise of Islam, places such as Cairo, Alexandria, Kanem-Borno and Timbuktu became centres of effusive philosophical activity.

Prof. John Mbiti, Christian Religious Philosopher

Besides all these, the main restraint of indigenous philosophy of the various African people with over one thousand ethnic groups was that it might sound contentious to talk about a single indigenous African political philosophy. In historiography, this has been amply recorded in the pioneering work *Primitives and the Supernatural* of the French ethnologist Levy Bruhl (1857-1939). As persuasive as they may be, these works have been well-counteracted by the Kenyan priest and philosopher, his Nigerian co-cleric of Yoruba extraction, Prof. John Mbiti, Prof. Bolaji Idowu, and Robin Horton who underscored the fact that Africa was not as dark as portrayed, but full of very dense philosophical traditions.

Although the issues of African pre-colonial state formation as well as its pre-colonial trend have been discussed separately in another work from ethno-philosophical point of view, it is important to show that perhaps some of the best state structures existed around the continent from monarchies to republican states, or what Prof. Horton has stated that a certain basic underpinning, existed in the states of Africa, irrespective of the group. This includes the fact that the state was seen as a continuum with an intrinsic metaphysical link among the past, the present, and the future.

Indeed, virtually in African people, the state and environment were seen as a gift from God and from the ancestors from the timeless past. Man is at the centre of this matrix and is seen to deserve the highest level of worth. The duty of any generation of leaders and citizens was therefore to preserve and ensure its perpetuity for the enjoyment of both the contemporary and those unborn.

Similarly, the task of its preservation was seen as a collective charge to all of which care, obligation, and responsibilities were ascribed. Society was an ethereal bond which seemed to involuntarily tie all to one; it is believed that clear sanctions which at most times were not determined by the living but consciously imposed by the pantheon ancestors and gods existed. In other words, there existed an involuntary 'social contract' with respect to the ordinary existence of society between those living and those on the other side of the divide, the unseen and others present in the society. It was a kind of social welfare system which African leaders such as Julius Nyerere (1922-1999), Kenneth Kaunda, Kwame Nkrumah (1909-1972), and Leopold Senghor (1906-2001) introduced into governance in the post-colonial era. Although they added neo-Marxian and socialist teachings to elucidate authentic African thoughts, their elucidation of the traditional African state was more of a social contract, which were involuntarily closely knitted by forces beyond the individual.

The coming of Christianity and Islam added great flavour to African thought as the thoughts of the two religions did not seriously deviate from African thoughts from the point of view of the individual and philosophy of the state. They all had great elements of reason acting within the confines of faith, although differing on many other issues, including content and liturgy. The similar way in which both world religions believe in the subject of human connection and man's material environment to some form of ultimate divine directive brought a great synergy with traditional African thought.

Part II

Nation-States and the Challenge of Integration

Chapter Four

Principles of the State and Symbols of Power

We have already seen that from the cradle of civic society, man was quick in devising some form of political organisation to ensure their enjoyable social existence or, as Aquinas considers it, 'for the need of proper co-ordination of social relations and managing of the common good'. Even if men were to have perfect moral chastity, English naturalist Charles Robert Darwin (1809-1882) maintains the fact that man's congenital imbuement with cognitive and free moral agency would still have compelled the need to have in place 'any form of political organization, rather than none'.[34]

British Naturalist, Charles Darwin

---

[34] Such a state of ethical purity would be supposedly something similar to what Adam was before the cataclysmic fall from the Garden of Eden.

On Governance and Civil Authority

Generally speaking, a large part of reasoning on the nature of the state is associated with the concept of 'Government'. As we have seen, most philosophers including Aristotle (384-322 BC) and George Wilhelm Friedrich Hegel (1770-1831) have suggested oneness in both ideas while others such as the father of classical liberalism, John Locke, and Swiss philosopher Rousseau hold that the state encompasses the government as it is the most prominent structure of human community.

Even if its main focus is 'legislative' as Locke sees it or 'executive' according to Rousseau, the state constitutes a fundamental means towards realising the raison d'être of civil society while government only deals with how the former is organised to attain the maximum goals. Notwithstanding this, it is relevant to point out that the state has its own corporate identity, which remains unfettered by changes in government. The contrary situation would only occur when a change leads to other political developments that eventually result in dismemberment of the state, as evident from several cases in the former Eastern Europe.

In some countries where parliamentary democracy is in place, the use of the vote of confidence results in frequent changes of governments without affecting in any way the perpetuity of the state. This is very common in Italy, South Korea, and Japan. Even the effect on the national economy is rather transient, lasting a few days or weeks. As one author said, 'Men are seldom unanimous in the means of attaining their ends, so their difference in opinion in relation to government has produced a variety of forms of it. To enumerate them, would be to recapitulate the history of the whole earth'. Let us therefore contend ourselves with the definition that has been provided by the same author, which simply renders the terminology precisely thus:

> *In general, it is the polity of the state, or an orderly power constituted for the public good, instituted for the preservation and advancement of men's civil interests and for the better security of life, liberties, and the properties.*[35]

The word 'government' actually comes from the Latin root *gubernare* which itself was borrowed from a Greek locution *kubernan*.[36] These all mean to steer or direct, in this case, the affairs of the state.

---

[35] *Encyclopaedia Britannica*, vol. ii, p. 726, 1768.

[36] A more detailed explanation on this can be found in Tom McArthur, *Oxford Companion to the English Language*. London: Oxford University Press, 1992.

German Sociologist, Max Weber

To enable effective discharge of this mandate of shepherding how men and their social institutions relate and yet 'keep at bay the inherent drift towards anarchism', German philosopher Max Weber (1864-1920) and a host of other thinkers have advocated that governments must always enjoy the monopoly of the use of force. In simple words, they put forward that all governments need a measure of *auctoritatis* and power of coercion in order to be effective and command respect.[37]

---

[37] Like many others, the ideas of Han Weber are reprinted in the *Great Books* by the University of Chicago.

The idea of 'authority' was developed in Ciceronian times to denote the capacity and empowerment to create, invent, counsel, establish decrees and where necessary adjudicate. The point is that the expectation of the government is to organise and control, in other words to 'rule'. But it is interesting that these related expressions 'rule' and 'regulate', which deal with this type of process, are again borrowed roots from the Latin *regula*, which means a big straight stick like a shepherd's rod!

Arising from such a rationalising over claiming coercive rights over others to some few, and the particular need to shelter it from abuse, another heritage of intellectual feud emerges—how should governments be constituted. Aristotle, for instance, had asked if such power should be shared between the 'multitude' and the 'wealthy' or between the 'good' or the 'best man'.

Ideas are diverse as others such as Hobbes favour an absolutist regime, whether vested in an individual (prince) or an assembly. Aquinas also shares through some of those ideas that he saw the 'public personage' as being above the law. But Rousseau has a more republican perspective in identifying the power base to be derivable from only the people. He relates the constitution of Government to the fact that 'no one can be put out of his own estate and subjected to the political power of another without his consent'. But many religious thinkers, including biblical traditions advocate 'servant leadership' where governance includes that the strong should serve the weak.

The pupils of the representative persuasion postulate that the sovereignty of the people and that of the government is consistent, as the former derives its strength from the latter. In this sense, the power base lies with the people. This is also the foundation of modern democracy.

The Constitution

Charles de Montesquieu,
French Philosopher and Jurist

The question of division of sovereign powers among various segments of the state is related to this discussion. These could be either between a central authority and constituent parts (states and regions) or among various arms (executive, legislature, and judicial). This latter trinity is sanctimoniously referred to as 'separation of powers' by the French social commentator and writer Charles-Louis Montesquieu (1689-1755), who called it 'the sacred maxim of the Government'. Modern political scientists have also come to consider it a critical element in ascribing value judgement as to whether a system of governance is 'just' or 'unjust'. But the relationships between these different components are enshrined in laws, more reverently called 'Constitution'.

In the tradition of the other political phenomena which had been considered earlier on, the signification of what a constitution is and the listing of its main elements remain open-ended matters. In the ancient past, it occupied one of the main treatises in both Plato's *The Statesman* and Aristotle's *Politics,* so it would be enough for now to remain with the lucid summation offered by Hobbes when he put it as 'that fundamental law . . . if taken away the commonwealth falls and is utterly dissolved'. Constitutions, whether unwritten as in the case of the United Kingdom or codified as in most countries, have to be made and accepted by the people directly or better still, as recommended by James Madison, delegated to a few (an assembly), on behalf of all.[38]

---

[38] See James Madison, *The Federalist*. But then it is practically impossible for all to sit and debate the Constitution.

More ahead, we shall attempt to set down some guidelines as to how this law-making process could be undertaken for the purpose of forming better integrated states. This is more so as it is the constitution that will determine the type of political system that the state adopts, whether it is 'monarchy', 'oligarchy', 'republican', or even 'military rule'. There are yet other constitutions which claim 'socialism', 'communism', or even 'theocracy', but one interesting factor is that all these systems claim to be democratic.

Democracy

As a matter of fact, democracy appears to be one of the most frequently applied jargons in political analyses of any form of government nowadays. Interestingly enough, the meaning and scope of this terminology changes as frequently as it is applied. The African statesman Julius Nyerere (1922-1999) once put it, 'in thinking of democracy, is the tendency to confuse one's own personal picture of which, if examined, will usually be found to include the "machinery" and symbols of democracy peculiar to the society which one happens to be familiar with.'[39]

---

[39] Julius Nyerere, *The African and Democracy* in *Africa Speaks,* by James Duffy and Robert Manners (eds.). Princeton: D. Van Nostrand, 1961.

He makes a historical critique of democracy, concluding quite rightly that 'to the Ancient Greek "democracy" meant simple government by discussion. The people discussed and the result was a "people's government"'. But not all the people discussed about it as the textbooks tell us: 'Those who took part were "equals" and this excluded women and slaves.'[40] Dr Nyerere identifies three critical factors which need to be in place to consider a system democratic— discussion, equality, and freedom. He concludes that democracy is simply government by the people.

John Stuart Mill, English Philosopher and Economist

---

[40]   Nyerere, op. cit.

This tallies largely with the much iconised version offered by the foremost American statesman Abraham Lincoln (1809-1865): 'Government of the people, by the people, for the people.' The most crystallised elaboration on the contents and practice of democracy which is today being set down globally had their origin in Anglo-Saxon traditions, particularly the United States. Between *The Federalist* and the works of John Stuart Mill (1806-1873), we see an evaluation of democracy as the most appreciated form of government since:

> *Sovereignty or supreme control of power in the last resort is vested in the entire aggregate of the community, every citizen not only having a choice in the exercise of that ultimate loyalty, but being at least occasionally, called on to take actual power in Government.*[41]

While not oblivious of the lack of infiniteness in the application of the thoughts of Mill and the founding fathers of American democracy, it is startling and worthy of much accolade that having been raised in a society where slavery was an accredited mode, they nonetheless harped on about the equality of all human beings at birth, hence the need for equal opportunity. It is for this reason that the effective workability was predicated on the sacredness of the right of

---

[41] Mill, Considerations on Representative Government, New York: Prometheus Books, 1991

suffrage and 'redemption' of the population from poverty and ignorance.

Indeed, Alexander Hamilton (1789-1795) argued that control over one's means of livelihood *ipso facto* constituted possession of his will. Mill, on the other hand, saw the fruits of democracy as derivable when all people are required and compelled to be educated and given some form of social culture. South American 'liberator' Simon Bolivar in fact brought this out more when he said in Lima, Peru, in 1825 that *'un hombre sin estudios es un ser incompleto'* and thereafter *'La salud de una Republica depende de la moral que la educacion adqueiren los cuidadanos en su infancia'.*[42]

---

[42] *Decreto sobre la ensenanza publica*, Chuquisaca (Bolivar), 11 December 1825. 'a man without education . . . The wellbeing of the Republic depends on the moral education of its citizens from infancy'.

Alexander Hamilton, American Statesman and First
Secretary of the Treasury of the United States

To these ideas from the other side of Atlantic, the
latter-day Prussian political economist and sociologist
Max Weber (1864-1920) suggested the need for a
democratic political system to have in place an efficient
and loyal bureaucratic apparatus. With accolades for great
intellectual prowess covering many disciplines including
law, economics, mysticism, and sociology, Weber was able
to underscore in his main works *Die protestantische Ethik
und der Geist de Kapitalismus*, and during his editorship
of *Archiv fur Sozialwissenschalf und Sozialpolitik* the
importance of ensuring that such a public service should

be devoid of politics and have clear-cut standards that permit upward progression by merit.[43] He argued that in a modern democratic setting, the office is run not through the capricious will of individuals, but through written documents that are properly preserved in files. The bureaucracy, better known as 'civil service' itself, is highly esteemed, maintains proper social distance irrespective of who is in political office, and is made to function under stipulated laws.[44]

In the entire Anglo-Saxon heritage, democracy has also come to include the existence of an 'organised opposition in government'. This is supposed to keep the government in power in check and bring about required moderation in decision taking. In fact, critical decisions cannot be taken without proper consultation and subsequent compromise with the opposition. Arising therefrom, democracy has come to be appreciated as a game with guiding rules that ought to be respected. In the same spirit of sportsmanship, it has also come to be appreciated that the acquisition and tenure in power must conform to lay down rules and standards.

---

[43] This work was published in 1904-1905, but Weber had another significant work that also covered some of these works, including 'Archiv ftir Sozialssenschaff and Sozialpolitik' (Essays on Sociology).

[44] These have again been reprinted by the University of Chicago, 1991, pp. 143-168.

Chapter Five

The Character of Civic Unions: Repulicanism, Federalism, and Unitarism

H uman society has built up its political character in many forms, ranging from the leviathan rule of a single 'sovereign' to the caucus rule of an 'oligarchy' and, as common nowadays, the more participatory rule of the people. In his *Commentaries on the Laws of England*, English Statesman Sir William Blackstone (1809-1898) says of this trio:

The political writers of antiquity will not have more than three regular form of government; the first, when the sovereign power is lodged in an aggregate assembly consisting of all the members of a community, which is called a democracy; the second when it is lodged in a council, composed of select members, and then it is stilled aristocracy; and last, when it is entrusted in the hands of a single person and then it takes the name of a monarchy. All the other species they say are either corruption of or reducible to these three.[45]

Republicanism

Two of man's most treasured political edifices both of which are derived from the above trilogy and form part of the basic concern of this study are the much paired concepts of the 'republic' and the 'federation'. We have already seen with similar concepts that a mass of definitions and characterisations do exist, but we can again describe some of the basic qualifying ingredients.

One of the most succinct yet replete definitions tendered for the expression 'republic' once more comes from the early writers of the first edition of the *Encyclopaedia Britannica* three hundred years ago, when they expressed it as a

---

[45] Jack Lively and Adam Lively, *Democracy in Britain: A Reader.* Oxford: Blackwell, 1991, p. 44.

'commonwealth, popular state or government; or a nation where the people have the government in their hands'. From this, it would appear that the original meaning of the term was associated with all political processes related to the state. But coming at a time when British political thought was occupied with drawing dividing boundary lines between absolutism, as represented by the Stuart Dynasty, and the winds of political liberalism then sweeping across Europe, the definition proffered by these early encyclopaedists could not have been better expressed than the comparative manner in which it was done.

But in the actual course of political evolution, the term has come to be limited to two sets of usage—i.e. as distinguished from 'monarchy' and as a prescription of the yardstick for measuring the extent of political participation in a given political entity. It is a kind of litmus test for the political ecology in which the people have the government in their hands relative to those in which political power is circumscribed to a few.

The term 'republic' has its origin in the Greek *politeia,* but it became popularised by the Roman jurist Marcus Tallius Cicero (106-43 BC). He translated it to Latin as *res publicae* (a public thing). Later, English writers paraphrased it as 'commonwealth'. In his work, *Historia,* the Greek historian Polybius cited the success of Rome as a republic to its prudent orchestration of monarchy, aristocracy, and democracy. To him, politics was not to be regarded as ethereal as men had been made to believe, but it was an unhidden *res publica* (a public thing).[46]

As a matter of fact, Roman republicanism had itself been inspired by Hellenic cultures before it. Not just the working of the Greek polis or the *metabolai* process of political adaptation of monarchy, but Rome also derived its political tutelage from the ideas of a succession of thinkers dating back to Herodotus, all of whom pointed to the wisdom of a mixed constitution. So what Cicero occupied his mind with in his most outstanding works—De *republicae* and *De lesgibus*—was to describe the working of the Roman political system in the light of Plato's thought as dilated in the latter's *Republic* and *Laws*. It should be added that, as a matter of fact, Cicero also derived titles for his praises from these works of Plato.

According to Cicero, the republic could endure because the constitution was mixed, balanced, and founded on the strictness of tenure for the elected officers.[47] The 'Senate' which had risen to over nine thousand at the time of Caesar developed over time as a permanent advisory council of state, while limited suffrage ensured the participation of 'all'. The Emperor himself did not owe his position to birth, but he deserved it through public approbation of his hard work and self-accomplishment.

---

[46] This is taken from *Encyclopaedia Britannica*, vol. xx, p. 143.

[47] Stockton, David, Cicero: *A Political Biography*, London: Oxford university Press 1988.

From the writings of Cicero and his contemporaries as well as William Shakespeare's epic drama, *Julius Caesar,* we see a fundamental attribute of the republic—'virtue'. What a person received pertaining to political reward was not basically hereditary, but on merit. This is because the republic or the modern state is not just any group of men, but those united together by a common agreement on law and rights and a common desire to participate in events.[48] The system was to allow for upward political mobility and the highest fulfilment of individual hopes and aspirations.

On the part of the individual, he owed it to the republic 'duties' and 'obligations' such as passion towards all that would bring honour, glory, and pride to the fatherland.[49] We shall see this in more detail later, but it is enough to say here that unlike the realm under monarchy, which had often been seen as pertaining to the proprietary rights of the sovereign or some dynastic guild, the *patria* (fatherland) which comes with the republic and indeed the modern state was for all worth dying for.[50]

It wasn't just the scores of Roman politicians, but their latter-day heirs like Florentian Historian and Diplomat Nicolo Machiavelli (1469-1527) and the great Latin

---

[48] Robert D. Putnam, *Making Democracy Work: Civic Traditions in Modern Italy,* 1993, p. 116.

[49] John Rawls, *A Theory of Justice.* Cambridge: Harvard University of Press, 1991, has many interesting articles on this, see pp. 333-382.

[50] Luis Castro Leiva, *The Opulence of Virtue and the Dictatorship of Commerce,* 1990, p. 211.

American Liberator Simon Bolivar (1783-1830) had at different times expressed their disposition to die for their republics if that became a necessary position to take. Bolivar wrote to his colleague, Colombian General Francisco Santander (1792-1840), saying, 'I will only want to live for the republic otherwise I die.'[51] In modern times we have heard Hugo Chavez (1954-2013), an acclaimed reincarnate of Bolivar, re-echo this passion.

Simon Bolivar (1783 - 1830), Venezuelan General, patriot and Revolutionary.

---

[51]   Romero Martinez, *Bolivarianism*, Caracas, 1995.

stuff virtue is made of; it is enough to agree with the French thinker and traveller Alexis de Tocqueville (1805-1855) that the distinct proprieties and eccentricities in a society would colour its political deportment.[52] For instance, Aristotle had in the *Nicomachean Ethics* associated the republic with the concept of *eudaimonia* (the well-being of man), and a virtuous act is one that leads to the attainment of this.[53] He then advises that acts which need to qualify as virtuous would be mindful in eschewing extremities of position. This clearly puts aside the rather jingoistic acts such as display of courage in the defence of the republic (as in the case of the alibi found for the treachery which prompted the gruesome events on the *Ides of March* when Julius Caesar was murdered).[54] Brutus and the other perpetrators justified their acts on the basis of passion, love, and pursuit of the glory of the republic. This rather ambitious clique related to the role of the individual and the republic then calls attention to another perspective of virtue—an outlandish showing of heroism when Marcus Antonius (83-30 BC) on that occasion swayed his listeners by asserting that 'not because I love Caesar less, but because I love Rome more'.[55] The scores of military purges, which till late plagued Latin America,

---

[52] Alexis Tocquevile, *Democracy in America* (reprinted), University of Chicago, 1991.

[53] Mackie, *ibid.*, p. 186.

[54] Van Doren, *ibid.*, pp. 44-46.

[55] Julius Caesar in *Great Work of William Shakespeare*, London, 1990.

Africa, or Asia, claim rather intriguingly 'love of fatherland' for their actions. Anything that would advance the course of a strong state was considered virtuous, but let us leave this for now and return to it later.

The republic also became synonymous with a political regime where things are discussed in the open and laws made by the people—*civitas libera quae possit sibi legem facere.* Political ideas, programmes, and issues of state to a large extent had to be discussed before the glare of everyone. Hence, ancient Greek and Roman politicians had to properly train themselves and be equipped enough to outwit one another in oratory.

In the process, the Senate emerged as the best talk shop the world has ever produced. So the de-shrouding of public policy and the open declaration of political postures and programmes became a well-developed republican tradition. Republicanism also developed to be prized as the political ideal for any group of people, denoting the equality of man and liberty and its attachment to the opportunity of virtuous public service as we have seen.[56] It is on this ground that Immanuel Kant turned his attention to the fact that the republic always provides an ethical regime where civic ethos is founded not just on the basis of pragmatism and utility, but also on reason, morality, fair representation, and openness.

---

[56] Robert Skinner, *Machiavelli and Republicanism.* London: Oxford University Press, 1992, p. 293.

The Federalist Victory versus Unitarism

With the 'federalist victory' after the American Revolution, as we shall see later, the use of republican rhetoric became increasingly associated with federalist political structures. The federalist system is easily distinguished from a 'unitary' form of government where power flows from one centre and from the looseness of a 'confederation' where power is consolidated and concentrated in the branches, thereby only leaving the centre to coordinate the resolve of the detached power centres.

Federalism itself has been defined succinctly by the *Dictionary of Political Science* as 'a form of territorial political organization in which unity and regional diversity are accommodated within a single political system'.

It is therefore a compromise between undue concentration of civil power or its debility at either the centre or the branches. In the words of Vincent Ostrom, 'It is a political arrangement to counterpoise the "centrist ambition" with "regional ambition."'[57] This is worked out through a convenient distribution of bureaucratic power between the central government and the corresponding subdivisions: states, provinces, regions, or cantons as the case may be.

Thereafter, civic authority is appropriately worked out again between the second tier and other relevant

---

[57] Vincent Ostrom, *The Political Theory of a Compound Republic.* Nebraska: University of Nebraska Press, 1987, p. 80.

levels, such as municipal and county components. Since it basically brings together separate political entities in a way that none will lose its distinctiveness and political integrity, basic policies that would affect all are negotiated and a margin of agreement reached. Special care is taken to allow the centre to focus on the common problems while the regions maintain enough autonomy to handle matters in a manner reflective of their diversity.[58] It is important to add for further clarification that in about the eighteenth century, i.e. the Age of Enlightenment, when most of the modern structures of statehood and civil organisation took place, federalism as a political credo was developed. It came out of the *E pluribus unum* to describe the existence of arrangements where 'one made of many', even if not in an organic manner, existed out of human construct.[59]

For the purpose of ensuring consistency and clarity of intention, most federative republics have a codified covenant which we earlier referred to as the 'constitution' spelling out the basic terms of their coexistence. Fundamental changes to matters that touch on constitutional law can only be brought about by the affirmative agreement of a stipulated majority in the national legislature. In the case of the United States,

---

[58]   *Encyclopaedia Britannica*, vol. iv, p. 712.

[59]   Cymhia H. Enloe, *Ethnic Conflict and Political Development.* Boston: Little, Brown, 1973, p. 89. Also see Omo Omoruyi, *Representation in Federal (Plural) Systems: A Comparative View.* Third Press International, 1980, p. 89.

for instance, issues of constitutional nature would require the confirmation of at least two-thirds of the states.

Cases in some other countries brought the principles to the fore. For entry to NATO or the European Union or accession to some far-reaching community policies, such as placement of foreign troops or monetary union, it is expected that some form of national referendum or some other forms of popular tallies in the units had to be taken. This is despite the fact that these issues fall within the ambit of foreign policy or national defence customarily reserved for the central government. In many countries, even matters such as privatisation of the vital national assets and mineral industries or the incurring of foreign debts have to receive the agreement of the representatives of the people as constituted in the parliament.

Furthermore, the system necessarily has a measure of non-centralisation, i.e. diffusion of power to units which should be fairly self-sustaining. As we shall see, this may differ from place to place, especially when it comes to implementation, but such an arrangement must be entrenched in the constitution. Besides, at the heart of it, there is the need to have some form of territorial democracy or what is also referred to as 'real division of power'. This means that at the centre there is neutrality in dealing with the component parts, and a fair margin of equality in terms of representation is maintained. This makes it possible for all interests to be taken care of and accommodated fairly at the national level.

The importance of fair representation or what has been called in Nigerian political circles as 'federal character' at the centre has been emphasised by most writers on the subject. In fact, it has been argued that fair representation is the most veritable exhibit of the plurality which seems to be the label mark of most federating states.

By way of digression, it would be relevant to mention that in societies where various forms of heterogeneity exist between units (as is the case in several Latin American and Caribbean countries), it has been suggested that unitary forms of political arrangements, a supposed structural integration, are a facade and do not reflect the actual diversity.

This is why in, say, Guyana and Trinidad and Tobago electoral results and the subsequent representation in government continue to be sharply divided along racial lines. At different times, when by electoral exercise Cheddi Jagan and Banseleo Panday, both of Indian origin, became the 'strong' men in their respective countries, most key appointments went to people of that ethnic extraction to the chagrin of those of African descent who had for long dominated the leadership. Again, in both countries, those of Indian extraction continued to monopolise and dominate the professions.

On the other hand, federal structures even as fragmentary as they may seem in countries such as Mexico and Venezuela have tended to produce more congruity; hence, despite the fact that they comprise a small percentage, people of African descent, such as Aristobulos Isturiz and Claudio Fermin, could not only emerge in the prestigious mayoralty of the national capital Caracas but also for a long time remained strong contenders for the country's presidency.

Approaches to Federalism

Contemporary Nigerian political scientist Omo Omoruyi illustrates the existence of an asymmetrical bond between pluralism and federalism by showing that it is the various races, tribes, and the like in the case of the latter that in most cases eventually dissolve to form the political subdivisions such as states and regions which make up the polity.[60]

The reality is that at the level of a mere plural society, it may be commonplace to draw these political subdivisions along ethnic lines. As the roots of federalism take hold, overlaps begin to occur, bringing clusters of ethnic groups together. And at the national level, the supposed equality or parity in representation becomes defined not by the clannish colour, but by statehood. This has been well depicted in Indian politics where most of the leading political parties

---

[60] See Omoruyi, op. cit. and M. C. Smith, *The Plural Society in the West Indies*. Los Angeles: University of California Press, 1965.

have increasingly come to represent collective ideologies and interests rather than sections. We shall return to this later.

Lastly, at the hub, there should exist common uniting factors which have to be well cherished by all, appropriately developed and instilled. In some cases, such as the German nation, this was an inherited language and culture; hence, what it needed was further cultivation, and it still remains strong even in the younger generation. This is why despite the tumultuous political history that the German nation faced in the course of the twentieth century, it was possible for them to come back together with relative ease. The factor of tongue and identification with a common civilisation could have also played a major role in the generally open-handed manner with which the Hong Kong people viewed their return to the motherland after over 145 years of separation.

This becomes more compelling when we realise that the former island colony in the actual sense needed absolutely nothing else from the mainland, and a unified voice in this direction from its inhabitants could have yet forced the international community to prevail on delaying the process of political transfer which took place there smoothly on July 1, 1997. No doubt some pro-democracy groups in Hong Kong strongly opposed the return to Beijing, but most of the leadership, including de facto Chief Executive Tung Chee-hwa, all stood for unification.

In the same manner, despite the weight of political repression and resultant expulsion from the homeland, the various tribal units that make up the Tibetan nation remain held together by the force of creed and cultural tradition. In some other countries, such as Israel and its Arab neighbours which we shall see in more details later, the bonds of religious fraternity and racial brotherhood are commonly identified as a unifying factor. In the case of Israel, this is why some ultra-right Jewish groups have in recent times begun to introduce legislation that could debar Christian groups which have lately bombarded that country with a wave of evangelism and proselytising. The Israeli government continued to encourage Jewish immigrations from all over the world back to the homeland to the extent that in 1978 it even violated the territorial integrity of a sovereign state by evacuating Ethiopian Jews through 'Operation Black Moses' after what was believed to have been three hundred years of separation.

Muammar Gaddafi, Former President of Libya

In contemporary times, in the Middle East, this has continued to play a major role both in Israeli politics and again in that of its Arab neighbours. Both ways, politicians continue to play on this factor to gain support. In some cases as with Libya and Iraq, a supposed aggression from the United States was used by rulers like Muammar Gaddafi (1942-2011) and Saddam Hussein (1937-2006) not only to survive in power but also to prop up national support. However, this factor has also been well narrated in the history of several other peoples, including the Swiss nation, where the endeavours to be unfettered from the German feudal ball and chain at the very beginning and later on from a French invasion in 1798 are easily referred to.[61]

In the cases of Switzerland, Australia, Israel, and Canada, some authors also put forward that the hostility may also not necessarily be human; it could be dictated by the common need to join forces to surmount the vagaries of nature and geography—isolation, inclement terrain, and climatic alterations. In another sense, the existence of a common national patriarch such as George Washington in the United States, Mohammed Ali Jinnah in Pakistan, or Simon Bolivar in at least five Latin American nations has remained a symbol of national identity in a number of federal states.[62]

This is why in some countries despite the 'triumph' of republican political institutions there is still a deliberate

---

[61] An interesting discussion on this can be found in George A. Codding, *The Federal Government of Switzerland*. Boston: Houghton Miffling, 1961.

[62] See Luis Castro Leiva, *Grand Colombia*, 1991; Augusto Mijares, *The Liberator*. Caracas: Ediciones de La Presidencia de la Republica, 1991.

choice to keep in place, even if only in the form of a fragmentation, a measure of monarchical tradition for the purpose of having in place a national rallying point as seen around the Scandinavian and some other places in Europe and Far East Asia. Despite these lofty factors, which seem to drive federalist-minded people to remain together, it is sad to say that in the majority of countries, including the United States and most especially the new states of Africa and Asia, such a common denominating factor is still being sought and seems far-fetched.

In its actual practice, different approaches have been devised to federalism. In some systems, such as the former Soviet Union, the centre was so powerful as to have the exclusive right to dictate and often overrule on matters that should have been the exclusive reserve of the regions or republics, as they were called. But then it must also be remembered that arising from the haunting reality of its tsarist historical ancestors, (which did not dismantle at the time when its Habsburg and Ottoman peers faded away), as we shall see, the entire federation was completely overwhelmed by the Russian Nation, which made up over 70 per cent of the population and land mass.

Federalist traditions in this category therefore operated more like a unitary system where there existed a hierarchical decentralisation of functions that necessarily drew strength and life only from the centre. This is why the Soviets could impose what those who opposed the system called 'Russianisation' of the Soviet Union.[63]

Many countries especially in Africa and Latin America consider themselves to be federative republics and have constitutional provisions devolving power between 'exclusive' and 'concurrent' issues, but in actual fact, due to either immaturity of the democratic process or some peculiarities of political history, social, or economic circumstances, the regions still remain mere appendages of the headquarters in terms of control and food.[64]

However, as we shall attempt to discuss in more detail later, in a second set of countries, such as Canada, the United States, and Switzerland, the federation principle has been very well developed. So the process of joint use of power between the centre and the subordinate parts is adeptly defined, respected, and functional.[65] Here the

---

[63] For more details on this, see Boladei Igali, 'Nationalism in the Soviet Union'in *Pakistan Journal of International Affairs*, Islamabad, 1991.

[64] For a detailed study on this, see Crawford Young, *The Politics of Cultural Pluralism*. Madison: University of Wisconsin, 1981, and Mae C. King, *Localism and Nation Building*. Ibadan: Spectrum Books, 1988, pp. 46-89. Also see Donald Smiley, 'Cleavages and the Canadian System', in Bolaji Akinyemi, Dele Cole, and Walter Ofonagoro (eds.), *Readings in Federalism*. Lagos: NIIA, pp. 233-335.

[65] Richard Simeon and Ian Robinson, *State, Society and the Development of the Canadian Federalism*. Toronto: University of Toronto Press, 1990, pp. 301-327 as well as Putnam, *ibid.*, p. 40 have given a rather exhaustive treatment of this.

guiding principle is that neither the centre nor the regions should be mere collaterals of the other, but the regions function as distinctive components and relate with the centre in a supplemental manner[66] on such issues as national defence, law and order, external relations, and control over natural resources.

Top legislative and judicial functions are also normally reserved for the centre. But interestingly, in countries like Canada, the provinces have the right to conduct international relations in a number of cultural, educational, and economic issues. In the United States, regions enjoy large margins of autonomy as it relates to justice, law, and order. Laws on control of natural resources are also flexible.

---

[66] See Federakust Papers and Nwankwo, 1998, pp. 151-171.

Chapter Six

Eclipse of the Old Symbolism
of Power and Statehood

O f all the forms of governance instituted by man, by far the most embraced both in terms of antiquity and spread was the 'rule by one man'. In virtually all human societies, a pyramidal chain of authority emerged, but the supreme power at the top of the obelisk was always vested in a single individual or what became known more popularly as monarchy. He was literally the owner of the realm, be it a small homestead, village, clan, tribe, or nation. Hence, most political historians are of the opinion that 'one man rule' was the first form of collective political authority. Exactly how and when the first man lifted his authority over others and what compelled or motivated them to accept is beyond the confines of this book, but it is thought by some writers that:

> the first government was arbitrary and administered by a single person; till it was found by experience that to live by one man's will, was the cause of all of man's misery; and this, he conceded was the origin of inventing laws.[67]

The practice of monarchy in a great number of societies is easy to understand when seen in the light of man's preoccupation, according to Aquinas, to build a bridge between the 'City of God' and the 'City of Man'. The submission to a political sovereign in the terrestrial realm was a kind of shadow of the perfectly everlasting supremacy of God. As the German historian Ernst Kantorowicz explains, the monarchy therefore had to build around itself some trappings of power through images and symbols that made the principal and the entire office objects of awe, reverence, and even fear. The easiest way to do this was to

---

[67] *Encylopaedia Britannica*, 1763, vol. ii, p. 253.

build a divine aura around the institution, i.e. a person with two bodies (a spirited one and a physical one).[68]

Accordingly, over time, traditions and customs were created which depicted the monarchy as either of divine origin or of some other form of supernatural authorisation. This was all the more well captured in Greek mythology, where gods, both female and male, were portrayed as involving themselves in libidinous obsessions with mortals and so producing super humans like Hercules.

Various people around Europe and other parts of the world had similar mythical traditions associating rulership with the divinity. For instance, in Japan, the Emperor was thought of as an heir of the sun god while in Imperial China, as we shall see more succinctly later, political authority was only meaningful if properly identified with the Confucian election. Among the Arab and Jewish societies, the cultural home setting of Islam, Christianity, and Judaism, respectively, civil society was intended as God ruled. The frontier of political leadership was therefore coterminous with the manifestation of the prophetic mantle.

In the case of the Jews, between Abraham and Samuel, God is recorded in the Scriptures to have been leading his people directly through the operation of prophecies of

---

[68] Such images and symbols of power became developed by the various societies.

Ernst Kantorowicz, *The King's Two Bodies: A Study in Political Medieval Political Theology.* Princeton: Princeton University Press, 1997.

various 'called' whose sole duty was to pass on His will to the people and be a mere shepherd for God. Moses is recorded to having been divinely instructed on the minutest details of the plans to leave Egypt, the journey across the Red Sea, and every step that he took during the years in Sinai. God ruled, made the laws directly, and even led his people to wars personally. This was the reason, when the people of Israel asked for a king during Samuel's prophetic reign, that God comforted him not to regard that act as a disaffirmation of his ministry, but a direct rejection of His divine governance. But even at that point, Saul, and later David, on both of whom the task of monarchy fell, had to receive the spiritual licence to rule by being anointed by Samuel, who was effectively God's superior envoy in Israel. The symbol in the choice of David, a shepherd boy, as king underlines that God just wanted somebody to help guide his people rather than rule.

This was why God's rejection of Saul was synonymous with a dethronement; hence, he could not raise a dynasty. And when David's son Solomon took over the throne, he had to make a covenant with God to the effect that his mandate was only to guide and he needed God to saturate him with His wisdom to do so since the people belonged to Him. This tradition was passed on to Christianity and Western political history as we shall see.

We have seen that with the Islamised Arab societies, this pattern was analogous. The community of Muslims which was called 'ummah' was regarded as a group of people held together not by any direct historical genealogy, but by the bond of the spirit, so they had to be governed by the Shari'ah—the laws of Allah, and by the 'Fiqh'—the body of Islamic jurisprudence. The life of the Muslim was to be guided by the Holy Koran, the 'Sunnah'—the practices and teachings of Prophet Mohammed, the founder of the religion, and his sayings or traditions called 'Hadith'.

The accounts of history show that during his lifetime, the Prophet Mohammed never took any position of secular leadership. Because the fact that God was the only sovereign, his duty was to teach and interpret the precepts of Allah to the people, of course with the help of the rest of the canonical retinue such as the Imam. After his death, Islamic societies established elaborate political structures called the 'Caliphate', all basing power on the spiritual authorisation traced back to the Prophet. One Islamic scholar explains this thus:

> *After the Prophet, four of his closest friends and companions . . . became leaders and heads of the Muslim, society and state with the title Khalifat Rasool Allah, that is, caliph or successor to the Messenger of God. They ruled scrupulously according to guidance of the Qur'an and the Prophet's example. After them the political leadership deviated markedly from the example of the Prophet.*[69]

---

[69] Suzanne Haneef, *What Everyone Should Know About Islam and Muslims*. Lahore: Kazi Publications, 1979, p. 24.

As European societies developed their civic tradition, this was the background. With the incursion of Judeo-Christian ideas and the spread of the religion among various Germanic groups, a new impetus for teaching became added to this in the continent. A major turning point in this regard was the conversion of Emperor Constantine (306-337), which now lent to Christian political dogma acceptance in all of Europe. European potentates in the Eastern Empire at Constantinople, therefore, concentrated both spiritual and temporal authority on themselves with the monarch considering himself as a direct successor to the ministry of Christ on the earth.

In the Western empire, the pattern took a slightly different form as political authority which was wielded by Rome faded, so in each place several local institutions developed around the authority of the local clergy, especially the bishop. Among this, the Bishopric of Rome, which had through many devices (both Scriptures and humanistic reason) traced its origin to the Apostle Peter to whom Christ gave 'the keys of the Kingdom of heaven', became a nerve centre.

Hence, papal power developed from Rome, which began to challenge Byzantine claim to dominance. With the conversion of the Franks and the consecration of Charlemagne in 718, the Church in the Western empire established itself and the monarchy which it approved as divinely enthroned.

Anyhow, the Eastern Empire soon fell to the Turks, and so only Rome continued and its influence spread quickly to cover all of Europe. As we see from the *Plowden Reports,* the royal dynasties that emerged in Europe, though under the spiritual influence of the papacy, were considered to be a *persona mixta* or in another sense *res mixta.* The king was thought to possess 'two bodies': the *corpus naturale* and *corpus ecclesiae mysticum.* It was a kind of Christology in which he was a man yet possessing a divine attribute. The idea of imperial *Christomimeles* that emerged was that the King, by virtue of his human nature, was in the form of flesh and blood, but he was the perfect personification of Christ and the Godhead on the earth. He was a *germina persona*—human by nature and divine by grace, and therefore could only be removed by God and could do no wrong in the sight of men.[70]

How Political Liberalism Started

Both in Constantinople and Rome, effective administrative structures were developed for the maintenance of law and order as ecclesiastical and secular authority began to complement and overlap each other. Of special significance were the king's informal advisers or council, who at the time when land ownership and clerical

---

[70] Kantorowicz, *ibid.,* pp. 42-88.

credentials meant all developed largely from the property estate magnates and senior clergy. These councils, assemblies, or great courts as they were called began to assume a more professional and independent outlook, especially during the thirteenth century.

Over time, these ad hoc gatherings of chief tenants were called 'parliaments' in England, while its German equivalent grew from *Diets* to take the name of *Reichtag*. In France, these exclusive convocations took the name *Etats Generaux* and developed to become a three-chamber parliament while in neighbouring Spain it became known as *Cortes*. They also began to assert a right to influence on matters of public policy within the realm. For instance, as early as about 1258-1265, the English parliament began to challenge royal exclusivity to state affairs, and the same happened in France in around 1356, and also in the same year in Aragon under King Alfonso III.

In the course of time, the assertion for power in these hitherto malleable bands, which took different subtle and inconspicuous forms across Europe, began to be more overt.[71] This was more inflamed by the upsurge of knowledge which came with the Renaissance, making room for civic humanism, collapse of religious orthodoxy, and the upsurge of urbanisation.

---

[71] Hugh Seton-Watson, *Nations and States: An Inquiry into the Origin of Nations and the Politics of Nationalism*. London: Taylor & Francis, 1977, pp. 22-87.

At the same time, the reanimation of classical studies and all its neo-liberal attraction by itself became commonly available to all, and a new commercial class who owed their holding to industrious sagacity rather than genealogical patrimony began laying claim to power. There was a new comprehension of individual identity and an inescapable itch for understanding the material world. Obviously, Europe and of course the rest of the world were at that time in a watershed between the dusk of the old imperial legacy and the rise of the nation-state still at dawn. Change in the political configuration of the state was inevitable, so absolutism either had to bend over to accommodate the forces of participation or get completely granulised.

As we shall see shortly with a few examples in Europe and North America, both alternatives occurring as a change in some countries led to a total overhaul of the political system. In other cases, a process of accommodation was quickly crocheted, thus allowing some of the medieval institutions to survive.

The Role of Florentine Scholarship

In Italy, considered the home of the rebirth of knowledge, the letting up of the veil of religious dogmatism began to pave way for attention being granted to the seemingly maverick but intellectually lush ideas of Niccolo Machiavelli (1467-1527). In both his best-known works *The*

Prince and others such as *Discourses on the First Ten Books of Livy*, the Florentine statesman applauded the quintessence of religion in the ordering of human existence, but objected to its rather ponderous control on statecraft.[72]

Similar to humanists before him, such as the Dutch scholar Albertus Magnus (1206-1280), he equated politics, just like medicine and jurisprudence, as belonging to the realm of scholarship and that it should therefore be left to its practitioners; while in his abstractions about power, he exalted the 'reason of the state' higher than morality.[73]

Niccolo Machiavelli

---

[72]   Maurizion Viroli, *A Biography of Machiavelli*. Princeton: Princeton University Press, 2002.

[73]   Skinner, 1989, pp. 122-142.

The ideas of Machiavelli and the influence which they wielded in contemporary Italy can only be better appreciated against the background of his claimed passion for his city, Florence, and for ultimate unity of Italy. He therefore argued for continuity of the Italian political legacy of the 'Republic' and tried to develop theories that would advance this. Like the politicians of Ancient Rome who had always tried to out-beat each other in the Senate by play-acting their presumed love for their 'polis', the vision of Machiavelli was to return to that setting under a prince. In contrast, neither Cesare Borgia (1475 or 1476-1507) nor the Medicis would take unbridled power for themselves, but would rather be the curator of the representative participation in politics. The mythical prince would in so doing help restore the Italian nation and well-being of its people to its glory. These ideas formed the bedrock for the declaration of a 'reason for the state', which deeply influenced not just Italian politics but spread quickly to the rest of Europe.

How 'The King in Parliament' was Born

In the rest of Europe, a new wave of change began to take hold. Let us start with England where monarchy had been perpetual even before the Norman invasion of 1066, which is considered an important landmark in the country's

111

medieval history.[74] It is not necessary to rehash the history here, but it would serve to mention that the branching of the parliament into the 'Lords' and, as the name would suggest, the more active and vocal 'Commons' had taken place during the Middle Ages.

As the Middle Ages came to a close, the parliament in England positioned itself so as to have a say within the scheme of things on such subjects as taxation. The stance and political posture of the Commons had already begun to be influenced by the writings of Sir John Frotescue's piece in 1469, which began to rationalise on the existence of a *dominium politicum et regale* in England and its absence in France where the monarchy was absolute. During the period of the Tudor reign in England (1485-1603), very little conflict surfaced between parliament and the monarchy, since the former always conformed to the wishes of the ruler.

---

[74] You can read more about this in Anthony H. Birch *The British System of Government*. London: Allen and Unwin, 1986, p. 30.

JAMES I.

King James I of England

However, things began to change quickly with the ascendance to the throne by members of the Stuart Dynasty (1603-1714). One writer sums up the new change as follows: 'James I outlined in his speech to parliament in 1610 the doctrine of the divine rights of kings, which combined assertions of the sovereignty of the crown, and the divine ordination of royal authority and the hereditary title of the throne.' Quoting ebulliently from Scriptures and natural law, James I (1603-1625) had on that occasion pressed home the point that the King was absolute, and he was firmly guided by these two sources of power in the administration of the people and dispensation of justice among them. But inasmuch as his power base was from God, by nature he had no obligation to be limited by parliament in the running of the state. He was above the state and could not be subject to laws made by constituents of the realm. Plainly said:

> *the state of monarchy is the supremest thing upon the earth; for kings are not only God's Lieutenants upon the earth, and sit upon God's throne, but even by God himself they are called gods.*[75]

Even though the King did not try to practice what he had so eloquently explained, as would be expected, members of parliament both individually and collectively reacted sharply to this. The reaction of the parliament called *Assertion of Rights of 1628* was sent to the successor to the throne—King Charles I. Although his father, King James I, had only theorised on these issues, the young monarch tried to implement them by raising taxes without turning to the parliament.

As the challenge from the parliament became more forceful, he went on to suspend it for a period of eleven years and ruled alone, thereby bringing about a civil war during the 1640s. By the time a settlement was arranged in 1646, the King lost more than a pound of flesh to the parliament which increased its power drastically, from mere advisory to

---

[75] King James I, Speech to Parliament, March, 1610.

consultative and thereon to law-making roles. For instance, besides having a say over taxation, the parliament added to its powers the approval of high appointments such as ministers, judges, and those of ecclesiastical echelon. They now also had a control over the maintenance of a standing militia.

In the ensuing peace process, King Charles I (1625-49) in his *Reply to Nineteen Propositions* of June 1642 conceded that 'in this kingdom the laws are jointly made by a King, by the house of peers, and by a House of Commons chosen by the people, all having free votes and particular privileges'.

Although these principles as conceded still produced much mopiness in the royalist camp, they have been used continuously to govern and order the British political system. It was in the refinement and fine-tuning process that the same King Charles I lost his own head to the guillotine in 1649. As events continued to unfold, a rather tyrannical rule of King James II followed after the short stay of King Charles II, leading to an invasion by the Dutchman William of Orange in 1688, then the passage of the Bill of Rights in 1689 and the eventual Act of Settlement in 1701. This was a kind of non-violent revolution in which the power of the monarchy to make and suspend laws or raise taxes or impair free speech in parliament were annulled. If it were to survive, the kingship would share power with the people as represented by their elected parliamentarians. It was after this event that British writers of the time could boast:

> *The governments of France and Spain are generally arbitrary; though they differ as much from the governments of Turkey and other eastern empires, where absolute despotism prevails, as they do from England and other European nations where liberty is said to flourish in its fullest perfection.*[76]

It is important to mention that the cultivation of this British system was also influenced by the ideas of social contract philosophers on the scene. The most prominent of these were Thomas Hobbes and John Locke, even though they were antithetical on their substantive philosophical thoughts. For instance, in contrast to each other, Hobbes with the confusion of the English civil war just before him abhorred the Machiavellian and Miltonian mode for civic enthusiasm while in both his *Second Treatise* and *Two Treatises of Government* Locke laid stress on what he called natural rights.[77]

Nonetheless, one uniting factor among these two thinkers is the recognition of human equality and individuality of man. Their ideas also coincided on the fact that political authority is not just divinely imposed but conceded by man. Freedom to them therefore was the 'absence of coercion or the absence of external obstacles'.

---

[76] *Encylopaedia Britannica*, 1765, vol. ii, p. 727.

[77] J. G. Merquior, *Liberalism: Old and New*. Boston: Twayne Books, 1991, p. 10.

Even after these events, Locke and others, such as Jeremy Bentham (1748-1842) and Tom Paine (1737-1809), continued to advocate for continued political liberalism, if not total republicanism. This is why most scholars hold the view that the Revolution of 1688 although thuggish in nature and spearheaded by Anthony Ashley-Cooper (1652-1699), 2nd Earl of Shaftesbury, could rightly be said to have been intellectually authored and masterminded by Locke, whose ideas formed the dictum of the revolutionary vanguard.[78]

---

[78] Van Doren, *ibid.*, pp. 216-223.

Chapter Seven

Birth of a New Reason for the State

I n some other societies, rather than make compromises with a supposed supernatural design of monarchy, the wind of change of the day recorded more far-reaching results. Men began to define sovereignty not in terms of an individual or a select group of persons, but as sourced from the people. The movement of neo-liberal ideas began to oscillate around different corners of what may be called the known world, which was susceptible to European influence. At the time, Europe already had strong contacts with various African and Asiatic people, but the nature of those societies made the penetration of such liberal ideas slow. The Ottomans were also neighbours of various kings, but the impact was again slower for cultural reasons. Of particular significance in this respect were Europe's colonial possessions abroad in North and South America.

Before considering the impact of the republican ideas in the 'New World', let us pause to comment on the debate regarding the exact directions in which the ideas moved. Some circles within the humanities schools in Europe, particularly Italy, are of the view that liberal ideas were solely exported from the source to these colonies. But a number of American researchers tend to suggest that at that stage of its crude beginnings such free thoughts were received on the other side of the Atlantic, where a kind of intellectual catharsis was applied to them and the refined ideas were re-exported back to the continent and thereon to South America.

Scholars from the United States who are of this persuasion have always tended to claim for themselves a kind of messianic calling towards giving assistance to prematurely miscarried European ideas, which were quickened, made to attain their proper intellectual formation, in this case its civic-humanist element, and then returned to Europe. Well, this is not surprising as the American State seems to have always had a philosophical foundation based on a kind of rationalism of puritanist fibre. After all, do not the history books show that the founding fathers of the American colonies had to leave the comfort of their homelands to unknown lands to escape the corruption and peccadillity of their people?[79]

Be that as it may, in one way or the other, what seems certain is that the influence and inspiration was not unidirectional but to a large extent was of dual carriage and mutual in impact.[80] In the same way, it would seem spurious for either *pax Europa* or *pax Americana* to claim for itself a kind of refining sanctuary and export platform for the republican thesis; *per contra* both the polishing process and the influence that republicanism sent forth were mutual.

For instance, the ideas of Machiavelli and later on Montesquieu, Locke, and Paine had become common handbooks in North and South Americas. At the same time, the thoughts of Thomas Jefferson (1743-1826), Antonio de Narino (1765-1823), and the much urbane Francisco de Miranda (1750-1816), among others, were the subject of attention among academic and political classes all over Europe. So actual enlisting in the wars of liberation or independence fought on both sides was not delimited by the Atlantic Ocean. If anything at all, that mass of water rather

---

[79] E. Brooks Holifield, *Era of Persuasion*. Boston: Twayne Books, 1989, pp. 79-85, 90-109 and see Richard Olson, *The Emergence of the Social Sciences*. Boston: Twayne Books, 1993, pp. 36-41.

[80] J. G. A. Pocock, 'Machiavellian Moment' and 'Between Gog and Magog'. See also Merquior, op. cit., pp. 15-36; Fred Sturm, 'Dependence and Ibero-American Philosophy', in *Journal of History of Ideas*, 1980; Holifield, *ibid.*, pp. 5-9.

served as a uniting bridge for rabidity of ideas and a pathway for republican zealots.

'In God We Trust'

It is not surprising that of all the main political revolutions that followed 1688, the first which had a global impact did not come from the land mass of Europe but came across from Britain's thirteen territorial possessions. Located along the Atlantic seaboard from New Hampshire to Georgia, these American colonies, as they were called, prospered tremendously and began to build a society that had great promises for the future. As their economic fortunes increased, the leaders began to seek some form of social and economic autonomy.

As these moves became noticed, concessions similar to those made by the monarchy to the parliament and other measures of autonomy were at this time granted to these colonies, but much areas of conflict still existed.[81] The problem was that like the rest of Europe of the time, Britain was not only entering into a phase of modernisation, but also stretching itself into a new wave of imperial expansion. In the international politics of the day, that was the main way of consolidating its mounting national prestige and integrity in the concert of Europe's fledgling nation-states. It was also

---

[81]   Seton-Watson, *ibid.*, pp. 198-219.

a time of intense diplomacy dominated by expensive wars and alliances. As a matter of fact, the Anglo-Franco War which led to the eventual acquisition of Quebec involved an annual budget outlay of about £14 million throughout the period. Since the home government was almost bankrupt, the burden of taxation fell on those rich colonists across the Atlantic.

The home government and the colonists also had other disputes over the need for a direct parliamentary representation back in Westminster and the lack of autonomy over a number of appellate judicial matters that could have been handled within the colonies. Maybe what Britain forgot at the time was that when a child reaches a certain age measures of autonomy have to be granted to him otherwise he begins to question the relationship. This was exactly what happened, as all these matters began to provoke thoughts in the minds of the colonists regarding the benefits from the attachment of the umbilical cord to Britain. On all counts, the relationship seemed to them to be parasitic.

With the home government's unilateral passage of the Proclamation of 1763 debarring further expansion by the colonists into Indian territories, the situation of tension and animosity became even more pointed. This move by the Crown made sense to both Britain and its third parties, as the need arose to have peace in the Americas, but to the land-hungry colonists it spurred open disagreements, leading to an armed conflict in 1775. By the following year, though still much divided among themselves on virtually every issue apart from the quest for liberty, the leaders went on to the Declaration of Independence, which was made on July 4, 1776, and also adopted the name United States of America. In the chapeau to the declaration, the orchestrators of the document clearly stated:

> *When in the course of human events, it becomes necessary for one people to dissolve the political bands which have connected with another, and to assume among the powers of the earth, the separate and equal station to which the Laws of Nature and Nature's God entitle them, a decent respect to the opinion of mankind requires them that they should declare the cause which impel them to separation. We hold these truths to be self evident, that all men are created equal, that they are endowed by their Creator with certain inalienable rights . . . That to secure these Rights, Governments are instituted among men, deriving their just powers from the consent of the governed.*

Like Locke, they repudiated the existence of an unjust government to be contrary to the designs of the Creator. Although the initial plan of the fifty-five signatories of this declaration and their other supporters was to have an autonomous state within the imperial fold, something similar to Canada and Australia today, by the time the war was over in 1783 it had given them total independence. The world's first modern republic emerged with a structure that emphasised that political power could only be exercised by the consent of the governed.[82]

Subsequently, the Americans elaborated on the detailed working of the system, including the 1788 Constitution which stressed on the need to have a federate structure. Though strongly opposed by many, a combination of adroit diplomacy and intellectual rigour invested by Alexander Hamilton and James Madison saw it through, providing for a strong centre with its exclusive powers and yet fairly autonomous branches on several issues. At the centre was the 'President'—something similar to a Hobbessian leviathan or a Prince who owed his position neither to birth nor to inheritance, but to the will of the people as collectively expressed through their elective power. In order to check his power, he worked closely with two chambers of lawmakers, none of whom again owed his position to patrimonial benefaction. In 1791, this constitution went through its first amendment, by embedding a Bill of Rights.

From Plato to Rousseau, men had always thought that pure republicanism and federalism could only work in a territorially circumscribed setting, or in order to be stable it had to be compromised with monarchy and aristocracy as was the case in Ancient Rome or Britain, still familiar to all of that day. The American Revolution and the system of an elected all-powerful 'prince' rule came to repudiate that notion. It was not necessary for the system to have

---

[82] Van Doren, *ibid.*, pp. 223-228.

a monarchical-type figure for the purpose of national unity, but a banner of liberty and common heritage of the organised society were intended as the binding factors.

This development had a blazon effect for the republican cum federalist credo. That is not to say that the new system did not have its own defects. As a matter of fact, its problems are today enormous and the promise of social justice and egalitarianism which it presaged still remains a chimera.[83] Francisco de Miranda who witnessed the actual formative phase in this model republic forebode in his diary as early as 1784:

> *I had the pleasure of communicating with the famous republican and very prominent actor in the recent revolution, Mr Samuel Adams . . . We had some drawn-out conversations regarding the constitution of this Republic. As for two objections which I raised on the subject . . . The first is that in a democracy the foundation of which is virtue, no position whatsoever indicated for it, and on the contrary all the dignities and the power was given to property, which is precisely the poison of a similar republic . . .* [84]

---

[83] Scheltens, 1977, p. 320. See William Bennett, *The Devaluing of America*. New York: Summit Book, 1992, p. 65; Nozick, *ibid.*, 1986, pp. 183-189, John Warwick Montgomery, *The Shaping of America*. Minneapolis: Bethany Fellowship, 1976;

[84] For a contemporary reading, among others listed above also see Francisco Miranda, *Travels in America*, 1784, pp. 163, 81.

The emergence of the United States of America on the global political scene, as it were, brought a new realism to the process of state formation. The United States entered the global scene as a sui generis state—none ever of its kind. The closest to it were the Roman and Greek city states, with a clear divergence from the latter. Unlike in the old realm, the 'prince' was to be universally elected with a fixed tenure and would rule under laws as enshrined in constitution. The process of building the state was not without its own problems both at the time of its founding and also now. The society remained fractious and polarised along racial, national, and sub-religious compartments (Protestants, Evangelicals, Catholics, Jews, Mormons, Muslims, etc.). The outbreak of Civil War (1861-1865), shortly after independence, showed that the centrifugal force inherent in the system was not only potent but also real. The war itself, known as the 'War between the States', engaged the north and south which was centred on various conflicting issues that claimed lives of at least 750,000 soldiers, excluding civilians. For the purpose here, it will be enough to surmise that it included such issues as slavery, centre-regional relationship, and other economic and social issues. The southern slave states also favoured confederal relations, i.e. a weak centre, and wanted the status quo maintained and possibly extended to other parts of the country. They threatened to secede in case of failure to do this. The then newly elected president, Abraham Lincoln, leading the unionists, rejected this proposal, thereby leading to one of the bloodiest but sadly fratricidal wars ever that was fought.

James Madison, American Politician and Political Philosopher, Fourth President of the United States

Abraham Lincoln, 16th President of
the United States of America

Like other countries whose political history has been
written on the blood of its people, the end of the war
brought the American State and people much closer.
Also having occurred at the time of the beginning of the
industrial revolution, post-war interaction, contacts, and
reconstruction became enhanced. The war also taught the

new American State a lesson that the interest of states is intrinsically determined by selfish factors. The southern states used what is referred to as 'King Cotton' diplomacy by shutting down export to the European countries of Britain and France in order to force them to support the secession move, because their industrial sector was highly dependent on cotton textiles. This move was unsuccessful because they had already stockpiled cottons and could not risk going into war with the United States. Europe therefore allowed their American partners to fight and sort out themselves. Americans also came to appreciate the importance and need to preserve their territorial integrity.

The American State came to appreciate more the virtue of being strong internally and that of building a stronger federation and republic. Although some of the legacy issues such as race remain critical factors, America has continued to promote free society where the best of humankind have found a home. The best in commerce and enterprise was easily attracted by the allure of its capitalism and free market. Similarly, the other virtue of freedom enshrined in the country's constitution and Bill of Rights (the first amendments to the constitution) adopted by the Congress in 1789 was magnetic in pulling to this country some of the best around the world.

It is a fact that the United States was not an acting combating state in both World War I and II but was dragged into the war; it ultimately determined how the war ended on both occasions. World War II also helped the United

States to come out of the worst economic depression in the country's history. The massive increase in government expenditure on military production for the war brought total recovery from the depression. In the post-war era, America became the sanctuary for some of the best intellectuals, especially people from the Jewish community in Europe, all of whom joined to build the country. America did not only determine the post-World War II order but also became the dominant power. Much more than any other human civilisation, it also became the world's superpower and a dominant welfare state in the midst of livid capitalism.

The country contributes only 6 per cent to the world's population but about 28 per cent to its GDP. Questions have commonly been asked about what has kept America strong and united and whether it will last longer. In answering this question, it should be noted that the American dream and ideal have been founded on certain virtues which still remain strong today. Despite some right wing tendencies which were borne out of ignorance of the historical antecedents of America's greatness, the process of aggregating some of the world's best into one political space has been this country's forte. Besides the great premium placed on agriculture, infrastructure, military might based on technology, scientific advancement, and huge expenditure on education, research and innovation will, for a long time in human history, keep the country dominant and internally strong. In terms of agriculture, the American farmers who make up only 2 per cent of the country's population cultivate an area of nearly 922 million acres of farmland but lead in the production of virtually every known crop and livestock. As a matter of fact, United States' farm production places her in a position to be able to feed the whole world uninterrupted for a long period.

Theodore Roosevelt, Former American President

Similarly, a major jinx, the racial barrier, seems to have been broken with the ascendance of the 44th President, Barack Obama, who is of African American descent. Notwithstanding this, the country remains on the precipice on many fronts. More so, from its founding the country has had a great propensity to remain on top, with great leaders such as George Washington, Abraham Lincoln, John Adams, Thomas Jefferson, Harry Truman, Dwight Eisenhower, Franklin Roosevelt, Theodore Roosevelt, John Kennedy, Ronald F. Reagan, and Bill Clinton. One of its founding leaders, Theodore Roosevelt (1857-1919) advocated the need for the pursuit of 'strenuous life'—one of physical agility, moral rectitude, valour, and heroism, a lifestyle of striving to remain on top. Besides these, America is perhaps the most endowed country in the world in terms of natural resources and has robust scientific knowledge to use them in sustainable manner.

Mi alma es La Republica

But it was much more than that, as the floodgates of liberal political thought and revolutionary zeal in the countries of South America, starting with Haiti and onwards to Venezuela, started to lead to strong independence moves. As former Oxford but Venezuelan-born researcher Luis Castro Leiva puts it:

> *France became an ideal abstract model, which mirrored the pitfall of the inevitable extension of republican faith or, at the very least, of liberal convictions.*[85]

---

[85] Leiva, *ibid.*, p. 208.

Having said that, it may be unnecessary to return to the argument as to how the wind of the liberal ideas blew between the south and north of the Atlantic shores. But it would be important to comment on the much generalised axiomatisation which tends to suggest that Ibero-American philosophy only occupies itself with problems generated within European and North American thought. It needs be accentuated that beyond the impact of the events in the United States and France and the 'instinctualism' which they may have had for Latin America, the birth of republicanism as a political credo was to a large extent home-grown in these countries, arising out of their own peculiar circumstances. Indeed, Fred Sturm argues that philosophical thought in *tierra firme* emerged as a synthesised synergism of a rather centrifugal interplay between Amerindian, European, and African cultures.[86]

Regarding political traditions, the emergence of well-linked republican perceptions by Simon Bolivar, Francisco Miranda, Jose San Martin, and the pro-clerical Miguel Hidalgo (1753-1811), among several others, was a precipitate of internal contradictions which arose after four hundred years of colonial rule—one of the oldest periods ever of alien rule in world history.

Furthermore, there is no doubt that several of these Hispanic American leaders had travelled widely within Europe and had been well nourished with liberal political

---

[86]   Sturm, *ibid.*

thought in leading intellectual circles in those countries. Related more directly to their own circumstances, they were also not unaware of the pro-liberal move in metropolitan Spain from the time of the bubonic ascendance to the period under Felipe V. During the reign of Fernando VII, a deep crisis of authority generated within Castile and Aragon, following the much abasing Napoleonic invasion. Some like Miranda who had even fought besides Napoleon and interacted with the leaders of the American Revolution were not oblivious of the republic ambience. To summarise, it is noteworthy to say that a distinct philosophical world view arose out of these events in their relation to the real situation on the ground in South America. It was also in this process that charismatic leaders such as Simon Bolivar emerged, vowing to liberate the entire continent and set up republics or rather a united confederation of the various states in the region. So between 1810 and 1830 through wars of independence and bloodshed, the huge colonial empire from Tijuana in Mexico to Chile which started way back in the fifteenth century by Fernando II and Isabella I collapsed, giving way to republics.

'Equality, Fraternity, and Liberty'—Social Contract in Practice

At a time when Europe was undergoing fundamental political changes, the appeal of a revolution in the Americas that based its doctrine on virtue, no matter how imperfect it seemed, was quick to spread, especially in France. The French nation itself began to take form, from way back in the first century when the land 'Transalpine Gaul' came under Roman rule, and steadily built one of the most influential and prestigious monarchies in Europe. The fact that France became the first locale for revolution and the impact it had on modern civilisation is not far off.

As we saw already from the medieval days of Aquinas, Paris had become the centre of knowledge and scholarship, particularly of radical thought in Europe.[87] The 'Age of Reason' itself could not have had a better end than with the contributions of the nearly contemporary thinkers—Louis Montesquieu and Jean Jacques Rousseau. The ideas of these political theorists and the French experience deserve a more copious review to better appreciate the French Revolution.

With the platform afforded for intellectual expression by the *Paris Academe* at Sorbonne and the encyclopaedia, these two philosophers began essaying on various topics on the political ideal. In the case of Rousseau, his ideas called attention to the natural purity of man, and particularly in his *Discours sur l' origine de l'inegalite*, he opened discussions on the inherent equality of mankind. He absolved nature for the ills of society and blamed the system for operating against the natural ordinance of order and fairness. With his later masterpiece, *Du Contract Social,* which came out

---

[87] Van Doren, *ibid.*, pp. 117-125.

in 1762, Rousseau both repudiated the existing ethical and juridical foundations of French and European society of his days and advocated that the legitimacy of government remained only valid in as much as it conformed to the *volonte generale*.[88]

The act of coming together brings about a course of superimposition of the collective moral will over that of all individuals, but in so far as they still have the prerequisite of bringing about the collective will or assembly, they in a way still retain the prerogative vested in them from the beginning. The process of coming together is simply a symbolic link between the public and the individual, so it is in a sense like each individual making a contract with himself. Rousseau argued that the sovereign or public regime created is therefore expected to be altruistic and entirely set apart for the collective and, in so doing, the individual. So to him, society ought to be a true republic that was held together by a covenant between the individual and the collective and between the ruler and the ruled.

The ideas of Rousseau laid the foundation for the French social democratic state and advocated for the change of social relations from the timeworn dynastic guild to the rule of moral injunction. However, the actual direct impact on republican postulations in France of the day came from Montesquieu. Towards the concluding part of the prologue to his classic *L'Espirit des Lois*, he described that grandeur

---

[88] Scheltens, *ibid.*, p. 232.

academic venture having the intention of persuading those who command, to increase their knowledge in why they ought to prescribe, and those 'who obey to find a new pleasure' resulting from obedience. Modern scholars rank *The Spirit of Law* as one of the masterpieces in the chronicle of political theory and in the annals of jurisprudence. Its significance lies in the fact that Montesquieu displayed both a high level of erudition in reference to virtually every known work before him and in a very ingenious manner developed his independent points of views. Chapters 2 and 3 of that work bring out a classification of government not just in terms of the rather familiar categorisation of aristocracy, democracy, and monarchy, but in accordance to three 'species' with rather anthropomorphic attributes which he ascribed to each. For a successful republic, he underlined the importance of ensuring the existence of virtue, which should include a transparent and unfettered procedure for the citizen to exercise his suffrage.

With regards to aristocracy, the philosopher reasoned that 'the best aristocracy is that in which those who have no share in the legislature are so few and inconsiderable that the governing party has no interest in oppressing them'. He impressed aristocratic regimes to endeavour to involve the people and operate as if they were in a democracy (republic).

Montesquieu, however, sharply censured absolutism. Unlike the other two categories to which he prescribed basic standards for success, his direct censure of despotism through words such as 'naturally lazy', 'voluptuous', and 'educated in a prison by corrupt eunuchs' clearly emphasised the shame against it and the passion for a republic. He sadly concluded that the monarchy could only work well in the 'orient' because of the inherent servility of the people and surmised that unlike the republic where virtue is supreme 'there is no great share of probity necessary' in a monarchy. In the rest of the work, Montesquieu described the ideal governmental setup as one in which a well-defined 'separation of powers' existed side by side with a proper foundation of 'jurisprudence'. The ideas of Montesquieu in various forms contributed in a great way to the understanding of the nature of government and sensitised the French society for change.

The 1700s were for the French people and their society a period of great intellectual exertion and social stress. The absolutism of the Bourbon monarchy combined with the appalling social inequalities expanded to create much social and political disaffection in between the reigns of King Louis XIV (1638-1715) and King Louis XVI (1754-1793). For instance, although Montesquieu had warned that 'no nobility no monarchy', from 1648 to 1789, the estates' general was not summoned. Just like England, as we have seen already, the price of war within Europe and the pursuit of external policy took a great toll on both nobility and peasantry alike. At the same time, the individualistic and rationalist tilt of political philosophy made both the monarchy and the Church lose much of the former aura.

The ensuing crisis and counter-reactions led to the chains of revolts that took place between 1787 and 1789. It was in August of 1789 that the monarchy had to concede to the new regime as expressed through the Declaration of the Rights of Man and of the Citizen, which professed equality, fraternity, and liberty of mankind.[89] A Civil Constitution of the Clergy was also made widely known in 1790, limiting the role of the priestly class in civil administration. The revolution which became dominated by the National Assembly and various vanguards or clubs, especially the Jacobeans and the less influential rivals, the Girondists, ultimately led to the fading out of the monarchy, feudalism, and clericalism. It should be mentioned that the Jacobeans were originally a radical political group called the Club Breton of Versailles. They changed their appellation in 1789 after coming into Paris and taking over the premises of the 'Jacobean' Dominican Fathers. Eventually, the club became associated with acts of terror, especially under the near totalitarian period of its leader, Maximilien de Robespierre (1758-1794). A republican state that was intended at being a model for the rest of the world was thereafter established.

---

[89] Leiva, *ibid.*, 1989, p. 208.

The Rest of Europe

True to the aspirations, the events in France spread to other places in nearby Europe, especially in the Lower Countries, the Iberian Peninsula, and Scandinavia. In all these places, political change led to the setting up of a constitutional monarchy, just like in England. In the very heart of Europe, change was less rooted as strong monarchies, such as Austro-Hungarians, the Ottomans, and Russians, tried reluctantly to share power. For instance, having just made the *Ausgleich* institute a dual monarchy in 1867, the Habsburg Emperors Francis Joseph (1830-1916) and Charles (1887-1922) adopted the economic and social reforms under the Emancipation of the Russian Serfs.

The abolition of this feudalistic guild gave the empire transitory social peace until the outbreak of the First World War (1914-18) and its eventual destruction. This event together with the simultaneous dismemberment of the Ottoman Empire, which also formed part of the central powers during that global conflict, provided the forerunner to a chain of developments. The Ottomans themselves had held sway over most of Central Europe since the thirteenth century. Though stopped by the Habsburgs and the tsar from moving south-east, they had a strong presence in the Balkans and Asia Minor.

The end of war in 1918 created a number of 'orphan states' in the Balkans and Central Europe. The Polish, Hungarians, Bulgarians, Albanians, and Austrians opted to be alone, but the Czechs decided to team up with the Slovakians. Believing that a united Slavic front would be the best bulwark against predacious neighbours, Croatia, Slovania, Dalmatia, Serbia, and Bosnia all came together to form Yugoslavia. In almost all these places, states were formed around some form of constitutional monarchy or outright republics.

The other main development that would be important to touch on is Russia where Tsar Alexander II (1818-1881) had languidly made political reforms in 1861, abolishing serfdom, but at a time when change and knowledge was so freely taking over Europe like a whirlwind, that large empire remained largely closed. Even further changes and liberalisation by Tsar Nicholas II (1868-1918) including the establishing of the 'Duma'—an assembly for the people in 1905, failed to assuage the revolutionary mood. In February 1917, a revolution led by the Communist Bolsheviks, which can be compared in magnitude only to the French Revolution, sacked the monarchy and established a socialist republic. This we will see in more details later.

Unlike the situation in the United States of America, state formation in Europe were around individual nations or at best a collection of nations, and most were mono-national in composition. For instance, United Kingdom comprised essentially the English, Welsh, Irish, and Scottish while Spain brought together Spaniards, Basques, Galicians, Catalans, and Octalians as dominant groups. But other states such as Germany, France, and Italy were essentially

Germans, French, and Italian in character. In a sense, and despite the level of homogeneity, pockets of minorities, either of nationality, sub-nationality, culture, or creed, exist in every European country. This is besides the variants of Romani (Gypsy) people who are indigenous and live all across Europe.

The process of consolidation of the state building in the modern sense was therefore free from some of the other ethno-religious divisive ingredient inherent in the United States and in some of the post-colonial states which we shall see later. The other advantage which Europe enjoyed was the fact that the actual experience of building modern states started on their land. Europe, unlike other parts of the world, entered the new global political system with broad experiences spanning many centuries. States in Europe were therefore not artificial creations, but arose out of many centuries of experimentation through conscious efforts at coming together. Indeed, most of the instruments forming their modern states are documented after atrocious wars and laborious peace and treaties. Europe was, therefore, largely politically mature and had long dealt with some of the splintering integrative issues which continue to plague much of the nation-states that emerged around the world.

In addition to this was the factor of robust social and economic advancement. For nearly two thousand years, Europe had dominated world affairs in virtually every area of human endeavour. As a matter of fact, by the seventeenth century, the entire world, including the rather infantile

United States, was merely the backyard of Europe. Social and economic development and advancement in science and technology and physical development in Europe towered several centuries above every part of the world. Industrial revolution itself was the last of Europe's great achievement, which moved the continent further ahead of other parts of the world. The profile of several European countries such as Vikings Scandinavia, Spain, Portugal, Holland, Belgium, Britain, and France shows that at different times, they ultimately passed the baton of global dominance from one to one another. The continent cumulatively benefited from the progress thus made in human development. What this meant is that Europeans entered the new global political order relatively comfortable and catered for. Although local expression of descent occurred intermittently, the main challenge unlike, say, the United States, Asia, or Africa was not a question of whether people should stay together but that of concerns on how to make life better for the people.

Still seeing further, having achieved a measure of domestic ethno-political comfortableness, European leaders such as Jean Monnet, Robert Schuman, and Konrad Adenauer, as early as the post World War II era began to think of how to galvanise regional integration. The European Coal and Steel Community (ECSC) was formed in 1951 (Treaty of Paris, July 23, 1952) while the supranational European Economic Community (EEC) was formed in 1958 (Treaty of Rome, January 1, 1958). As the body continued to grow both in membership and scope and bound of relations, the Maastricht Treaty of November 1, 1993, gave birth to the European Union, and the Lisbon Treaty of 2009 gave it a legal or rather constitutional framework for the existence of a union, a community, and a common continental government. In between, the numbers increased from the initial six to twenty-eight. A common monetary union (Eurozone), though still holding grudge against some Euro-sceptics like Britain and Sweden, came into place in 2002. The combined population of Europe is 503 million people according to the 2012 estimate and the GDP is $16.54 trillion, i.e. 20 per cent of the world. Europe also has a common foreign policy, a common external defence policy, a common parliament, a common court of justice, and commonly harmonised policies on almost all internal affairs. Even more than the United States, the citizens of the European Union continue to enjoy the highest per capita income in the world and the best standards of living. Unlike in the United States, the brand of capitalism in Europe appears to have a greater human face, to the extent that extremities of existential conditions between the poor and the rich are reduced.

In Scandinavia in particular, a model of social welfare is practiced through the instrument of taxation to ensure that the societies are kept free of the extremely poor as much as possible. A few countries in Europe, such as Sweden, officially have no poor person by the United Nations standard. Europe therefore continues to stand at par with the United States in terms of investment in research, innovation, and science and technology. The European Institute of Technology at Budapest is one of the world's leading centres for development of all branches of human knowledge in science.

This has taken the whole discourse of integration to a level that is beyond this study and indeed offers a challenge or paradigm for Africa where states are still dawdling, though undauntedly instilling international cohesion and regional integration. But whether this will spare the gigantic Europe from the blight of an echo of internal grumbling and grumpiness, especially on the morality of what some consider an effort in eclipsing their heritage of pseudo identity and in reducing poverty through a 'neighbourhood' policy, remains to be seen.

Chapter Eight

Integration and Pluralism in Western Democracy: Switzerland and Canada

T he emergence of the United States of America as a unified entity came to represent the iconoclastic modern state. It was federal, racially diverse, a republic, and democratic. But it was also a largely and openly negotiated union of federative units.

In the rest of the world, rather than form a home for a people of a select ethnic or religious extraction, the modern states largely came to represent a place of diversity. There exist very few countries in the world today where homogeneity of human groups in sociological and ethno-demographic terms could be claimed. In places like Tibet where religious congruity could be claimed, it is known that much diversity of ethnic expression exists.

Similarly in Somalia there is a fair level of ethnic, linguistic, and religious monotony at the national level, but some other forms of insular variations ranging from clannish doctrine and religious non-conformism express themselves, thereby keeping the country in contemporary times in persistent political and social commotion. Accordingly, what the modern state has preoccupied itself with since its emergence, and like a growing child continues to aspire to do, is to keep balancing the needs of various forms of diversities which give to it a defining characteristic.[90]

A few examples of the exact process of state formation and the taking on of the gauntlet of national integration around the world would be useful to explain some of these phenomena.

---

[90] The people are all Somalis and 99.9% Muslim.

The Helvetica Federation of Switzerland

1 APPENZELL AUSSERRHODEN
2 APPENZELL INNERRHODEN
3 BASEL-LANDSCHAFT
4 BASEL-STADT
5 NIDWALDEN
6 OBWALDEN
7 SCHAFFHAUSEN
8 SOLOTHURN

Detailed Vector Map of Switzerland
with Administrative Divisions

Unlike much of the rest of Europe where the phenomenon of nationalised states started, the political history of Switzerland remains as peculiar as its geography. Isolated within the continent's main mountain ranges, the country's small terrain in the centre of Europe comprises nearly as many miscellanies as ethnic and linguistic diversities. As one publication puts it:

If one were to try to capture in one word the essence
of Switzerland as a whole, it would surely be the word
'diversity' that would be most appropriate.[91]

The great ingenuity which the Swiss adopted in turning
the challenge of a rather difficult topography with only water
as a natural resource into one of the world's most affluent
societies was also distinct in the formation of one of the
world's most prided multinational states, and for about
seven hundred years, this country has also maintained what
is termed 'the world's oldest democracy'.[92] It is on account
of all these that some authors insisted on referring to the
Swiss example as not a multinational state but instead a
'multilingual nation'.[93]

The nearly eight million population mix is defined
according to language groups, consisting of about 65 per
cent German, 18 per cent French, 10 per cent Italian, 2 per
cent Spanish, and about 1 per cent Rhaeto-Romanish. All of
the first three are recognised as official languages, while the
fourth or fifth, which is a Latin dialect, has been given the
status of 'national language'. These are, besides the various
less significant dialectic variations, spread across the country.
The religious complexion is equally orchestrated, with 41.8
per cent Roman Catholics, 35.3 per cent Protestants, 4.3

---

[91] Kummerly, *Switzerland*. Bern: Publication of the Ministry of
Foreign Affairs, 1992.

[92] *Encyclopaedia Britannica*, Macropedia, vol. xxviii.

[93] Seton-Watson, *ibid*.

per cent Muslim, 1.8 per cent Orthodox, and 0.2 per cent Jewish. These diversities have a serious reflection on the cultural life which combines what is seen as the serenity of the Germanic traditions and the much resplendent ebullience of Latin heritage.

Years of Transmutation

The integration of the Swiss Confederation, however, goes back to several hundred years of metamorphosis. Previously a small country of agriculturists, farmers, and fishermen, this region earlier referred to as 'Helvetia' had at different times received waves of migrations. In the course of history, the country had also fallen under various forms of alien rule including Roman, Germanic, and Frankish rules. Even the Muslims and Magyars (Hungarian) had at some time raided and exercised some form of influence on parts of the territory.[94] The largest group of immigrants was, however, the 'Alemanians' who settled along the Rhine valley, followed by the 'Burgundians'. It is recorded that at each point, there was strong resistance from other groups, such as the Rhaetia, who were already settled, but in most cases, they were overpowered and eventually a cross-ethnic mix happened.

---

[94] *Encyclopaedia Britannica*, Macropedia vol. xxviii.

The actual move in favour of desegregation began in 1291, when leaders from the three mountain cantons of Uri, Schwyz, and Unterwalden came together to form the *Bundesbrief* or *Federal Chapter*. This design for mutual aid was primarily fronted against the Habsburg dominance, but its consequence was the laying of the foundational stone for the creation of the 'Helvetica Confederation'. In the initial stages, this union recorded much success, especially in defending the autonomy and traditional rights of the territory.

In the centuries that followed, the union either attracted or coerced the membership of thirteen of the cantons that existed then. The resilience of the federation even in those early years was demonstrated by its survival of a lot of centrifugal pressures.

First came the large-scale internal disagreement and a divergence of interests between the cantons and European principalities. Thereafter, during the years of intense diplomacy in Europe leading to the emergence of the nation-state, the various cantons disagreed on such issues as the service of Swiss mercenaries in foreign armies. How could the various ethnic groups in Switzerland be able to divorce themselves from the attraction and emotional appeal of nationalism, war, and ethnic chauvinism then rife in Europe?

Of particular significance was the conscious abstainment from being dragged into a series of ethnically divided Franco-Germanic Wars and the increase of ethnic reversion all around them which followed the collapse of the Ottoman, Prussian, and Habsburg empires. The Swiss therefore witnessed and, in most cases, provided the conference venue for the process of redrawing and redefining Europe's territorial cartography along language lines, but stayed indifferent and unrepentant of its political form.

The second major problem was the Reformation and Counter-Reformation. This country became the centre of some of the most extensive and perhaps debilitating strains experienced by Christendom. It provided the launching pad for the propagation of the most dogmatic and fervent ideas of Protestant proselytes, especially Ulrich Zwingli (1484-1531) and John Calvin (1509-1564). Conversion to the new body of teachings, as well as the Catholic Counter-Reformation which followed, became divided along language lines, thereby accentuating the potentially explosive ethnic imbalance. The consequences were bloody religious wars during the sixteenth and seventeenth centuries.[95]

A further consequence of these zealot-motivated feuds was the persistence of disaffection between various groups that became politically divided along federal and confederate positions in the union. The inability to resolve this immediately dragged on, and another brief civil war was fought as late as 1847 between the seven Catholic cantons who preferred more autonomy and their Protestant

---

[95] Kummerly, *ibid.*, 1992.

counterparts whose ideas of a union at the time were the exact opposite.

Economic and Social Well-Being

Over the years, various factors of geography and political voluntarism have come into play to give this country its peculiar national character in the midst of deep-seated heterogeneity. Modern analysts have cited as evidence several factors and varying reasons for the level of success of the Swiss model of state formation. In search for explanations, Professor Seton-Watson gives primary place to an advantageous geography, pointing out that the country's central location along major trade routes in Europe engendered wealth creation, which in turn diverted attention from bellicosity or hostility.[96]

In the course of time, Switzerland has also been able to maximise its economic fortunes by turning itself into one of the most important banking and financial centres in the world. Several light industries such as chemical production, pharmaceutical and cosmetics, food processing, and watch manufacturing have all been cornered by the Swiss economy.

With economic prosperity comes the issue of social welfare. The Swiss social welfare system and the dispensation

---

[96] This is not withstanding the fact that the country continued to be the main exporter of mercenaries in Europe.

of social infrastructure are believed to be one of the most efficient and far-reaching in the world. An economy that relies enormously on tax regimes, the social welfare system is well subsidised by the central government, thereby helping to bring about a fair level of equality at the national level.

Diplomatic Neutrality and Political Nicety

Many other writers have, however, given primary importance to the country's policy of neutrality. Starting from its neutral stance in the Thirty Years' War which engulfed almost all of Europe, the eventual truce in 1648 granted the country sovereignty from the Roman Empire. Perceiving the mood of belligerency in contemporary Europe and the implications for its unity, Switzerland officially declared its neutrality policy in 1674. This was respected by everyone and was formally recognised by the Congress of Vienna in 1815 and later by the Treaty of Versailles at the end of World War I.[97] This policy of neutrality by itself helped in further enriching the people, as normal economic activity and 'national self-satisfaction' strove in the midst of wars all around the world. Furthermore, many associate the success of the banking sector in the country's economy as an attribute of the relative stability it offers to investors.

---

[97] Kummerly, *ibid.*, 1992.

An additional factor which has often been identified and lauded by many commentators is the ingenious political system adopted by the country. Apart from the fact that the canton system facilitates easier administration in the mountainous regions, recognition is given to the individuality of component parts—'cantons'—which are allowed a high degree of autonomy and freedom on a wide range of issues. Furthermore, two plebiscites and a 'right of initiative' are instituted to give everyone a fair chance of participation in law-making. The national government itself is run by a seven-member council, one from each of the cantons that make up the country. The presidency is rotated within these seven cantons, with each person holding office for a one-year term. Besides presiding at meetings, the presidency carries no extra privileges. Professor Max Frankel concludes that the federal government has never been a threat to the cantons, as it has been safeguarded against the latter by such constitutional measures and the rather forceful voice of public opinion.[98]

For a long period, mutual confidence and trust has been built between various institutions at different levels of authority and various groups. The system is intricate, and even at the level of partisan politics, parties are expected to form alliances and coalitions based on their correspondent voting power. It is concluded:

---

[98] Max Frankel, *Partnership in Federalism*. Bern: Peter Lang, 1977, p. 26.

The words that are so important for American politics (and in many countries)—leadership, conflict, and excitement—have no positive values in Swiss politics, which are so far as possible depersonalized, geared to compromise, and like the Old Romans, suspicious of new things.[99]

Neither the Swiss nor the admirers of their model have in any way ascribed to this system any eulogies of perfection, but it is true to say that the system has helped to assuage the levels of cultural, religious, ethnic, and partisan political division. It has, on the contrary, been very effective all these years and has served the purpose of enhanced national harmony well in the midst of diversities.

Accounts have emerged in the world media on the role of Switzerland as a country during World War II, pointing to the fact that her self-imposed neutrality was much coloured with anti-Semitic biases. But then this issue which could have led to a major political crisis in other countries became contained, and ways for resolving it were easily worked out. This is why many authors and political scientists, in general terms, feel safe to continue parading the Swiss experience or rather experiment with integration as a model for other countries.

---

[99] Frankel, *ibid.*, p. 26 and also see J. Peter Meekinson (ed.), *Canadian Federalism: Myth or Reality*. London: Methuen, 1968.

The Canadian Federation

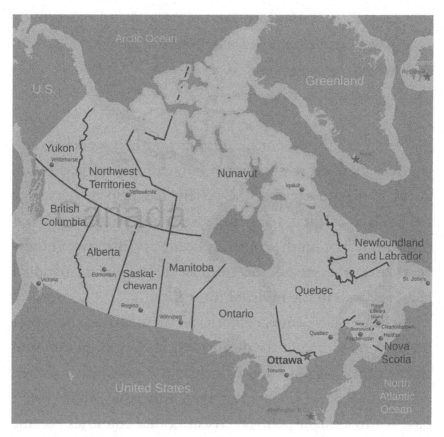

Map of Canada showing its Provinces,
Territories and Capital Cities

While the political history of Switzerland has easily been pointed to as a success case of unity in diversity, Canada has been referred to by one author as a land of great contrasts and oddity—in geography, demographic distribution, and cultural aggregation. From the point of view of land mass, for instance, the country is presently the second largest in the world, coming just after Russia, hence its national motto—*A mari usque ad mare* (from sea to sea). Its size of 9.984 million square kilometres is about two-thirds of the earth's total area. However, the country's inhabitants of just about 35 million are barely 1 per cent of the world's population. But by nature of the physiographic diversity which it exhibits, even much of that vast expanse of territory is stored up in water—lakes and wetlands.

The more intriguing part of the divergence comes from the fact that there exists no 'compact, homogenous people'; rather the country is an agglomeration of a multiform of national and social groups, each with its own forms of cultural and religious expression as well as legal and educational traditions. Hence, it is one of the few countries in the world, if not the only, where the world's two most popular international languages—English and French, are both common languages. There also exist lots of Germans, Italians, Chinese, Ukrainians, and Jews.[100]

Deriving there from and because of sharing an amazingly large 8,895 square kilometres border with the United States,

---

[100] Later, immigrant populations in Canada have also tended to maintain their distinct cultural identities due to the fact that they tended to live together in colonies. A good example are the Ukrainians, many of whom settled around the prairies where the climatic conditions are similar to Eastern Europe. Similarly, those from Holland settled in the Southern Ontario area, where they could continue the tradition of vegetable and fruit farming. Please also see *Encylopaedia Britannica*, vol. xv, p. 229.

it is again one of the only countries where the struggle for a distinct national identity has to contend with the persistent combat by each of mankind's three leading cultures— British, French, and America, to instil its influence. The half successful struggle for a distinct Canadian culture vis-à-vis these pressures, especially the American weight, animated a leading politician in the country, Samuel Jacobs, to say sarcastically:

> *The United States makes a rule today and we follow it tomorrow; or to put it differently, they take the snuff and we do the sneezing.*[101]

This is why many have recurrently seen Canada as a second-rate provincial version of the United States. In fact, the attachment or 'marriage of convenience' to Britain was because the francophone elements saw this as the lesser of two evils. This is why Professor Smiley concluded that any attempt at understanding Canadian politics would only be meaningful if tackled from the point of view of the duality or multi-party of 'cleavages' among others, between languages and cultures, central and peripheral parts, rich and poor provinces, and oil-producing units

---

[101] Samuel Jacobs, *House of Commons Debates*, 30 March 1997, quoted in McArthur, p. 177.

and non-oil-producing ones.[102] No wonder the country's political characters had to settle for the rather sweet-sounding mixture of Franco-American liberalism and British conservatism—a democratic state voluntarily submitted to the authority of the British Matriarch and belonging to the Common wealth of Nations.

The irony is that the country derives its name from the Huron-Iroquois (Native Indians) word *kanata* which literally means a village or settlement.[103] So besides the ethno-national miscellany of human exodus that constantly streams into the country, the cross-cultural kaleidoscope is further enriched by the presence of more aboriginal populations—the Native Indians and the Eskimos (Inuits), whose tribal and language groups are placed at a minimum of fifty-three distinct groups. This in another sense, why it would be unhistorical, in fact, unapprised, to propose that the history of this great land began with the derivation of the name Canada.

However, the point at which French explorer Jacques Cartier arrived at the Gulf of St Lawrence in 1534 has always been suggested as a convenient point to consider

---

[102] Donald Smiley, 'Cleavages and the Canadian System', in Bolaji Akinyemi, Dele Cole, and Walter Ofonagoro (eds.), *Readings in Federalism*. Lagos: NIIA, pp. 233-335.

[103] See McArthur, op. cit., p. 17, also see *Encyclopaedia Britannica*, vol. xv, 1993, p. 440.

its modern history.[104] Even before then, several European fishermen and explorers, including English-sponsored Italian, John Cabot, had traversed the littoral provinces, but no effective efforts were made to establish a firm presence. Although Cabot had landed on Newfoundland and Cape Breton, his benefactor, King Henry VII, at the time took very little interest. A small French-based community was thereafter established in Nova Scotia in 1605 and thereon in Quebec.

As the land was discovered to be lucrative, especially for trade in fur, the French formed the Company of New France in 1640 and subsequently serious and conscious immigration started. Although several English sailors including Henry Hudson had landed on the territories during the early 1600s, no serious follow-up was made until the French fortunes began to increase in the mid-seventeenth century and began to arouse envy and competition.

By 1670, the latter had formed the Hudson Bay's Company, poised to control as much of the fur trade as possible. As would be expected, this combined with other developments in Europe resulted in an antagonistic Anglo-Franco rivalry for much of the next one hundred years. Occasional skirmishes and armed hostilities, including the War of Spanish Succession, took place in 1713, in which France forfeited Nova Scotia and Newfoundland. With this

---

[104] Seton-Watson, p. 194, also see *Encyclopaedia Britannica*, vol. xv, p. 458.

great blow, the French tried to push towards the Ohio and Mississippi valleys, but got held up and were defeated by Native Indians in the Seven Years' War. The final blow was their eviction from the North American territory in 1763.

Background to the British North American Act (BNA), 1867

The parody was that as the French were withdrawing, the successful outcome of the American Revolution and War of Independence forced large communities of English-speaking monarchical devotees to cross over to Canada, settling in Nova Scotia and New Brunswick in 1784. With this upsurge of loyalists, London decided to break up the territory into the two provinces of Upper and Lower Canada in 1791, but had to unite them again in 1841 and then gave Canada the right of self-governance in 1848. Thereafter, all the efforts at constitutional reform have been directed at installing harmony between the two main ethnic, linguistic, and religious components which make up the country.

With an increasing move towards its internal consolidation and confederacy, the British approved the Dominion of Canada or British North American Act in 1867, thereby bringing together New Brunswick, Quebec (formerly Lower Canada) and Ontario (formerly Upper Canada) under the British North American Act (BNA), much later Alberta. British Columbia, Manitoba,

Newfoundland, Saskatchewan, as well as the Yukon and North-west territories joined.[105]

Since the Hudson Bay Company which had a *de facto* control of the territory was by that law required to be sold, some authors suggest that it represented the turning point for the establishment of the Canadian state. By the same token, most writers on Canadian politics believe that the genesis of the nation's economic headway as well as the present problems of political integration also had their roots in the 1867 Constitution; hence, it would be imperative to shed some light on this.

The orchestrators of the BNA who met at the time in Quebec and Charlottetown were primarily preoccupied with two visions: one, to bring into being a nation where despite the intergroup scuffle a framework could be found to create collective political identity and a common ardour at the national level could be developed. The second imperative or vision was the need to lay a solid economic base for the creation of a prosperous union which would engender sustained economic development, especially as the former Hudson Bay Company was to be dissolved.[106] While British parliamentary democracy and American civic liberalism were all there to adopt, they were especially mindful in not wanting to repeat the developments in the

---

[105] Florence Elliot, *A Dictionary of Political Science*. London: Penguin, 1969, p. 75.

[106] Simeon and Robinson, *ibid.*, p. 20.

south that led to a civil war. This was why that constitution was deliberately ambiguous on a number of issues to make it flexible enough for amendments and had to be more firm on other matters in order to ensure that the aspirations of one community could not be overruled by another. Unlike the American Constitution where general authority in all matters not specifically assigned was left to the states, it was the opposite in the case of Canada which has been referred to as a 'centralized quasi-federal model'.[107]

Nationalism in Quebec

Throughout this period, much disaffection existed between the English—and French-speaking communities. Besides the open rebellion in Lower Canada in 1837, in the late nineteenth century, Louis Riel had been martyred, and much antipathy existed over the supposed relegation of French language and culture.[108] Moreover, as a member of the Commonwealth, despite its multinational composition, Canada had been a part of various British military adventures to the embarrassment of the French sections of the population.

---

[107] Simeon and Robinson, *ibid.*, pp. 31-56.

[108] Louis Riel (1844-1885) was a Canadian lawyer, political activist, and leader of the metis who were people of French and Indian descent, whom he also represented. In a largely political trial, he was charged with treason and hung.

From the 1920s, Canada started to plan an independent outlook in foreign policy, and by 1931, Britain had made laws entrenching the legal equality between its colonies and the mother country, but these could not easily appease the deep-rooted quandary of national aversion. However, during the period of the Great Depression, the characteristics of the 'cleavage' changed from the earlier ethno-religious formation to a linguistic tilt, while the territorialisation of French nationalism became focused in Quebec. Even though in the World War II era, the federal government displayed considerable strength in being able to rapidly mobilise national consensus, this was short-lived as the increasing ascent of political doctrine and separatism in Quebec continued to pose a deep apprehension, indeed irritation, on national politics.

Through the conservatism of leaders in Quebec, such as Maurice Duplessis, and the adoption of the 'Quiet Revolution' (which by the way was not so quiet), the 1950s and 1960s bore witness to the consolidation of francophone schismatic activism, including shedding off the wrap of its previous regional locus in the pursuit of a 'fighting back' course at the national level.[109] At this time, Quebec had also become enriched by the willing acceptance of investments from American capitalist enterprise, so *nouveau riche* emerged, bent on hoisting their collective identity.[110]

---

[109] Simeon and Robinson, *ibid.*, pp. 137-142.
[110] Seton-Watson, *ibid.*, p. 229.

Every parallel effort of the national government towards integration was, however, to the *Quebecois,* seen as already coming too late as French ways of life and language were treated as second fiddle and could ultimately be wiped out. For instance, despite these separatist enumerations for the purpose of enhancing Canadian nationalism, the central Government set up the 'Massey Commission on Defending of National Cultures', and despite the confrontational attitude of the *Quebecois,* it went ahead to implement several pro-francophone recommendations, such as the opening up of more French language radio services. In 1965, the Royal Commission on Bilingualism and Biculturalism had already recommended the need for equal status for both cultures.

Moreover, the French elements could not be appeased by just these moves because there were other social issues which fuelled the wind of discontent, such as the high unemployment rate in Quebec and low standard of living in comparison with Ontario.[111] They saw a solution only in the creation of a separate state which would be unilingual and bring in all the francophone communities in the neighbouring provinces. Things were made worse by the visit of French President Charles de Gaulle (1890-1970) to Quebec in 1967 who just attended an International Exhibition in Montreal.

---

[111] Seton-Watson, *ibid.,* p. 229.

People demonstrating in favour of French President,
Charles de Guille during his official visit to Quebec
in July 1967 when he made a speech on independence
of Quebec saying vivre le Quebec libre

During that visit, an *entente culturelle* was signed
between the two sides (even without turning to Ottawa),
and President de Gaulle continuously addressed his crowd
with the words *'vive le Quebec libre'*.[112] The truth is that
France had, as it were, abandoned those kith and kin in
Canada during the period 1763-1783, which did not show
much official imprest in their lots. France therefore had to
revamp the broken contacts for the fact that if eventually
Quebec becomes a state, as it is being proposed, it would
be the world's second purely French country. So the visit

---

[112] See Seton-Watson, p. 229 and also Elliot, p. 77.

of President de Gaulle did not make much official efforts to dissuade the rise of nationalist rhetoric. Although Quebec had as early as 1882 sent Hector Fabre (1834-1910) to represent it in France, it was the resumed contact with that country which spurred them to open an office for international relations that same year (1967).[113] It would be useful to mention that right now Quebec has a 'network of representatives in each of the world's main regions'. These include in 'general delegations' in Brussels, London, New York, Paris, Tokyo, Abidjan, and Munich. Quebec also has commercial representation offices in much of Latin American and several French-speaking countries, especially in Africa.

It was against this background that the extremist Parti Quebecois (PQ) was formed a year after the visit in 1968, which gradually rose to take control of provincial power in November 1976 against a platform created for achieving independence for Quebec while retaining some form of political association with Canada. However, its plans could not receive support at two referendums held in 1980 and 1995.[114]

The federal government thereafter legislated on the bilingualism of the country, enforcing the use of both languages at all levels of government. Prime Minister, Elliot Pierre Trudeau (1919-2000), himself of French extraction but

---

[113] See the web page on 'Quebec and the World'.
[114] Quebec and the World, *ibid.*, pp. 249-254.

bicultural in breeding and urbane in vision, tried to focus on what became a 'new federalism' which summoned forth diffusing nationalism by encouraging a more centralised, unilateral, and competitive pattern.

'Canada Act'

A major turning point for the integration of the country occurred when the British Government by the hand of the Queen Elizabeth II eventually proclaimed the 'Canada Act' on April 17, 1982, thereby passing on to the country total control over its constitution, *pari passu* severing the statutory bond between the two countries. This new document incorporated the original law of 1867, the various amendments made by Canadian parliament, and the results of several rounds of talks between London and Ottawa for more years. The main objective of the negotiations was to give form to the vision of those like Prime Minister Trudeau who wanted 'one Canada with two languages' and at the same time also rule lines to show the relationship between the provinces and the centre.[115] It is unnecessary to go into the details of this law, but important to pinpoint the main denominating factor which was the proviso for a Charter of

---

[115] This new document incorporated the original law of 1867, the various amendments made by the Canadian Parliament, and the results of several rounds of talks between London and Ottawa for more than two years.

Rights and Freedom, setting down thirty-four rights to be observed.[116] It should be mentioned for the purpose of clarity that this Canadian Charter of Rights and Freedom was different from the American Bill of Rights. In the latter case, it is part of the Constitution, but with Canadian, it is limited by a 'notwithstanding clause'. This clause allowed both federal and provincial parliaments to set aside some provisions of the charter. Besides, its provisions would be revisable every five years. This was not only to give the parliament the assumed power of supremacy, but also by account of the country's peculiarities make it possible for amendments.

Furthermore, the constitution can only be amended by a resolution of parliament agreed by two-thirds of the provinces and must make up not less than half of the national population. Other parts relate to special provisions for the protection and preservation of the rights of the aboriginal Indian and Eskimo (Inuit) populations, the accentuation on the right of provinces over the natural resources, and education. However, under a complex arrangement, the federal government is involved in the development of such mineral wealth all across the country.

The latter two provisions (mineral resources and education) are worthy of special attention because in many other multi-ethnic states the binding factors are the exclusive control of the federal government over natural resources

---

[116] More details could be found in Eugene A. Forsey, *F. I. Sistema Politico de Canada*.

which are exploited and the proceeds put in a common purse for some 'equitable' form of distribution.

In the case of Canada, to mitigate any possible pauperisation of some regions not endowed with natural resources which may arise as a result of the effect of these special 'owner takes it' kind of law, the federal government is obligated by law to provide social welfare, social security (including pension and veterans funds and unemployment benefit), and health care. For the purpose of equalisation of the regions, the federal government also ensures the remission of funds for the balanced provision of public services all across the country.

With regards to education, again in many countries, there is the emphasis on enforcing uniform educational standards to ensure equal development, but it is the opposite in Canada due to the special circumstances of differences between French and British/American education systems. However, there is again a provision for children from one language who happen to be a minority in another province to receive education in their mother tongue if the numbers permit.

It was on this account that the Supreme Court of Quebec rejected the region's disputed Bill 101 which tried to force English-speaking parents educated outside Quebec to send their children to French schools if they moved there.

At the time of Prime Minister Brian Mulroney, a policy of 'cooperative federalism' was brought forth. It was intended to persuade the government of Quebec to endorse the 1982 constitutional amendment and increase support for Quebec to remain within Canada. Many Quebec nationalists were willing to be part of a Canadian federation with a more decentralised government. This formed the content of the Meech Lake Accord.[117] This accord clearly stated Canada's dualism and defined Quebec as a distinct society within the confederation, of which Quebec has a duty to preserve. The veto on constitutional change held by Quebec was partially restored again by the extension of the list covered by it, and it was established that each time three of the Supreme Court judges must be members of the Quebec bar.

Brian Mulroney, Former Prime Minister of Canada

---

[117] The Accord emphasises more regional autonomy to stem down the tide of separatist rhetoric, *ibid.*, pp. 315-327.

Still in search of an acceptable national integration framework, Canadian leaders again convened at Charlottetown in August 1992, emerging with the document called 'Shaping Canada's Future Together' or Charlottetown Accord. This basically re-emphasised the provision of the Meech Lake Accord, such as the distinctiveness of Quebec, and added provisions to a number of provisions for the rights and possibility of negotiation of internal self-government for the Aboriginal groups and an elected Senate. However, in national referenda held in October, this again failed.

Conscious Policy versus Divergence

It would appear that, by the events of its history, Canada was not able to do more within the existing circumstances to blend itself into one homogenous society, while still retaining individual cultural and historical identities. As has been shown, the result achieved has so far come out of deliberate policies which emerged through years of negotiations. The approach has not been in one direction, neither has it been for the majority English-speaking population to persistently impose its will on the French communities.

It would be important to mention that for a long time the English-speaking populations had refused to see Canada as a state comprising two nations. Though not stated in exact words, there had existed a presumed reasoning by the Anglophone that the country was made up of a single nation to which French-speaking Canadians belonged and had to agree to be integrated into it in a subordinate fashion. This is what the French elements have rightly refused to accept, because there were really two nations in the territory until the Treaty of Paris and since then they have continued to live in a politically passive but culturally vibrant environment under the patriarchal banner of the Church. So the approach had to change to dialogue and negotiation for the enhancement of collective interest.

Another point of value is that efforts were not limited to a given or presumed set of variables but multifocused both on the substantive issues and on the strategies. Hence, the efforts have cut across human, cultural, economic (fiscal), and legal/institutional perspectives. Policies therefore had to be deliberately conceived and implemented to take everyone along. For instance, in the federal civil service, bilingualism became a basic prerequisite for upward movement initially and right now for recruitment. As far back as 1974, as much as 93 per cent of the 963 'executive positions', which existed just five years after the passage of the Bilingual Act, have been classified as bilingual.[118] It is also noteworthy to say that some of those that have stood for the national integration have themselves been of francophone ancestry.

---

[118] Smiley, *ibid.*, p. 326.

Besides, common national institutions such as the Canadian Broadcasting Corporation (CBC) had to be well funded to ensure effective national coverage and run programmes that would facilitate integration. Even private radio and television stations, without being censored, are under the close surveillance of the Canadian Radio-television and Telecommunication Commission (CRTC) to ensure that they are 'effectively owned and controlled by Canadians so as to safeguard, enrich and strengthen the cultural, political, social and economic fabric of Canada'.[119]

The Ministry of National Patrimony was set up to encourage a distinct Canadian culture. It has been giving out free national flags and has been at the centre of promoting social and cultural activities in the provinces.

Finally, the political tools and stability as we have seen also played a very important role. At the centre, legislative power is in the hands of the 104 members of the Senate appointed at the provincial level, who may hold office until they are seventy-five years old. The 219-member Lower House is elected by direct election, and the leader of the winning party forms the government. Besides the PQ, formation of political parties was across provincial or ethnic backgrounds. The seat-in Governor General appointed by the Queen, as the title suggests, only serves as a nominal head of state, and in each of the ten provinces and two federal territories, a Lieutenant Governor is appointed in addition.

---

[119] Forsey, *ibid.*, also see McArthur, p. 178.

Former Quebec Premier Jacques Parizeau waves to
supporters during YES rally in Montreal to convince
voters to back independence referendum

These have however not been without challenges. The
question of Quebec still remains. The PQ was re-elected
to power in the 1994 election under Jacques Parizeau.
Following a presentation made by Hardial Bains, the party
leader of the Marxist-Leninist Party of Canada, Premier
Jacques Parizeau promptly called for a referendum in 1995
at the Royal Commission on the future of Quebec. After
leading all night in the referendum and very confident of
victory, the final count only showed 49.6 per cent of votes
supporting negotiations that could lead to sovereignty.
Following the defeat, Premier Jacques Parizeau resigned
and was succeeded by Lucien Bouchard, a former member

of Prime Minister Brian Mulroney's Cabinet, as the PQ leader and abandoned the call for a referendum. The PQ was re-elected in the 1998 election but still did not call for a referendum due to the low level of support. They, however, increased their pomposity on the possibility of secession without necessarily holding a referendum. The Quebec government also warned that it is not obliged to comply with court injunctions raised by some of its citizens debarring possible fissures through non-constitutional means.[120]

Lucien Bouchard resigned from office in 2001 and was replaced by Bernard Landy. In 2003, the PQ launched 'Saison des Idees' (Season of Ideas), which is a public consultation aimed at gathering opinions of Quebecers on the sovereignty project. But unfortunately, the party lost power to the Liberal Party in the 2003 election. A polling data was carried out in June 2009 on the support for Quebec separation by Angus Reid. The result of this poll was very weak, showing 32 per cent of Quebecers believing that they had enough sovereignty and should remain part of Canada, 28 per cent thought that they should separate, and 30 per cent believed that Quebec did not need greater sovereignty but should remain part of Canada.

This raises a fundamental question as suggested by Ruth Lapidoth—if separatist groups insist on getting

---

[120] Guy Bertrand, a prominent lawyer from Quebec, has since 30 August 1996 obtained court injunctions on this. With the ruling, Canadian courts would have the right to define if a unilateral declaration of independence is legal.

independence even against the will of some who may want to stay back, what moral excuse could be given to prevent further splintering?[121] In a visit by former President of France Nicholas Sarkozy to Quebec City in 2008, he praised Canada and said, 'The world does not need another division', thereby breaking the long-standing 'non-interference, non-indifference' stance of France towards Quebec. But during a visit by the Premier of Quebec Pauline Marois to France in October 2012, President Francois Hollande went back to the long-standing 'non-interference, non-indifference' stance by stating thus, 'This policy has existed for thirty years. It has been carried out by all successive (French) governments. This formula prevails today, I am for continuity.' However, analysts have said that the formula will allow France to continue with its subtle support for independence of Quebec, thereby confirming that the search for a solution still continues.

Relatively, the fairly balanced standard of living propelled by economic development also facilitated national integration. That is why Canada continues to be listed among the world's index of top ten affluent countries, having one of the highest gross domestic product (GDP) per capita.[122] Canada has some of the best social services in the world. Despite the vast and irregular topography, its road and railway network in the populated areas are among

---

[121] Lapidoth, *ibid.*, p. 21.

[122] *Encyclopaedia Britannica*, vol. ii, p. 785.

the highest in terms of mileage per capita in the world. The country's economic lot has been better enhanced by the fact that somehow every region has some economic merit either in agriculture, forestry, fishing, energy, or mining. What has helped the country to become one of the world's leading producers in all these sectors is the massive influx of capital from the United States and some measure of investments from Britain. These have also boosted the country's export industry, which had from the time of Hudson Bay Company always represented over 50 per cent of the GNP.

No doubt Canada has achieved much, yet more challenges remain ahead. But one lesson which it easily teaches is that the task of national integration is continuous and needs a lot of patience and cutting of compromises.

Chapter Nine

Mega States in the Orient and Peaceful Coexistence: India and China

While Switzerland and Canada may have had to build their federations and political cultures around unfolding circumstances created by external imperialism and linguistic diversity, respectively, the experience of state building and integration on the Asian continent has remained intriguing. This is due to the complex historical, cultural, and religious peculiarities which countries in the area face.

The two cases of India and China however stand out.

Bharatavarsha Sovereign Socialist Secular Republic (India)

Map of India

The Indian Republic (Bharatavarsha in Hindi) has grown out and remains affronted by the matrix of profound religious and cultural plurality and discord. For one, broad linguistic differences exists all across the country, but the symbolism and prominence of this phenomenon as a determining instrument of political behaviour (or in the synergy of national integration and state formation process) is rather dwarfed in juxtaposition with the religious variable. Even when one returns to ponder on the course of this country's pre-colonial history, what is demonstrated is the prevalence of an outlet of diverse currents of creed. Unlike many other places not supplanting each other with each new influx or excrescence, they are generally cohabiting together and mutually tolerant.

Furthermore, India's pluralistic setting, which easily lends to it the rating as one of the world's epitomes of cultural diversity, is yet exacerbated by its mammoth population of nearly over 1.2 billion people, the second most populous country in the world after China.[123] The country's land mass of about 3.29 million square kilometres, even though it makes it only the seventh largest country in the world, cannot by any means be underestimated, especially as its distinct geographical form is marked out by the fact that it covers much of South Asia and is cordoned off from the rest of the Asia continent by the lofty Himalayan mountain

---

[123] Young, *ibid.*, p. 349.

ranges and by the Indian Ocean (between the Arabian Sea and the Bay of Bengal).

The various people that make up this vast country in different forms trace their history to the metropolitan civilisation, which had its setting around the Indus Valley about the third millennium BC. It may not be necessary to bother about the details of the historical evolution, but it is enough to establish that most of the early past was marked by a continuing osmotic movement of human populations and the ebb and tide of the various political establishments and fragmented state structures which they formed. These included the Bihar-based Magadhan around which the Mauryan Empire took off. This expanded greatly during the reign of Emperor Asoka, the Great (321-185 BC); later on, the Gupta empire (320-540) sprang up.

It was in this process that the parents of the modern-day Hindu religion and Hindi language—i.e. Vedic religion and Sanskrit language which came with it arose. Subsequently, the religions of Buddhism, Jainism, and Sikhism also sprang up around the area. From about AD 1000, invasions by the fourth religious group—Islam, began to take place, leading ultimately to the establishment in 1206 of the long-lived Delhi Sultanate and bringing much of the present South Asia under its cover. By 1526, the Sultanate itself was replaced by the expansionist Mughal Muslim emperors.

The arrival of the Portuguese explorer Vasco da Gama in 1498 and the subsequent contact with Europe not only weakened Mughal hegemony but led to the introduction of another religion—the Christian faith.[124] There is no doubt that resistance to European attempts during the establishment of political control was very firm, which included a major defeat of the Mughals in 1757, Hindus in 1818, the Sikhs in 1849, and again the Hindus in 1857. But with the ensuing creation of the British East Indian Company in 1858, the whole territory came effectively under colonial rule for the next ninety years.

The Problem of Faith

As noted already, India is made up of a very diverse and multifarious religious pigmentation, permeating into every facet of national life. Religion determines everything from culinary habits to education expectations and social relations. Even the resistance against alien rule, which continued in the form of modernised and better organised nationalist activities, began on a semi-religious platform with the formation of the largely Hindu Indian National Congress Party in 1885 and the parallel coming together

---

[124] For instance in 1757, Britain defeated a combined force of the Mughals and France, thereby allowing her to consolidate and set off a process of political balkanisation among the various people. It is true that the Hindu Marathas have before this same defeat also gone against the Mughals in the seventeenth century and set up their own empire. See Seton-Watson, pp. 271 and 290.

of Muslim leaders in 1906, leading to the formation of an analogous body called the Muslim League.

From early times, the likely role of this religious diversity in the country's politics and national integration had been very obvious. This was why as early as 1888, Lord Dufferin, Frederick Hamilton Temple-Blackwood (1826-1902), the British Viceroy in India, had declared that the Muslim community in India was a nation of 50 million, with their own monotheist traditions and iconoclastic fanaticism contained in the form of periodic animal sacrifices. He had further written that the practice of social equality among these Muslims and their memory of the history of their splendour as rulers from the Himalayas to Cape Comorin continued to imbue in them a distinct sense of national pride.[125] This pro-religious distinctiveness of identity was further corroborated extensively by the statement by Ali Jinnah, who later became the Pakistani national hero:

> *It has always been taken for granted mistakenly that the Musalmans are a minority. The Musalmam are not a minority. The Musalmans are a nation by any definition . . . What the unitary government of India for 150 years had failed to achieve cannot be realized by the imposition of a central federal government. The Hindus and Muslims belong . . . to two different civilization which are based mainly on conflicting ideas*

---

[125] Quoted in Young, p. 295.

and conceptions . . . To yoke together two such nations under a single state, one as a numerical minority and the other a numerical majority, must lead to growing discontent and final destruction of any fabric that may be so built up for the government of such a state.[126]

Muhammmad Ali Jinnah, Leader of Indian
Muslim League and Founder of Pakistan

---

[126] From Young, p. 296.

Although Britain went on to give limited internal self-government by 1919, Indian politics had already become clearly divided along religious lines. At the dawn of independence in 1947, on the insistence of the Muslim population, the country was divided into two—India and Pakistan. Although the intention was to make Pakistan, which was then north-western India, an essentially Muslim state, the realities of human population distribution made it largely unfeasible to have a mathematically neat division.

Accordingly in both countries religious numerical minorities exist, despite the fact that at independence almost 10 million Hindus and Muslims each bitterly transmigrated from their homes to move to the other country.[127] At the time, very bitter Indo-Pakistani riots took place, during which about 2 million lives were lost both ways. This was particularly more for India where the Hindus make up 80.5 per cent of the population, but due to the large number of inhabitants of religious minorities, such as Muslims who make up 13.4 per cent, Christians 2.3 per cent, and Sikhs 1.9 per cent each, Buddhists 1 per cent; Baha'i faith, animists, and several other lesser-known groups still go into several millions. Seldom spoken about, but economically significant, the Jewish community also live around the coastal areas bordering the Arabian Sea.[128] For instance, the

---

[127] Seton-Watson, pp. 290-297.

[128] *Encyclopaedia Britannica*, vol. xxl, p. 14, *India Yearbook 1995*. New Delhi: Government of India.

162.1 million Muslims in India are almost the same size as the entire population of Pakistan itself, making India the third largest Islamic country (coming just after Indonesia and Pakistan).

It would be safe to suggest that the usage of the terminology 'religious minorities' as it relates to India is a misnomer if left to stand alone, as it does not imply paucity in numbers as is customary in other places. The word 'minority' therefore only becomes relevant as a sociological terminology when it is viewed in relative comparison with the greater number of adherents of the Hindu faith.

The implication of the country's political and social growth and change has been twofold. First, the preponderance of religious multiplicity came with consequent diversity of cultural viewpoints and refinement on almost every issue at the macro level, thereby giving rise to much civic disquietude. Unfortunately all the main religious groups in India are highly ritualistic, each claiming for itself the appellation of 'purity'.

Yet, as we shall see with some specific instances, within each religious group existed a succession of sectarian slivering as well as a rather acrimonious internecine combativeness. In most of South Asia, there exists a caste system of 'jatis' by birth. One's birth regulates him strictly to a particular social community, occupational specialisation, and overall aspirations in life. For instance, among the Hindus and the other more oriental religions, there existed an intricate system of rigid and prescribed segregation between the Brahmans—priests who occupy the top of the pyramid and other castes down to the Panachamas or 'untouchables' at the very bottom.[129] As the name would suggest, the untouchables literally meant those not even reckoned as worthy of classification. However, in the new republic, the caste system did not only expose itself as patently inequitable and old-fashioned in a modern state system but also constituted an in-built volcano for violent social dissent and political disruption from the less privileged castes. This was inevitable as the access to Western education became available to all and the attempt to uplift their lots was resisted from the orthodox establishment in the upper castes and it was bound to create a counter backlash. This may not have been the case at the beginning, but as it is common with every oppressed people all across the world, this was certainly bound to happen.

This internal divergence was not just restricted to Hinduism. It may be suggested that among the Islamised sections of the population the snobbish and inhumane caste system did not exist, but in actual fact, they were not much better because they remained much feudalistic, divided, and ranked among princely estates and their subjects. In addition, within the Muslim fold, the problems between the Sunnis and Shiites have been the basis for much civic unrest.

---

[129] For more details on this see Young, pp. 60-64, 274-326 and also Daniel Patrick Moyniham, *Pandemonium Ethnicity in International Politics*. Oxford: Oxford University Press, 1993, pp. 159-164 and Seton-Watson, p. 435.

Religious Egalitarianism against Inquietude

On attainment of independence, the first thing the government had to do was to tackle this potent religious keg of gunpowder by declaring India as a 'secular state'. Despite the preponderant majority of the Hindu religion, this meant religious egalitarianism for all and sectarian neutrality at the centre. As a matter of fact, one of the country's early leaders, Prime Minister Jawaharlal Nehru (1889-1964), based on the philosophies of non-violence, moderation, and tolerance of his guru Mahatma Gandhi and his own cosmopolitan disposition, began to embark on deliberate policies to do away with the centuries-old dynastic guild of caste. For the purpose of creating a sense of belonging for all and more peace and harmony between various religious groups, disadvantaged groups in the lower castes whom Mahatma Gandhi (1869-1948) preferred to call 'Children of God' were specially protected under an arrangement called 'Scheduled Castes' and 'Scheduled Tribes'.

Mahatma Gandhi Speaking to the crowd on a makeshift
stage during a rally in Peshawar in July 1938

By 1955, beyond the detailed constitutional provision to
ensure the welfare of these groups, the government passed the
Untouchability (Offences) Act under which penalties were
made more stringent for acts of discrimination by virtue of a
person's 'untouchable' status. In order to fence off a Pakistan-
type fragmentation along religious lines, Nehru ensured
that the establishment of new states did not take a religious
line. Hence, the former province of Madras was in 1953
divided into two: Tamil Nadu and Andhra, and similarly in
1960, Bombay was divided into two with respect to religion
as the key factor of worth. This policy was to bring about
immediate end to clashes between the Hindu political elite

and the Sikhs. On the same account, Nehru refused the creation of a Punjabi state, even though this was later done by his daughter, Indira Gandhi (1917-1984), when she became the Prime Minister, but she was still cautious to keep the Sikh sacred town of Chandigarh as joint capital for another Hindu state. It is suggested that Indira Gandhi did this as a compensation for the Sikhs who had fought faithfully and gallantly during the war with Pakistan in 1965.

India's first Prime Minister, Jawaharlal Nehru (1889 - 1964)

However, this move and the subsequent appointment of a minority Sikh Zail Singh as nominal Head of State (President) of the Republic still failed to appease their separatist demands. By the early 1980s, during which period a rich middle Punjabi class sprang up thanks to the results of India's 'Green Revolution Programme', Sikh vociferations had moved from mere demand for regional exclusivity to requisitions for actual sovereign autonomy of their homeland Sikh Khalistan—Land of the Pure.[130] In the ensuing events including the takeover of the Sikh's sacred 'Golden Temple' in Amritsar by some insurgent and radical elements and the government-led invasion which took place, Indira Gandhi herself was murdered in 1984 by her Sikh aides. This by itself sparked off the worst national religious upheaval since the country's separation from Pakistan.

Another connotation of this religiously pluralistic state of affairs, though of little relevance to this exercise, is that it has been the root cause for much pusillanimity and diplomatic squabble in India's relations with most of its neighbours, especially Pakistan and to a lesser extent Sri Lanka and China. This situation and the fact that Kashmir, a largely Muslim territory and geographically contiguous with Pakistan, was left in the hands of India, instead of being allowed to join their religious kinfolk, has led to three

---

[130] While the cow is sacred to the Hindu and cannot be eaten, the pig was to the Muslim unclean and cannot be eaten. By calling Pakistan as a land of the pure, there was implied imputation of impurity in this context on the other side.

wars between the two countries. The war of 1971 led to the release of Bangladesh out of Pakistan to form another dominantly Muslim state.[131] Of all the potentially explosive religious issues, the most challenging remained Hindu-Pakistani relations. Although Pakistan was separated from India, the potential of Hindu-Muslim clashes remained potent. The mere fact that the choice of name for Pakistan meant 'Land of the Pure' for the other side had a strong religious connotation. From the early 1920s when the riots at Malabar took many lives, the diatribe that Muslim communities desecrated the sacredness of the cow, which for them meant good meat, or on the reverse that Hindus littered everywhere with carcasses of pork, which to them was also good nourishment, remained an issue of conflict and kept the inter-communal atmosphere tense and suspect.

Besides, India inherited the troubled land of Kashmir, and despite the separatist agitation from the outset, it has remained adamant on allowing a split along religious lines, due to the long-term implications for its unity. Though inhabited dominantly by Muslims at the time of independence, the Hindu minority who had exercised traditional political rule in the region opted to join India instead of Pakistan. This situation has kept the relations between the two sibling countries sour and in rivalry during the past sixty-five years, including three wars—1947, 1965, and 1971. Though not known much for wealth in terms of

---

[131] See Seton-Watson, pp. 290-297.

mineral resources, Kashmir's location in the proximity of the Himalayas has made it a point of interest for streams of tourists and researchers, but both activities have suffered following the spate of terrorist activities associated with this struggle.

Another moment of great tension between India and Pakistan was again witnessed during the twelve coordinated shooting and bombing attacks across Mumbai in 2008 by Islamist terrorists who were alleged to have been trained and come in from Pakistan. According to one of the survivors of the attack, they purportedly received reconnaissance assistance from Inter-Service Intelligence (ISI), a premier intelligence service of the Islamic Republic of Pakistan. The twelve coordinated attacks led to the killing of 164 people and wounding of at least 308. The attack was carried out by Lashkar-e-Taiba, an Islamic terrorist organisation based in Pakistan with links to Al-Qaeda. Though the Pakistani government initially denied the involvement of any of its nationals, it finally accepted the only survivor's nationality as Pakistani. Pakistan has always vehemently denied use of proxy terrorist groups to achieve its foreign policy goal in underscoring the issue of jurisdiction over Kashmir.

Possibly inspired by the *Intifada* against Israeli occupation in the West Bank in the Middle East and with covert Pakistani support to Kashmiris, the problem has turned to that of demand for the right of self-determination arising from within the territory. This remains a problem to India, as concession to Kashmir would open a Pandora box, yet the spate of nationalist fighting and acts of terrorism have intensified and the subject continues to receive greater international attention. Delhi has since then continued to resort to ruling Kashmir directly by Presidential emergency powers.

The other main problem which highlighted the tense Muslim-Hindu relation was the contention by some ultra-right Hindus regarding the presence of the Babri Masjid Mosque built by Mughal emperors in Ayodhya in Uttar Pradesh state. This mosque is now considered one of Islam's most holy shrines in India. But since that same site is historically considered to be the birthplace of the deity 'Rama', during the early 1990s a movement was started by some Hindu groups who were bent on erecting an ancient Hindu Temple in that location.[132] Despite the efforts of the central government, the mosque was eventually demolished in 1993, thereby creating disaffection among the Muslim community in not only that part of India but also in the entire country.

Overcoming the Goulash of Tongue

Language and the monomaniac overlap which often occurs between it and religion have always been vital factors

---

[132] This makes very good parallels with the views of some ultra-right Jews whose ideas point towards the re-enactment of the temple of Solomon at the present sight of Temple Mount, where Islam's sacred 'Al Haqq Mosque' still stands.

in the national politics of India, including the events leading to the 1981 assassination of Prime Minister Rajiv Gandhi (1944-1991). This may be why from the very beginning the government had tried to address the language problem. The manifestation of religious diversity, though substantially cancerous and noisome in their interaction with one another, becomes trivial when considered from the vista of the country's linguistic assortment.

In pre-colonial times, Hindi had in some sense already been the most widely spoken language in the entire subcontinent. Besides, there are some other languages which also had much lexicological resemblance to each other. However, the government took chances in shying away from allowing equanimity of tongues by imposing it on others. The government therefore had to declare Hindi and English as common languages, but it was also wise to designate fourteen other languages as 'national languages', thereby creating a wider feeling of belonging. Some of the main ethnic and language groups which are recognised as official languages at the regional levels and the percentage which they make up are Bengali 8.1 per cent, Marathi 7 per cent, Telugu 7.2 per cent, Tamil 5.9 per cent, Gujarati 4.5 per cent, Urdu 5 per cent. Others are Oriya 3.2 per cent, Kannada 3.7 per cent, Malayalam 3.2 per cent, Punjabi 2.8 per cent, Assamese 1.3 per cent, and Maithili 1.2 per cent.[133]

---

[133] McArthur, *ibid.*, p. 503, see also *India Yearbook 1995.*

Although Hindi speakers make up 35 per cent of the population, the overall ethnic composition is equally diverse comprising about two hundred languages; hence, when the States Re-organisation Commission was appointed in 1953 and the linguistic consideration was to be the weight by which requests for state creation were to be considered, over 150,000 petitions were received![134]

Democratic Peculiarity

With regards to the political organisation, post-colonial India was by the India Act of 1935 handed down the Britain political tradition of parliamentary democracy. But in view of the country's special challenges of state building, its early leaders incorporated aspects of American separation of power and federalism. By 1950 when the country took on a republican polity, conscious efforts had been made to lay the vertebrae for a governmental structure which would engender national unity and at the same time accord as much autonomy as possible to the various regions.

Accordingly the country is headed by a nominal President whose position is by selection through an electoral college of the legislatures of the various regions,

---

[134] See Young, p. 281 and also Seton-Watson, pp. 291, 297-302. It would be important to note that many of these languages are from language families such as Indo-European, Dravidian, Austro-Asiatic, and Sino-Tibetan.

his position is merely ceremonial and expected to be a rampart for national unity, especially at times of collapse of the democratic process or in the event of war. The President is therefore expected to rule on the advice of and in strict deference to the actual political power expected to be wielded by the elected Prime Minister and his Council of Ministers.

In order to maintain further balance, check, and stability in the system, there also exists an 'Official Opposition' maintained at public charge. The pattern at the centre is further replicated in the twenty-five regions, where the boss is the Delhi-appointed Governor although the actual executive power is only employed by the Chief Minister, who is elected for a four-year term. Due to their special developmental needs, an additional seven regions are designated as 'Union Territories' and are administered directly by the President through an appointed administrator.

It is important to observe that although such a political habitude has become a common substance of most democratic political structures, it has all the more become useful in alleviating the pressures that could otherwise have been generated by pluralistic Indian life. The legislative arm of the government at the centre comprises the *Rajya Sabha*—a 245-member upper chamber indirectly picked by state legislatures and the central government in Delhi. The 545-member *Lok Sabha* or lower chamber is directly elected, apart from two seats that are reserved for the representatives of the Anglo-Indian community to be nominated by the

President. The fact that the constitution gives residual power to only the national legislature and the power which it has to overrule the regional legislature have helped eliminate a situation where some of the unit parts could turn themselves into pests. Furthermore, the power of the national legislature to create new states without turning to receive the sanction of other units has helped reduce and diffuse tension and nationalist jumpiness.

There also exists an American-type Supreme Court comprising a Chief Justice and twenty-five other justices handpicked to reflect the country's juridical diversity. Besides this, the government also recognises and encourages the activities of some voluntary agencies called *Lok Adalat,* which engage in peaceful resolution of conflicts. The role of this latter body in the informal resolution of various forms of conflicts at the incipient stages has been very effective.

Unlike many other multinational countries, the unity, integration, and political stability of India have been enhanced further by the relative national spread and centrist ideological demeanour of its main political parties. Professor Crawford describes this phenomenon thus:

> *The nature of the party system is a second variable. Political competition and electoral campaigns are structured by an array of parties whose labels and formal symbols capture ideological difference, and not cultural pluralism. This symbolism is of very great importance; we may suggest that it represents a*

> *normative formulation of what the political system ought to be. The ideological connotation of the parties create a collective image of a political system whose policy choices are governed by contending social philosophies.*[135]

Crawford argues that the ideation of political parties on an ideological pedestal rather than on religious or linguistic 'cleavages' has made it possible for rather sensitive national issues to be discussed in the open, free of intergroup irony and intimidation. Even the *Jana Sangh* regarded by many as the Hindu nationalist party denies this claim, but then it remains mainly regional in spread. Hence, political parties in India generally help in diffusing the deism which from time to time comes with cultural pluralism by acting as bridge menders between cultural segmentation at the mass level and with ideological debate among the political elite.

This may be because the national political elite across different cultural and pietistic offing share common class interests and therefore 'have neither political incentive nor ideological predisposition to advance their claims through invocation of a communal constituency'. Religion to that extent only remains a social factor with respect to interaction between the rank and file at the bottom. At the top, the interests are more converged. In fact, this leads some authors to suggest that the political elite would prefer to allow the diversities to continue to perpetuate their class dominance.

---

[135] Young, *ibid.*, p. 310.

Sound and Visionary Political Leadership

It would be incomplete to mention this indisputable role of political institutions in the politics of India without singling out the role of the Congress Party and the calibre of political leadership which it produced. From its inception, despite its dominance by Hindu literati, which was historically spontaneous given the obscure advantage which they commanded at the time, it is on record that Mohandas Karamchand Gandhi better known as Mahatma Gandhi (1869-1948), despite his profound Hindu religiosity as well as many of his contemporaries, tried to serenade as much of the other groups as possible. They also unfettered the party from any leaning towards Hindu iconoclasm or intolerance of other cultural groups, portraying itself as a national patron or benefactor for Indian unity.

Under Jawaharlal Nehru (1889-1964), who was much more urban and cosmopolitan, the emphasis became more on national catholicity of faith, better transcultural symphony, and civic equanimity. Fortunately, the religious pluralism did not take on ethnical or linguistic localism, but was fairly trans-cultural and territorially diffused. At a time when the whole world was torn apart in two competing camps, due to his country's peculiarities, the visionary Nehru and later his heir Indira Gandhi (1917-1984) insisted on 'non-alignment'—a policy which kept India out of a lot of trouble.

It would also be very useful to comment here on the agricultural and educational policies. Realising the fact that starvation could be the best lightning bolt for agitation and division, which could engulf the very harmony of the political entity, these early Congress leaders emphasised on the 'Green Revolution'. This has paid off well as India is completely self-sufficient in food production. In the educational sector, the danger of illiteracy (analphabetism) was identified early and Mahatma Gandhi, even while directing the effort against British rule, came up with what was called an 'alternative community-based system of education'. At independence only 14 per cent of the population was literate; hence it became enshrined in the constitution that primary school education, or rather between the ages of six to fourteen, literacy was universal with the emphasis placed on the disadvantaged segments of the population. By 1986, under the Revised National Policy on Education, primary school education became free and compulsory.[136]

Bureaucratic-military Fidelity

The role of the Civil Service and the military has also been broached on often in the formation of the Indian state. Besides the special recruitment drives arranged for members

---

[136] *India Yearbook* 1995, p. 80.

of the disadvantaged castes, efforts are made to ensure a wide national distribution in the public service. India is well respected within the Commonwealth of Nations, indeed globally as having one of the most thorough and well-developed public service apparatus. The Indian military has also shown much discipline and respect for the national constitution.

In defiance of the wave of military unrest and political avarice in Pakistan, Burma, and other places in Asia, the Indian military, which has seen four of the country's key leaders being killed under circumstances that would have created pretences for intervention staved off politics. The military has also displayed much morale and preparedness and also developed a strong nuclear capability and leadership in the country's space programme.

There is no doubt that the political evolution of India is still in progress. The country still remains divided on so many things, and much splintering and in-fighting goes on especially within the regions. As the Congress Party which had provided the platform for national unity begins to wane in influence, it remains to be seen if Priyanka Gandhi will come back to restore the charisma and mere messianism which the Gandhi race had lent to the country's politics[137] or

---

[137] This psychology graduate is the great-granddaughter of Nehru, granddaughter of Indira Gandhi, and daughter of Rajiv Gandhi. She is already being looked upon as heir apparent after her Italian born mother refused to take over the reigns of power after her husband, Rajiv Gandhi, was killed.

whether the experiment of the coalition will provide a more durable political order.

With regard to the centrifugal nationalist and cultural forces, not only the Kashmiris are asking for freedom but also the same has been going on in Nagaland, Punjab, Tamil Nadu, and in the north-east where Bodo tribe separatists are struggling against poverty. So even though India is the world's tenth (third by purchasing power parity) largest economy according to 2012 ranking, much economic and social misery and illiteracy still loom all across. Its large bureaucracy has taken pride in its size and the elaboration of its procedures, thereby literally stifling accelerated economic growth and instituting a regime of corruption.

It is however, predicted that it would be the world's fourth largest economy towards the mid-twenty-first century, coming after USA, China, and Japan, and this would go a long way to pull the integrative units together, as social welfare (as in the Canada and Switzerland or the Nordic countries) has been a strong element of national unity. On the social front, there is still much to be done. Although for the first time since independence, in 1997, India had a President who was from the lower castes, the fact remains that India's law books are dotted with legislation underlining the human rights issue, especially on the caste situation which shows the profundity of the matter. As the wording of the Civil Rights Act of 1985 seems to imply, there is still more need for compliance, as the problem does not seem to lie with the legislative realm.

In all, one cannot but appreciate the persistence of India's leaders in keeping and welding the various units that make up this massive country, which many professed would waste away or, as Professor Crawford puts it, remain one of mankind's most watched experiments at 'pluralistic festivity'. While conjectures on political matters could sometimes bring a precarious consensus, in the case of India, it would be worth the risk to admit that seeing its resilience for survival during the past years, beside areas such as Kashmir and Jammu, much or the rest of the country is likely to remain intact.

After the United States of America, India has the next largest number of scientists in the world; if its economy maintains the growth rate of 5.9 per cent and thereby creates wealth, there is likely to be a greater season of political peace.

The State and Political Evolution in China

Provincial Map of China
(Picture from chinahighlights.com)

Referred in the past as the 'sleeping giant', China has developed to be the most dominant state in world history. Up to contemporary times, events in China have always been of great interest and enigma both to its people and students of political history around the world. This may obviously arise from the fact that China has, for most of the recorded human history, stood out among all other nations as the most populous. It is still among the largest nations, demographically and territorially, presently estimated at 1.35 billion and a size of about 9.6 million sq km. It is the third largest in the world in terms of land mass.

In history, it occupied much larger areas that extended over most of South and Central Asia; in economic terms, China is today the world's second largest economy with GDP of over 700 billion dollars. Its external reserve stands at 500 billion dollars and enjoys a balanced trade of over 800 billion dollars.

In cultural terms, Chinese ancient civilisation flourished and came to its apogee much before other known human political structures and other parts of Buddhist and Confucianist philosophies. The states under these dynastic structures were seen as religious communities with great metaphysical content in the practice of politics.

The emperors under the Qin and Han dynasties saw virtues such as heroism and individualism, which were a critical element in governance and state building. This led them to pursue expansionist policies in Korea, Vietnam, Mongolia, and almost all of Central Asia. Chinese history was largely influenced by monarchy of various forms that were often extremely bellicose, ruled from as far back as 2000 BC. In later history, other dynasties such as Tang (618-907), Song (960-1279), Qin (1644-1911), and even the Ming (1368-1642), which is recorded as one of the most famous, began to bring in Neo-Confucianist thoughts into the body politic. In its encouragement of literature, philosophy, and bureaucratic finesse and statecraft, early-day Chinese philosophers such as Zengzi and Chuang, going back to the thoughts of Confucius, focused much of their works on political unity and identity. The state was seen as being arranged in a well-structured hierarchy with merit, valour, honour, and loyalty as its basic defined ethos. The rule by these hereditary monarchies continued until 1911 when the wave of republicanism blowing over the world resulted in a series of events, leading to setting in of a new political era in China.

From the turn of the twentieth century, politics in China moved towards a republican trend, abolishing some of the old institutions and philosophies, increasingly resulting in what was termed a new 'policy'. Although Buddhism and Confucian thoughts continued to underline statecraft and politics, a great premium began to be accorded to studies and discourse on mathematics, geography, astronomy, natural sciences, and even classical Greek philosophy.

What appeared to have emerged this time was a kind of amalgam that blended the conservative rigor which the indigenous religious world view imposed on public order with elements of Western liberalism. One of the leaders, Sun Yat-sen (1866-1925), who played a significant role in final capitulation of the Qin Dynasty, was therefore greatly influenced by American republicanism through his reading about Abraham Lincoln and other renaissance philosophers such as Descartes, Hume, and last but not the least Karl Marx. He therefore proclaimed three principles of the people, dwelling on the following:

1. principle of nationalism;
2. principle of sovereignty;
3. principle of people's livelihood.

More radical ideas came from the thoughts of Roman Catholic jurist John Chu (1899-1986), who expounded clearly that the metaphysics brought into the process of state building was coterminous with Christian thoughts as espoused in the Bible in the works of Thomas of Aquinas. Clearly Aristotelian, he worked closely with Chang Kai-shek (1887-1975) the nationalist leader of Kuomintang Party and later on founder of Taiwan. He not only translated the Bible to Chinese but also created the basis for bringing in the need for full interaction of Chinese life and political mainstream Western thought. It is against this backdrop and the efforts of many other philosophers of this period that China prepared for a new wave of state formation and Cultural Revolution.

Chairman Mao and New Cultural Revolution

Although Western thoughts had crept in aggressively into Chinese philosophy at the beginning of nineteenth century, it should be understood that this was not without its measure of opposition. Although Sun Yat-sen who undoubtedly was pro-West got easily elected as President of the new republic, he soon gave up power, and thereafter followed a series of internal political squabbles. There was an appetite to return to imperialism, and Chinese cultural revival began to emerge with the University of Peking becoming the epicentre of very combative debate on the state of the nation and its philosophical foundation. Obviously, this itself led to various forms of political in-fighting among the leadership. It was this process that led to the emergence of Mao Tse-Tung (1893-1976) and his communist movement.

Mao Tse-Tung (1893 - 1976), Chinese
Communist leader addressing a meeting

From a purely Marxian point of view, Chairman Mao dwelt his ideal of society on the basis of collectivisation of agriculture and industry. He played a leading role in the formation of the Communist Party of China, which from 1944 put behind what was a republican state that had existed. He espoused a new revolution and sociopolitical theory that believed in total state control and ownership of industry. With great influence of the Marxist-Leninist Russia, he introduced a brand of proletarian ownership of government with a great flavour of military strategy.

Mao's brand of socialism was hard-lined and strongly people-based that some called it '*Maoism*'. Though raised in a wealthy agricultural background, from an early age Mao was known to have been anti-imperial. His presence at the university provided a chance for recruitment into Marxism. Leading the Communist Party of China in 1922, he went into a strategic partnership with the Kuomintang—the Nationalist Party, to play a critical role in formatting the emerging political direction of China of the day.

This alliance lasted for five years with Mao leading an army mainly of peasant farmers which took the country through a civil war that culminated in the '*long match*'. This was soon followed by wars with Japan and a series of civil wars which strategically ended in his victory over erstwhile allies of the nationalist (Kuomintang) who fled to Taiwan. It was in 1949 that Mao proclaimed a formal foundation of a people-based government in China which became, for many decades, an authoritarian state that consistently kept at bay all that were regarded as counter-revolutionary.

The Cultural Revolution

The enunciation of what was termed as 'Cultural Revolution' in 1966 was essentially a step taken to purge the country of elements that gradually arose in veiled opposition and were regarded as counter-revolutionary. The Cultural Revolution was, as it were, directed at taking away from Chinese body politic, with the rise of a new class of communist elites, a new favoured class. Mao had observed what was happening in neighbouring Soviet Union where some in leadership became as it were a new dominant class (we shall see later on). Mao espoused in this direction a move to install a perpetual revolution expressed in the Cultural Revolution. The Cultural Revolution further focused on obliterating the traditional religious and cultural norms and legacies that tended to stratify the society and created group interests which were inimical to protecting his revolution.

Mao's revolution went a long way, in his words to give China 'a great leap forward' industrially and developmentally. Although on the flip side of history some prefer to remember Mao as one of the greatest dictators ever, his role as a philosopher, strategist, and statesman is unparalleled. He was unapologetically revolutionary and directly led wars of liberation. Hence in 1927, he was quoted as saying, 'Revolution is not a dinner party, nor an essay nor a painting nor a piece of embroidery: it cannot be so refined, so leisurely and gentle, so temperate, kind, courteous, restrained and magnanimous. A revolution is an insurrection, an act of violence by which one class overthrows another.'

Mao held tenaciously on to political power until 1976 when he died. However, as would be expected, great internal rivalry had existed among his close lieutenants for much of the twenty-seven years he ruled China. The two main combating groups were the so-called 'gang of four' whose emphasis was on continuity with revolution as espoused by Mao. The other group was made up of those that were more liberal, led by Deng Xiaoping. One of the closest to Mao, Deng favoured a shift away from the structured form and rigidness of both politics and economy. He averred his mind more to reform which was already being surreptitiously wooed from the West, and rising to permanence under the struggle for power, he started a series of policies in China.

Deng Xiaoping and Consolidation of Chinese Reform

The reforms and the rise of Den Xiaosping, in actual sense, could not be detached from Maoism. The making of a new phase in Chinese political history goes as far back as 1963, when Chinese economic planners led by Zhou Enlai had espoused the need to focus on four areas of interest. These were agriculture, industry, national defence, and science and technology. These were already being implemented in various ways under Chairman Mao, but with his ascension, Deng Xiaoping, who was part of the initial reform clique, enacted this as major developmental platforms in 1978 at the Third Plenum of 11th Central Committee of Government Platform. These reforms as now articulated stressed not only on economic reform but also on more openness in the entire body politic in the country.

Deng Xiaoping, Reformist Leader of the
People's Republic of China

Trade was more open with all countries, including the United States, education was massively expanded with higher academic standards, the old leadership system and tradition of bureaucracy were restored while government was devolved, allowing a few elections and autonomy at local levels. Although decisions were still largely decentralised and the Communist Party dominated all these, a high level of autonomy was introduced. However, with the experience of the Tiananmen Square incident of 1989, it is known that popular sociopolitical movements that aimed at change and transformation or aimed at greater religious, political, and social change in China still have a long way to go.

But one thing is that unlike the Soviet Union, which collapsed and disintegrated in the face of political change, China has remained strong. As a matter of fact, in the wave of market reform and liberalisation, Chinese state-owned companies continue to transform themselves into leading global players, now competing among themselves in a peculiar style of capitalism.

Ethnic Unity

One other reason that has kept China united is the fact of its largely monopolistic ethnic structure. Unlike the erstwhile Soviet Union or many other states that emerged out of unwieldy imperial states of conquered people, China is essentially constituted of one ethnic group, i.e. Han. The

Han group makes up 92 per cent of the Chinese population. The other ethnic groups totalling about 55 in number include Zhuang, Hui, Manchu, Uyghur as the largest with over 10 million each, and Dai the least with barely one million people. The ethno-linguistic unity is therefore solid or posed little challenge to the country's unity and integration. Although expressions of irredentism of various sorts exist from time to time, they pose little challenge for China's immediate national cohesion. Unity therefore seems to exist in the face of diversity and change. As a matter of fact one of the greatest legacies of Maoism was its conscious policy of weakening sub-national identity into uniformism of socio-cultural ideology through various movements within the country.

Although inimical to what some may call growth of cultural heritage and legacies, the deliberate suppression of local identities since the time of the Cultural Revolution has played a main role in diffusing the survival of individualism as it pertains to diversities and the growth of pan-Chinese identity. These came under the rather utopian slogan of great unity believing that 'everyone and everything is at peace'.

What the experiences of India and China show is that no one paradigm exists for building stable states. But political leaders and thinkers on whom the crafting of best models of state building rests have adroitly used a basket of choices as dictated by change and time. Even as unwieldy as both countries are and having experienced rather far-reaching political changes and socio-economic transformation, they have managed to remain strong and fledging. However, the seeds of internal dissent and potential assault on peace have in no way themselves to be totally disquieting.

Chapter Ten

State and Integration in the Middle East: Israel and the Arab World

As the modern state system went through its process of evolution in Western Europe, largely distinctively, the Mediterranean world and the Arabian Peninsula, also referred to as Middle East or Western Asia as seen earlier, were themselves the epicentre of an exuberant intercourse between religion, philosophy, and science during the period. The flurry of philosophical inter-exchanges in this part of the world could, to a large extent, be regarded as arising from indigenous processes of growth of civilisation. It is also easy to give a place to the role of their strategic geography which people of this area took advantage of.

Spread out in an area equidistant from Europe and Asia, the Middle East has three distinct geographical areas: Northern Arabia has the Syrian desert as its outward confines, while the south extends towards the Red Sea and the Persian Gulf. Indeed, the most southern part of the area was bounded by the Indian Ocean with rather effusive early trade and social economic links with people across these waters. The Arabian Peninsula particularly was therefore easily a mid-point between the fledging world of political philosophy and state formation which were experienced by Europe on the one hand and the Orient on the other. The traditional link between the people of the Arabian Peninsula and the classical culture of Phoenicians, the Greeks, Etruscans, and Romans were of particular significance.

The supra ethnic influence of the Roman Empire and the expansion of Hellenic political thought which went with it, as well as its proximity to the Egyptian civilisation, were of special significance. It is known that fledging trade and rich demographic exchanges existed between the area and Egypt from the earliest times. In the accounts of Ptolemy and other writings of the time, a good portion of the Arabian peninsula were referred to as Arabia Helix because of the wealth of the inhabitants, derived from long-distance trade mainly in spices from India and ivory, gold, and other products from Africa as well as local luxury items such as frankincense and myrrh much prized in Egypt and the Roman world.

In a situation where Arabia and other neighbours such as Jews, Turks, Kurds, and the people of the area found themselves as major trading hubs of great neighbouring civilisations, it was easy for some form of comprehensive political systems to emerge in order to control and regulate both commerce and interpersonal relations.

The Zionist Nation of Israel

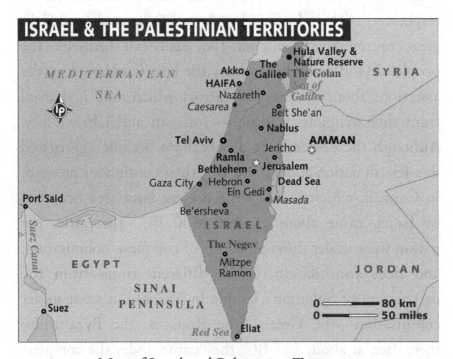

Map of Israel and Palestinian Territories

The nation of Israel located in the southward precincts of the Arabian Peninsula is perhaps one of the most controversial political enclaves in the world. They refer to themselves as the Zionist nation, and many of them would like to hold fast that it is a nation of entirely Jewish people. As a matter of fact, a popular quotation has it that 'Israel is the very embodiment of Jewish continuity, it is the only nation on earth that inhabit the same land, bear the same name, speak the same language and worship the same God that it did 3000 years ago'.

The Jewish people who make up Israel trace their origin to Abraham, his son, Isaac, and grandson, Jacob, respectively. Their history has however been shrouded in great controversy and enigma. They easily call themselves the people of God and their country the holy land based on the assertions about their secular history which itself is derived from their religious tradition—Judaism and Christianity. Although the descendants of Abraham became aggregated in a Jewish nation about 1300 BC, their continuous presence in Canaan, which today is the present land area occupied by Israel, came about around 1800 BC. Thereafter, the nation went under different forms of conquest, colonisation, and near annihilation. So at different times from the destruction of Solomon's temple in 587 BC, it went under colonisation—the Greeks, the Romans, the Byzantines; thereafter, at about 637 BC, they came under the conquest of the Arabs and the brief takeover of The Crusaders from AD 1099 to 1291, and the Arabs and Islamists returned

(Mamluks and the Ottomans for about three hundred years). It was after then that the British ruled between 1917 and 1948, when the nation of Israel was created from Palestine. But one fact of history is that people of Jewish origin even in forms of remnants have always lived in Canaan continually for over three thousand years.

Jewish people started to return to their homeland at different times to join those that were left over. Monolithic entry particularly from North Africa and Europe started to take place in the first half of the twentieth century. It is noteworthy that, in different nations where they had been scattered or dispersed at different times, they displayed unimaginable enterprise, scholarship, and dexterity for survival. This achievement has even made several of their adversaries and traducers to accept that these 'are the people of God'. But their return from different parts of the world to the land of Israel itself brought them under great attack and tribulation. Starting with the war of independence in 1948 against the Arab states who are their neighbours, they have fought a series of declared wars with the Arabs over the Sinai in 1956, the six-day war in 1967, and the Yom Kippur war in 1973. Yet, in all its existence from 1948 till date, the nation of Israel has been in a state of 'bellicose peace' with its Arab neighbours.

The Place of Economic Boom

Though a relatively small country with an area of 22,072 km², which can be crossed from its Mediterranean coast to the eastern end of river Jordan in only two hours, it is one of the greatest countries on earth. Israel can boast of a well-developed economy with a gross domestic product (GDP) of $247.9 billion and a per capita GDP of $32,200 in nominal term according to the 2012 estimate. With a population of about 8 million people, it has a labour force of 3.268 million out of which 2.5 per cent are engaged in the agricultural sector, 31.4 per cent in the industry sector, and 66.1 per cent in the services sector. Israel is ranked among the topmost countries in the world in terms of money spent in research and development in relation to GDP. This has no doubt propelled its ranking to fourth place in the world of scientific activities. Israeli scientists have immensely contributed to the accelerated progress in the areas of medicine, solar energy, computer science, genetics, and other areas of scientific endeavour. In the beginning of 2009, 63 Israeli companies were listed on the NASDAQ, which is more than the aggregate of those from Europe, China, India, Japan, Korea, and Malaysia.

The robust economic development has enabled the subsequent governments to build a world-class capitalist but equally social welfare state. Israel enjoys the best standards of living in the world like Canada and Switzerland. This is a major uniting factor.

The Place of Religion

Many have also described the key factor for the success of Israel as largely traceable to its compact and exclusive religion of Judaism that bonds them together. Judaism is egregious and creates an ethereal bond among the Jews. The Jews also claim to have a strong sense of ineluctable bond with God due to the promises He made to Abraham, Isaac, Jacob, and David and that no nation can be better than them. This from the religious point of view appears to have some implications that have contributed to the success of Israel.

First, the feeling of being in partnership with the divine and omnipotent creator of the universe has always spurred the Israelis in whatever they do. While this may be viewed as a mere religious dogma, it conjures within the Jewish people a drive towards determined national accomplishments and upliftment. The national morale at any given time exhibits the expectancy of a metaphysical intervention that is always accompanied by positive results. Military strategists often posit that the greatest battles recorded in human history have always been won when the physical strength of soldiers is combined with the feelings of such supernatural favouritism. This sense of feeling has motivated Israel in all its national challenges and battles which they have won with ease.

Second is the collective natural psyche and discipline which is perhaps more than any other religion. Judaism is based on set dictates and norms which traverse and encompass every aspect of human life. It is based on very strong emphasis and responsibilities on its adherents. It further imposes a very strict moral code that guides every aspect of life. This norm of living and its implication became visible during the time of post-Egyptian liberation, the wilderness years, as well as during Joshua's adventures in Canaan and the takeover of the 'Promised Land'. It has been maintained since that time till the formation of Israel in 1948 and till the present day. The Israelis at different times met very hostile neighbours at all times, who were already occupants of the land. However, they always showed strong discipline and strength in maintaining their homeland. The feeling of discipline that the religious life ingrained in them was accompanied by strength, courage, and unusual presence of mind to withstand most eventualities.

Last, irrespective of their origin, the Jewish people have the feeling of oneness with purpose, shared religious brotherhood, national vision, and aspirations which are superior to pseudo cultural interest by being averred to 'as the people of God'. Their lifestyle is always targeted at staying on top in everything they do. They also have the feeling of superiority complex, a feeling that they are better than any nation, thereby compelling the need for hard work.

Holy Land Syndrome

The nation of Israel is an entire site of religious activities for persons of different faith. Besides its very prominent religious symbolism, Israel remains among the most liked tourism destinations around the world. It has the most visited sacred and treasured sites of Judaism as well as those of Christianity, Islam, and the Baha'i faith. Some of the holy sites include the Western Wall, Dome of the Rock, Al Asqa Mosque, Church of the Holy Sepulchre, Mount Olives, Baha'i shrine and gardens, and Mount Sinai. The other most visited tourist destinations are Masada, Caesarea, Jerusalem Biblical Zoo, Zoological Centre of Tel Aviv-Ramat Gan, Hamat Gader, Coral World Underwater Observatory in Eliat, Banis, Yamit 2000 in Holon, Luna Park in Tel Aviv, and Qumram. In 2012, an estimated 3.5 million tourists visited Israel, i.e. almost half of the country's population.

Besides the contribution of other economic activities to the GDP of the country, tourism and the multiplier effects which it creates contribute hugely to the economic fortunes of Israel. Every year and virtually all seasons, this country attracts huge amount of foreign exchange by way of tourism.

But more like that, the 'Holy Land' syndrome unwittingly calls for, from both its nationals and friends of the country, the need to uphold and present its sovereignty. For example, Proselytes of the Christian and Judaism religions are enjoined to continuously pray for the peace of Jerusalem and by so doing receive blessings. So there is a collective demand to support and preserve this Holy Land spiritually and physically and support its survival, as an act of faith.

Conscious Policy of Integration

Although most of Israel's citizens speak Hebrew and profess Judaism as their religion, yet the Jewish people could be called 'many in one', as its citizens come from far and wide from different cultural backgrounds and experiences, each having its own pseudo culture. For example, the Jews from Latin America speak Spanish as the first language and have Hispanic culture. On the contrary, European Jews speak mostly Yiddish in Germany, Slavic in Czech Republic and rest of Eastern Europe, Yevanic in Greece, Zarphitic—an extinct language spoken in Northern France etc. These various cultural groups also practice their own type of Judaism which is slightly different from the rest. The Sephardi and Mizrahi Jews, for example, are people who have grown up for centuries in the Arab world and come from countries such as Morocco, Egypt, Yemen, Iran, and Iraq and speak Arabic, and their social interactions have tendencies that portray their origin.

Last but not the least are the Falashas who are the 'Black Jews' raised in Ethiopia, Eritrea, and other places in the horn of Africa with Amharic as the first language and have Judaism practices which they claim are superior to others.

The Ethiopian Jews also boast of the possession of the 'Ark of the Covenant'—a symbolic sacred representation of the presence of God in their midst, which disappeared after the destruction of the first temple. It should be also added that Israel is also the home to about 2 million Arab Muslims who have lived there before the time of the first exile of the Jews in 70 BC and are bona fide citizens of Israel with representation in the Knesset (parliament). There also exist the descendants of the Arameans, the Greeks, and other smaller racial entities who are not Jewish but are bona fide citizens of this kaleidoscopic nation.

From the time of its inception, Israel has therefore remained an immigrant-based society which was more or less a coat of many colours which its ancestral progenitor, Jacob, gave to his son, Joseph. Since 1948, its population has increased from 700,000 to 8 million people. Hence, immigrants make up the dominant part of the population. The society therefore found itself at the centre of various matrices flowing from the tide of human egress and ingress. In such a situation of social, economic, cultural, psychological, and ideological divergences, conflicts of various forms have always created rift.

To make matters worse, various Jewish groups settled in patterns that displaced their origin, i.e. religio-national background. The task of managing immigrants and of integrating these people was one of the most daunting challenges of the government at every stage.

The government of Israel therefore had to embark upon conscious policy instruments to promote the growth of a unified homogenous and integrated society. With the 1950 law of return (stipulating that every Jew world over has the right to return on equal basis) and the law that followed two years later on the (law of citizenship), a grand norm as it was provided guaranteed equal rights for all immigrants. Indeed, by 1973, these laws were further modified to allow even non-Jewish relations of such immigrants to obtain Israeli citizenship without hindrance. There was also the policy to avoid discrimination of women and other minority groups like the Arabs.

The succession of governments of Israel also tried to put in place other proactive policies in integrating immigrants into the society. It is perhaps the only country that has a ministry known as Ministry of Immigrant Absorption. This institution is charged with the responsibility of offering government assistance to new immigrants and thereby propelling their full integration into every facet of the society. Some of these policies cut across areas in education, language, employment, and housing. In the area of education, immigrants are encouraged to pursue higher education through financial assistance by means of scholarship, loans, and grants. Intensive language courses are also provided for immigrants that have no knowledge of Hebrew. Employment opportunities are made available for immigrant professionals in the areas of science and research and development engineers. Subsidised loans are also provided for the self-employed who participate in specialised business development courses. The Government also assists immigrants in the area of housing through the provision of subsidised rent and mortgages. These policies which have made it easy for the integration process of immigrants have continued till today.

The Role of Diaspora Community

Biblical and historical accounts show that the splintering and dispersion of Jewish people into different parts of the world occurred as a result of conscious divine action intended at creating reprieve. But then, the promise was also that whichever nation they were dispersed to, the God Yahweh would not leave them abandoned. True to this biblical belief or some may call a myth, the Jewish people from different parts of the world have proved to be most outstanding in science and technology, commerce and enterprise, industry, politics, entertainment, etc. Some of these great Jews especially in recent history and contemporary times include Karl Marx, Albert Einstein, Henry Kissinger, Kurt Eisner, Ben Bernanke, Dominique Strauss-Kahn, Mark Zuckerberg, Steven Spielberg, Roman Abramovich, Joseph Liebermann, etc.

Indeed, the progressive march of humanity into knowledge, science, and technology as well as culture and literature is all attributed to the works of prominent Jewish

Diaspora. But due to the homogenous structure of their religion and cultural setting, the Jews around the world, most especially in the Western democracies, have all seen Israel as their central homeland. They have therefore placed their collective intellectual and material fortune into the survival of Israel and striven to put in the best at any time to sway global activities in favour of Israel. Many Jewish Diaspora, also, directly commit their own wealth into the advancement of Israel in various areas. For example, the Jewish lobby in the United States under the name Jewish Congress and other Zionist movements have continued to ensure that the political and economic structures are formulated in such a manner to accord to Israel the most favoured nation's status in almost everything.

The Diaspora also plays a major role in the huge number of offshore transfers which they make to Israel's economy. Furthermore, the Jewish people in Diaspora play a major role as contact for their kith and kin in Israel in opening opportunities for the participation of economic activities in other countries. This has significantly helped in improving the economy and by implication the social well-being of the nation.

Good Leadership

David Ben-Gurion, Founder and First Prime Minister of Israel

A discussion on the experience and fortunes of Israel will be incomplete without a look at the leadership pattern of the country. The country has been blessed with many focused leaders that have ruled since independence in 1948, starting with David Ben Gurion (1886-1973), Golda Meir (1898-1978), to the present Prime Minister, Benjamin Netanyahu. Statesmen in Israel have remained committed to the survival and growth of the nation in very uncommon manners.

Those in politics and power have always seemed to accept it as transient. It is the only country in the world where a former Prime Minister could revert to serving as a minister or an ambassador after leaving office and later become Prime Minister again. The Israeli politicians do not therefore seem to see power as an end but as a means in helping to diffuse tension and bringing about rapid socioeconomic development in the nation. The celebrated Simon Peres moved from the position of Prime Minister to minister and then became President of Israel. Benjamin Netanyahu has also served as Prime Minister and later as minister and then became Prime Minister again.

State Formation in the Arabian Peninsula

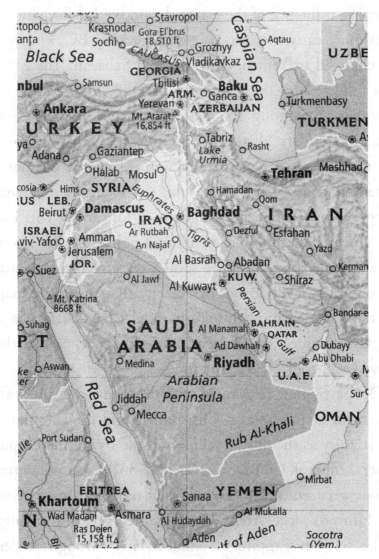

Map of the Middle East

States ruled by princes easily arose along the southward areas of the Arabian Peninsula, especially on the Red Sea, the Persian Gulf, and the Indian Ocean. Even the middle areas where the people were more nomadic and pastoral, the operating influence of the external world aided formation of states quite early. As early as eighth century BC, kingdoms had emerged in Yemen; Minaean and Sabaean. These were soon followed by the kingdoms of Had, Hra, Maut, and Quataban.[138] Among the pastoralists and nomads, state formation efforts also showed up early, centring round the tribal structures of the Bedouins. Towards the north-western portion of the Peninsula, the Deds state emerged and grew to become the Kingdom of Lihyanite. This itself later emerged as the more structured political order known as Labataean Kingdom. The solid nature of the Labataean kingdom was underscored by the fact that they were major city builders, leaving behind a mass of iconoclastic legacies that also flaunted the opulence and prosperity which they enjoyed and controlled at the time.

Of particular relevance to this study are the early conversion of Ethiopia to Christianity and the adoption of Christianity as the official religion in the Byzantine Empire. Under Emperor Constantine II (317-361), two missionary bishops were sent to convert people of the kingdom of 'Azum and Himyrts' (the Arabs). Christianity was also brought to the Sassian Empire of the Persians through traders, prisoners, and other freewill travellers. Of great significance

---

[138] *The Arabian Peninsula before Islam* by Abdulrahaman R. al-Ansari in UNESCO History of the World.

were the Christians of the Sassian Empire who took the task of conversion of the Arabs to the new faith as a cardinal objective, leading to the establishment of a Nestorian Bishop of Oman.

There also emerged during this period the Himyrts Kingdom which adopted its own brand of monotheist religion and political philosophy. The expansion of political power by these Himyrts Kingdom from Yemen and its inevitable clash with Axumite power in Ethiopia, though much drenched in blood, appears to have had a very positive influence in the process of state formation in the area. Steadily, other kingdoms started to emerge, for example, in Central Arabia occupied by the Kinda tribe. Towards the eastern fringes, the Arabian-influenced states started to emerge, though getting into a bellicose relationship with the Persian potentates. The Sassian Empire which had emerged around the Persian Gulf made various efforts to subdue the Arabs but ended up in creating relationships which helped in bringing about fusions even among the nomads. On their part, the nomads, especially the Bedouin tribes, remain largely warriors, most times providing the fighting force for the spurt of Arab kings providing escorts and guards to long-distance merchants.

The Benefit of Theocratic Foundation

As seen earlier, from the time of Prophet Mohammed and his successors, the form of governance established was regarded as Islamic in character. In other words, the foundation of the state was ingrained in religious dogma which provided basic philosophical foundation for existence. Under the constitution of Medina established in AD 622, the Muslim nation—umma, which literally means a brotherhood established under the reign of Califs (Rashidun Caliphate), was supposed to be rightly guided by the Koran and Hadith. Thereafter, there emerged the Arabian empire which, over time, came to encompass most of the area, starting initially with the Ummayad Caliphate (622-751) and then a series of dynasties, i.e. Mamluk and Othman (1299-1924), Ummayad of Cordova, Spain (756-1031), and Abbasid Caliphate (750-758). Some other expansive Islamic potentates also ruled outside Arabia and Persia in such places as Russia, Central Asia, South Asia, South-east Asia, China, and Africa.

The fundamental view as taught was the concept of the Government founded on the basis of consultation on the teachings of the Koran and Sunni, the election of a leader, fair opportunity of expression, and non-dominance of the views of the non-political majority groups. The Prophet Mohammed himself is recorded as having strictly abided by the majority view. This political structure held sway over much of the Islamic world in the course of history until their capitulation to European imperial rule in eighteenth, nineteenth and twentieth centuries.

The Art of Faith

The rest of Islamic countries mostly centred around the existing tribal and clan structures. States of various sizes were formed, all practicing at various levels of Islamic political structures. This varied in political traditions, ranging from the big imperial structures earlier mentioned to confederations, federations, unitary governments, absolute, and constitutional monarchs, but the state was founded on the reliance on the Koran. But then, while some practised direct and representative democracies others were simply absolute and constitutional monarchs. In other cases, various forms of oligarchies held to power or grew into authoritarian regimes that sprouted all over.

Rather than view the state as a social contract or artificial creation by the capricious influence of man, Islamic jurisprudence attributed its existence to supernatural design. It was a gift of the Almighty for people to live in harmony following divinely prescribed precepts. Sovereignty is therefore seen as belonging to Allah, who is also the source of power and the laws that govern rights and obligations at various levels. Although the ruler derives power from the people, it is primarily responsible to Allah to whom he also accounts. To that extent, the ruler himself is a servant of the people and has a duty to ensure that the state performs the welfare of all and guarantees the basic needs and existential requirements of all.

This faith-based Islamic philosophical premise of the state, while not perfect, helped Islamic states to thrive around the world and helped contribute to human civilisation in virtually all areas.

The Gift of Economic Well-Being

The economic and social systems were also religious in character, but while promoting true enterprise and entrepreneurship, the Islamic social and economic system is strongly welfare. The economy of the Islamic states with the rule of 'Zakat' is intended at ensuring free enterprise but inimical to property accumulation. It was strongly welfarist and egalitarian in ensuring that the rich were not inordinately carrying out commerce, industry, and wealth to the detriment of the poor. Indeed, exploitation of man and the debasement of the poor and needy were seriously sanctioned. The state, therefore, has spiritual and political obligation to protect the poor and ensure the full creative potentials of all.

Often because of great influence of global free market capitalism or erstwhile socialist and communist tendencies, most Islamic states survived till contemporary times have straddled in the middle. But the question that has often been crucial is to what extent has the state protected the poor and averted the exploitation tendencies of modern global economies.

In all this and with the discovery of a huge amount of hydrocarbon around the Arabian Peninsula, most of the Islamic world, especially the Arabian Peninsula, has shown one of the most profound levels of economic and social growth. Added wealth and attainment of high levels of sophistication in terms of consumption have helped the countries to enjoy relative peace in political terms.

During the period of East-West rivalry, various states pitched camps and therefore held greater areas of focus. A few others stood in favour of pan-Islamic nationalism based on needed unification of Muslims and a return to an imaginary supra-Muslim state which never existed. This is more so as Islamic states found their way of life increasingly forfeited by Western civic humanistic and neo-liberal thoughts. In places such as Iran, revival of teachings of anti-secular statehood had become amplified by some of its leaders who taught revival to strict Islamic dogma.

But more than that, one contradiction that many modern Islamic radicals question is the fact stated earlier that the Prophet's teachings insisted on consensus and fairness and whether this still exists in the present state system.

The other critical query which is extended and is being raised by some contemporary Islamic radicals is the role of Western adulteration of Islamic ways of living as the main argument to return to a more puritanical Islamic dogma lost over the years. The issue is whether the so-called 'Islamic' states or Muslim-dominated communities in multi-ethnic states practice tenets of religious injunction for governance as entrenched in canon. For example, they raise issues over the fact that whether in many Muslim-dominated states various forms of government from military-related autocracy, monarchy, or political monopoly truly promote a right environment for perpetuity of true spiritual growth and existence of equity and fairness. This gives a better understanding of the present wind of instability and violence being unleashed on the people.

The age-old philosophical dialectic on the proper balancing of faith and secularism has remained a potent force for internal implosion and external fight for survival as it were. These forces now seem to have come afore both within the Muslim world and in a more militant fashion around the world.

The aspect that relates to fight for survival in an age of 'clash of civilisation' became more pertinent with the end of the Cold War. From the Cold War period, students of political history, especially American political analysts, watched with worry the burgeoning rise of radical Islamic groups in the Middle East. The war against the Talibans in Afghanistan was therefore quickly referred to as a manifestation of the new direction of global conflict. The subsequent adventurism of Muammar Gaddafi (1942-2011) and Saddam Hussein (1937-2006) of Iraq did not seem to have helped matters as this quickly attracted the ire of dominant Western coalition of military power. The unsalutary results of the development of various sorts. Iran and Iraq War also helped create a mass of tension in the region. By the time Iraq rivalled and attempted to annex Kuwait in 1990, it only underscored a heightened political mood in the region. Indeed, the Iraq-Syrian relations saw no less amount of tension and escalation. Worse still was the radicalism of political processes in Iran. With the rise of Ayatollah Khomeini and the courage to try to confront the dominance of America and the spread of values and norms that were at variance with doctrinaire, Islam created the background for eventual clash. Unfortunately, American consumerism depended essentially on oil from the Middle East. So also the need to protect these strategic interests formed the gravamen of United States interest in the region.

Saddam Hussein, Former President of Iraq, Waving to Supporters During His Visit of Kirkuk, North of Baghdad

The other factor that created an unfortunate motif in the area was the Civil Wars in Lebanon (1975, 1982, 2006). With its origins founded in East-West rivalries, a breeding ground for proliferation of all forms of radical thoughts began in the region. This was especially so as Beirut was a major centre of Arabian learning and civilisation.

Above these, the other destabilising factor that remains is the unsolved Palestinian question and relation with Israel. The Palestinian question in elementary term finds its origin in the foundation of the Jewish state of Israel and the non-creation of a corresponding independent Palestinian state. This is in addition to resolving various straddling issues such as the question of inherited and shared historic and religious assets in such places as Jerusalem, mutual recognition, settlements, and hydrological questions. There is also the question resolving the issue of refugees and above all violence. These issues despite various peace efforts around the world, especially the Madrid Conference (1991), Oslo Accord (1993), Camp David Summit (2000), Taba Summit (2001), have remained stranded. The Palestinian resort to Intifada and existence of extremist faith-based groups such as Hamas and Islamic Jihad have rather inflamed the situation and created breeding grounds for the raising of dissident groups and global 'war'. While the Cold War lasted, this had been properly managed by the United States and Soviet Union with great amount of success.

Global and Religious Zealotism—Al-Qaeda

Towards the end of the twentieth century, there arose some form of agitation from fundamentalist Islamist groups for the establishment of an Islamic state across the Muslim territories with strict compliance to *Sharia*. This has notoriously been led by Al-Qaeda, meaning 'the Base'. Al-Qaeda was founded about 1988 by Osama Bin Laden, a claimed millionaire citizen of the Kingdom of Saudi Arabia who brought together his Arab Mujahedeen, who were all veterans of the war, against Soviet Union's occupation of Afghanistan, to fight a new jihad.

Bin Laden was actively involved in the war against the Soviet invasion and occupation of Afghanistan, which lasted for about nine years, that is from 1979 to 1988, with the Soviet Union suffering defeat in the hands of militias of Muslim Mujahedeen supported by the United States, Saudi Arabia, and Pakistan. However, the attention of Al-Qaeda and Bin Laden shifted to the United States, who was a former ally of Bin Laden following the invasion of Kuwait by Iraq and the subsequent involvement of the United States in the war tagged 'Operation Desert Storm' in Kuwait. The involvement of the United States in this war led to the stationing of its troops in Saudi Arabia. Al-Qaeda and Bin Laden saw this action of the United States as a desecration of the holiest land in the Islamic world. This led to the re-direction of Bin Laden and Al-Qaeda's antagonism towards the rulers of Saudi Arabia and the United States through an extended period of terror campaign. The main aim of this campaign was to dethrone the Saudi Royal family and install an Islamic regime on the Arabian Peninsula. Not pleased with the motives of Bin Laden, the Saudi authorities deported him and subsequently revoked his citizenship.

Al-Qaeda considered these Western nations and institutions as an impediment to the realisation of the establishment of a pan-Islamic nation. Owing to this belief and the desire to achieve the goal of establishing an Islamic state, the group had directed a holy jihad (a war of terror) against the United States and other Western countries. This, in their belief, would cripple the United States both economically and politically and would force it out of all Muslim lands.

The group's leadership structure at inception was made up of veterans of the war against Soviet Union occupation in Afghanistan. It was commanded by Osama Bin Laden and deputised by Dr Ayman al-Zawahiri until the assassination of Bin Laden in May 2011 by the United States. It operated through a coalition of terror organisations known as *International Islamic for Jihad against the Jews and Crusaders* to coordinate activities through a council known as *Shura* led by Bin Laden. Their operational base is not permanent, but in the earlier years of its formation, their headquarters was based in Afghanistan until the overthrow of the Taliban regime in 2001 by the United States led allied forces following the 9/11 attack of the World Trade Centre in New

York. It is currently headed by Dr Ayman al-Zawahiri, an Egyptian by origin.

Al-Qaeda is said to be currently made up of networks of terror organisations and affiliate groups like the Egyptian Islamic Jihad, Al-Qaeda in the Arabian Peninsula, Al-Qaeda in Iraq, Al-Qaeda in the Islamic Maghreb, the Libyan Islamic Fighting group, Lashkar-e-Taiba and Jaish-e-Muhammad of Pakistan and Kashmir, Islamic Movement of Uzbekistan, Armed Islamic Group of Algeria, Abu Sayyaf Group of Philippines, Jemaah Islamiya of South-east Asia, Harak al-Shabaab al-Mujahedeen of Somalia, and Jamaatul ahlil sunna lidawati wal Jihad known as Boko Haram of North-eastern Nigeria—all fighting for the same cause.

Among others, the following attacks are accredited to have been carried out since its formation: Two bombs were detonated in Aden, Yemen, in 1992 targeted at Movenpick Hotel and Goldmohur Hotel that killed two people and injured seven others; the 1993 World Trade Center bombing that killed six people and injured 1,042 others; the 1996 Khobar Towers military complex in Saudi Arabia that killed nineteen U.S. servicemen; the 1998 bombings of the U.S. embassy in Kenya and Tanzania that killed 300 people and injured several others; the 2000 suicide bombing of U.S.S. Cole that killed 17 U.S. servicemen; the 2005 London attack that killed fifty-two people and injured seven hundred others; and other attacks.

On 11 September 2001, it carried out the most devastating attack in the history of America, when four commercial planes were hijacked and two flown into the World Trade Centre and a third into the Pentagon, killing three thousand people and injuring several others. A fourth plane targeted at the Capitol Hill was crashed in a field in Pennsylvania. This singular attack stepped up the momentum of the U.S. fight against Al-Qaeda and terrorism, leading to the invasion of Afghanistan, dethronement of the Taliban regime, and the dislodgement of the operations of the group's activities from Afghanistan. It also culminated in the assassination of Osama Bin Laden during a covert operation carried out by United States in Abbottabad, Pakistan, in May 2011, almost ten years after 9/11. The killing of Bin Laden came as a devastating blow to the group.

However, the activities and objectives of this group transcend the attacking of United States and its allies, but it is rather directed at achieving far greater goals as its end result. According to a series of statements credited to the group's leader, al-Zawahiri, al-Qaeda is actively pursuing the liberation of Muslim lands from the occupation of both non-Muslims and apostate rulers, imposing their own version of *Sharia* on Muslims and non-Muslims in these lands, erecting then a state that they will call the *Caliphate*, and eventually making God's Word the highest.

The question then arises if these objectives can be achieved. Though the group has pursued all their goals with so much vigour since its formation, but it is yet to achieve them. It has however succeeded in fighting a long war in

Somalia and has seized control of some parts of the country where they have imposed *Sharia* as the prevailing law. They also took over some key towns in Northern Mali, including the historic town of Timbuktu in collaboration with some of their affiliate groups in North Africa, where they seek to establish an independent homeland for the Tuareg people called Azawad, governed by *Sharia*. The reign in Northern Mali only lasted for less than a year following the French-led offensive supported by Malian and African Union troops. As of today, there is no known state that is called the 'Caliphate'. But all are still waiting to see if their objective can be achieved in this twenty-first century or in centuries to come.

The Arab Spring

Another factor which was time bound was the threat of internal implosion within the Islamic world, especially in the Arab Peninsula. Towards the end of 2010 and the beginning of 2011, there were a series of protests and demonstrations that enveloped the Arab world, specifically originating from Tunisia in North Africa and spreading to other countries in the region and the Middle-East in quick succession. These protests were coined the 'Arab Spring' by Marc Lynch in his article on foreign policy. It was sparked off in Tunisia following the self-immolation of Mohamed Bouazizi after the confiscation of his goods and the harassment and humiliation he also suffered in the hands of local officials thereafter. This singular action of Bouazizi sparked off greater demonstrations and riots in Tunisia in protest for reformation of political and social issues in the country, which eventually led to the stepping down of the then President, Zine El Abidine Ben Ali on January 14, 2011, after spending twenty-three years in office.

The protest quickly spread to neighbouring North African and Middle Eastern countries like Egypt, Libya, Algeria, Bharain, Syria, Yemen, Jordan, Algeria, Morocco, Kuwait, Oman, Jordan, and Sudan. The protest in Egypt which lasted for about two months eventually led to the overthrow of President Hosni Mubarak, who had stayed in office for about thirty years. He was later sentenced to life imprisonment for ordering the killing of protesters. In Libya, the scenario was different as the protest led to arms struggle that later blossomed into a civil war between the loyalists of President Muammar Gaddafi and the rebel forces supported by the United States, France, United Kingdom, and a coalition of twenty-seven Arab countries through aerial bombardment. This brought the forty-two years' reign of Gadaffi to an end. He was eventually killed by rebel forces on October 20, 2011, in Sirte.

Arab Spring Protest in Tunisia

The situation in Yemen was not different as the series of protests also led to the end of President Ali Abdullah Saleh's reign in power on February 27, 2012. He had ruled Yemen since 1978 until its unification with the south in 1990. In Syria, the protests also led to a full-blown civil war between government forces and the rebels. Bashar al-Assad, who had ruled for over twelve years, succeeded his father who ruled for about thirty years until his death in June 2000. All overtures to Bashar al-Assad to relinquish power have failed as the war still rages on in Syria.

Libyans Protest Demanding the Removal of
Muammar Gaddafi

In this midst of uncertainty and turmoil, in the Arab world, the situation in the Gulf states, Saudi Arabia, Iran, Iraq, Kuwait, Bahrain, Qatar, and Oman remains delicate.

A critical look at all these countries only shows one pattern of leadership as synonymous with what was earlier highlighted. It is a common phenomenon that all the leaders of these countries had ruled for a long time without creating a healthy political environment for opposition to thrive coupled with dictatorship, human rights violations, and increased level of corruption and poverty in some cases like Yemen. As can be seen from some of these instances, rulership was seen as a succession of family dicta.

In Syria, Bashar al-Assad took over from his father after his death. In Libya, Gadaffi was also grooming his son to succeed him; the scenario in Egypt was also pointing towards the same direction. People were dissatisfied with all these and took up the sovereignty to bring the desired changes to most of these countries. Though they came with grave consequences, it eventually brought a lot of reformations aimed at creating a conducive environment for better political existence, something alien to the Islamic state as dictated by the Holy Prophet. This easily informed the election of 'Islamic Brotherhood' in Egypt. However, as the world expected, the appetite for change remains ominously as an ill wind and the pursuit of the ideal remains a mirage. What all these show is that these processes must be pursued with patience and perseverance. If done hurriedly, we could get a failure of states or total collapse as we shall see next.

Chapter Eleven

How States Disintegrate: A Post-Mortem of the Soviet Union

Having seen how states come about and stay together, it would be important to see what makes them disintegrate. Where it occurs, several states from Roman Empire, Ottoman Empire, British Empire, and its kind have failed. In recent times, Yugoslavia, Czechoslovakia, and Sudan splintered before the eyes of the world. This is crucial because during the past eighty years, world history saw the episodic rise and equally sudden collapse of one of the most prominent political edifices ever erected by man. In a contrast of wits, Vladimir Lenin, who founded the Soviet Union, and Mikhail Gorbachev, who led in signing its *nunc dimittis*, stated separately thus:

> *We want a voluntary union of nations, a nation which precludes any coercion of the nation by another, a union founded on complete confidence, on a clear recognition of brotherly unity on absolute consent.*
> (V. I. Lenin, 1917)

Versus

> *There are historical and religious reasons for the present problems. And of course, we are now having to pay for past crimes committed against entire nation.*
> (M. Gorbachev, 1990)

The idealism of Lenin and the realism of Gorbachev are the factors which characterised the history of the Soviet Union during the seventy years of its existence. The Union of Soviet Socialist Republics, as it was officially known, was not only a superpower in global politics but was also the single largest political entity in the world. Its geographical extent spread out from the north-eastern extremity of Europe to parts of Central Asia, the Polar regions and the North American continent, while its size was over 17 million square kilometres, i.e. one-sixth of the earth's land mass.

The population was nearly 300 million, which was the third largest after China and India.

The sheer geographical size, pluralistic human composition, and wealth of natural resources made the Soviet Union a land of intense centrifugal resilience and ascribed to it rightly a deserved place in global affairs. It shared common borders with over fifteen countries, thereby bringing it more under the focus of various interest groups.

Moreover, since it emerged from World War I as one of the allied powers and its subsequent acquisition of unprecedented military might, technological development and relative economic power gave it a place as one of the two superpowers in the bipolar world order that ensued after 1945. This is why even after its official demise, the influence of its successor state Russia has not been obliterated in the comity of nations, not at least until its leading stockpile of nuclear warheads is reduced.[139]

---

[139] J. R. Reshetar, *The Soviet Union: Government and Politics in the Soviet Union*. New York: Harper Publications, 1978.

Before the Soviet Union and the Bolshevik Conquest

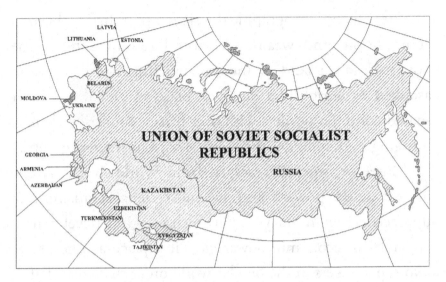

MAP of USSR Until its Collapse

By the beginning of the twentieth century, the tsarist empire of Great Russia along with the Ottoman Empire, the Prussian state, Ching Dynasty in China, Imperial Japan, and the colonial powers in Europe dominated the international scene. Diplomacy at the time was dominated by wars, alliances, truces, and the still creeping nation-state trying to consolidate itself. The Great Russian Empire was by far the most extensive, having been formed over several centuries of expansionism. Historians cite inordinate military adventurism, pursuit of economic interests, especially eastwards, and the protection of security interests in Europe as the reasons underlying the excessive expansion of the empire.

The heartland of the empire was dominated by the Russians and about twenty-two other smaller ethnic groups. The rest were 'colonies', also referred to as ethnic minorities (as compared to Russia)—Ukrainians, Belorussians, Uzbeks, Kazakhs, Kyrgyz, Lithuania, Finnish, Latvians, Polish, Estonians, Turkmens, Kurds, Gypsies, Jews, Germans, and Koreans.

It was against this background that World War I broke out in 1914 resulting in the collapse of the great powers. In the course of the war, the Soviet Union emerged as a successor of the tsarist empire, inheriting a multinational state of over one hundred different nationalities. The collapse of the old empire itself was not a direct consequence of the war, but was built around internal dynamics that led to the Bolshevik Revolution of October 1917.[140] The monarchy was sacked and replaced by the Bolsheviks whose perception of society based on historical dialectics (materialism) was a dramatic antithesis of the 'ancient regime' and indeed any other political or social system that had ever existed. It was the birth of the first Communist system of government, which hitherto had been on paper.

[140] G. A. Hosking, *A History of the Soviet Union*. London: Fontana Press, 1989, pp. 30-40. Also see D. Lane, *Politics and Aid Society in the Soviet Union*. London: Martin Robertson, 1978, pp. 21-53.

Valdimir Lenin, Russian Communist
Revolutionary and Premier of Soviet Union

On November 2, 1917, the Bolsheviks or Communists publicised a Declaration of the Right of the People of Russia, in which it pledged the equality, sovereignty, and the right of self-determination of the non-Russian nationalities. Accordingly, Ukraine, Finland, Poland, and a few others were granted independence in December 1917, but as it turned out Ukraine, Belorussia, Georgia Azerbaijan, Armenia, and others were soon invaded and reoccupied by Moscow in the same month of December 1917.[141] In December 1922, most of these different nations and states

---

[141] Reshetar, *ibid.*, p. 19.

came together to sign a treaty forming the Soviet Union, and in the years that followed, more republics were annexed including the Baltic states.

During the drafting of the first constitution in 1924, most of the constituent fifteen republics which made up the union were believed to have expressed preference for a confederation, but Moscow imposed a federation on them.[142] So the Soviet Union was formed as a nominal federation of diverse people surviving out of the remains of an old colonial empire. The Communists therefore embarked on what they termed a development of socialist nationhood through the establishment of political 'equality of nations without which as demonstrated by history, it is impossible to ensure the actual equality and friendship of nations'.[143]

Although the Bolsheviks had a very good idea of the ideal state, it turned out that they had inherited more than just land mass from the imperial courts of the tsars, but the whole apparatus of state structure and the model of administration used by them. The organisation of the old empire was characterised by a concentration of power at the centre, and it was exercised with autocratic and absolutist disposition. Another feature of tsarist Russia was its isolationism. Scholars have trailed this political behaviour of Russian monarchs to the influence of contemporaneous oriental despotism of the Mongols and Mughals of Central

---

[142] Reshetar, *ibid.*, p. 20.
[143] A. Lashin, *Socialism and State.* Moscow: Progress, 1978, p. 115.

Asia and of Byzantine monarchs (especially the aspects of divine investiture and sanction of regal authority).

Although the tsars participated prominently in the European diplomacy of their times, the rest of the empire and its people were isolated and were never in the stream of economic and political changes that swept across the continent in the few preceding centuries. The British Ambassador then in Russia, Giles Fletcher, wrote in the sixteenth century that Russians 'were kept from travelling and that they may learn nothing, of other countries'.[144]

Against this strong influence of tsarist bequeathal, the Communists embarked on establishing their ideal of 'not a casual or ephemeral conglomeration, but a stable union of people'.[145] The Communist commitment was based on the need to abolish oppression of any of the constituent 'nationalities and establish a union based on equality, fraternity and friendship as "domination of one group by another is the product of imperialism".'[146] Soviet scholar A. Lashin articulated the cardinal principle of the union as follows:

Resolute renunciation of coercion in the relation to nationalities. Recognition of equality and sovereignty

---

[144] *Tune Magazine*, 5 July 1991, p. 38.
[145] Lane, *ibid.*, p. 469.
[146] Lashin, *ibid.*, pp. 116-145.

*and self determination of nationalities. Firm union of
nations achieved by volunteerism.*[147]

The Bolsheviks were determined to change the
foundation of the state to a close economic and cultural
union, through the integration of the non-Russian
nationalities into the mainstream. Although Lenin had
personally cautioned on the need to mollify the non-Russian
nationalities due to their colonial experience, he at the same
time often touched on the possibility of cultural national
autonomy in such a multinational socialist state. Lenin and
his counterparts in the Communist Party believed that the
people could be brought together and fused into one under
a different kind of dictatorship—of the proletariat.[148] Josef
Stalin, who took over the Soviet leadership in 1929 after
the death of Lenin, gave way to these ideas of 'inescapable
fusion' of the various nationalities.

---

[147] R. Hill and Peter Frank, *The Soviet Communist Party*. London:
Allen and Unwin, 1986, pp. 76-106. Also see A. Shevtsov, *The State
and Nations in the USSR*. Moscow: Progress Publishers, 1992, pp.
55-74.

[148] Lane, *ibid.*, pp. 1-5; Reshetar, *ibid.*, pp. 62-77; Shevtsov, 1992, pp.
36-54.

Josef Stalin, General Secretary of the Communist Party of USSR

How Did the System Work?

Similar to the policies of all totalitarian structures, the style of administration adopted by the Communists succeeded in allowing them to keep this unwieldy country and its satellite states in Europe in line and under control. It also enabled them, especially under Josef Stalin and Nikita Kruschev, to carry out massive economic and social transformation programmes.

However, the style of administration was history repeating itself to the Soviet people, as Communist rule was a virtual replication of the tsarist system with all the attributes of despotism, territorial expansionism, centralism, and isolation. Again, the process of forming the Soviet Union did not follow the egalitarianism and voluntarism copiously exposed by Lenin and the party; hence, after the formation there was stiff opposition to Communist rule, leading to civil war (1918-1921). Central Asia and some of the Baltic Republics were annexed forcibly by the Red Army. Western Ukraine and Belorussia were annexed as late as 1939, followed in 1940 by the other Baltic states and the northern half of east Prussia (Kaliningrad) and parts of Finland. The expansion was in all directions, and even the attempts made from the beginning to have a looser federation or confederation were suppressed.

Since Communist rule in the republics came about as a result of the gallantry of the Red Army, it was logical that these republics had little choice than to accept full membership of the Soviet Union. The fact is that the Union was only kept in one piece by the Commissars and the Red Army!

On the political structure of state, a single party dictatorship was accompanied by actual suppression of all forms of multiplicity of political expression, contrary to the establishment. The gathering was emergent party elite that supervised an intricate bureaucratic apparatus. Like old Russia and all colonial empires, power was concentrated at the centre (Moscow) with the republics completely marginalised to the status of implementing decisions.

The non-Russian Communist Parties were treated as branches of the Russian Federation Communist Party. The various constitutional amendments, often done unilaterally by the *Presidium* of the Party, over the years removed the independence and little autonomy reserved for the republics. For instance, the 1924 and 1936 Constitutions in theory mentioned such things as 'Sovereign Rights and Right of International Relations' between the republics and other countries, but the 1977 Constitution only mentioned such issues with respect to the centre. It is important to mention that during the process, attempts were made to eliminate the republics in order to form a unitary state.[149]

Mikhail Gorbachev, General Secretary of the Communist Party of the Soviet Union, attends the party 27th Congress

---

[149] Reshetar, *ibid.*, pp. 214-218.

With regards to representation in the Government, the republics had proportional representation in the 'Supreme Soviet', the highest body of state, but their membership and influence in the *Presidium* of the Supreme Soviet, the de facto top executive, legislative, and judicial body, was minimal. As Soviet leader Mikhail Gorbachev admitted, the *Presidium's* General Secretary, who automatically held a similar position in the Communist Party committee, 'was a dictator like nobody else and has greater power'.[150] In the other bodies of government, such as the powerful State Planning Commission, the high command of the military, KGB, the Council of Ministers, The Party Central Committee (Politburo), and the Party Secretariat, the other republics were equally under-represented.

Related to this was the process of 'Sovietisation' through 'Russification', which was said to have become necessary since the European areas of the union were relatively developed in social and economic terms and could adapt more easily to the process of reform, but the rest of the union was still semi-feudal, in some cases pastoral and culturally assertive.[151] It was therefore well intended and considered a necessity to introduce European educational

---

[150] Mikhail Gorbachev, *Newsweek Magazine*, October 1991.

[151] See D. Simes, 'Gorbachev's Time of Troubles', in *Foreign Policy*, Spring 1991, p. 101; E. Allswith, *The National Question in Soviet Central Asia*. New York: Praegis, 1974. Other details can also be found in Shiner Atiner, *Islamic Peoples of Soviet Union*. London: Kegan Paul Press, 1989.

development patterns with a mixing of the rather atheist Marxist-Leninist ideals and sociocultural values. The idea was to over time remove the manifestation of cultural identity and expression based on ethnicity.[152] The system sought the utopia of an unexampled cultural unison of ethnically distinct people, upholding only the aspects of their unitary and collective values that emphasise proletarianism and the gains in building a Soviet. This entailed the dispatch of Russian skilled, technical, and administrative manpower to the less-developed areas.

There should be no revisionism as regards the economic impact of this policy because it actually brought about the visible economic development of these former less-developed areas. However, the process termed 'Russification' involved huge population movements, sometimes involuntary as with the 400,000 Crimea Attars in 1944 and the resettling of Russians in various republics. In this respect, the aspects of the policy relating to education, religion, and culture in general terms were most contentious. Initially, the educational system in the republics allowed the use of their language at primary and secondary levels. However, this had marginal relevance because higher educational opportunities were concentrated in only the Russian Federation, thereby making it imperative for others to go through the process of 'Russification'. With further reforms in 1958, Russian became favoured as a compulsory second language in the

---

[152] Shevtsov, *ibid.*, pp. 160-187.

school curricula and later in the overall administration. The study of Russian and its literature became emphasised in the course of time at the expense of the other languages. Similarly, studies on history and culture of the various people became revised to emphasise friendship of the Soviet people and history of the Bolshevik Revolution.

Another characteristic of the Soviet system just like Old Russia was isolationism. While the state pursued an active foreign policy abroad, internally, a command and circumscribed social system was introduced. In an era of communication technology, the Soviet people were isolated from both within and the outside world. Geographic mobility within the various republics and sometimes cities within the same republic were officially disfavoured.

As a matter of fact, the prescribed and systematised routine of living made it difficult for close interaction at an interpersonal level or spontaneous and natural growth of human relations. Exposure to the outside world in which the Soviet Union participated so aggressively was restrictive and censored, including Ukraine and Belorussia, who were full members of the United Nations but never participated actively in international relations in that capacity. Basic ingredients of the modern state system, such as fundamental human rights acceded to by Moscow in various conventions including the Helsinki Final Act of 1975, were denied to the people. Such incarceration was accepted with much indignation and rashness by the various republics, which had historic, cultural, and religious affinities with their neighbours in other countries in Asia and Europe. The Jewish dissent, for instance, centred around the right to emigrate to Israel or visit their various relatives in the West.[153]

This leads us to the related Soviet attitude to religion, which was another area that created a lot of irritation in the union.[154] The Russian empire under the tsar was a land rich of religious diversity—Christianity, Catholicism, Islam, Judaism, and Buddhism. The Slavic and Baltic republics were tenacious Catholics and Lutherans with a very popular but rich liturgy, while the Russian Federation was dominantly composed of Orthodox Christians. In the case of Islam, it had been established in Central Asia area for several centuries and, before the collapse of the union, accounted for about 55 million of the population—the fifth largest Islamic nation.[155] The cultural influences on these areas were therefore Arabic and Persian. The Jews on their part were concentrated around the Russian Federation and some of the other European republics.[156]

Since the Communists saw religion as an instrument of exploitation, a steady but stern suppression was embarked upon; even though Lenin was somewhat accommodative, the repression heightened with Josef Stalin. From 1928, churches were closed and converted into public buildings, factories,

---

[153] L. Kochan, *The Jews in Soviet Russia State since 1917.* London: Oxford University Press, 1978, pp. 410-412.
[154] Lane, *ibid.*, pp. 446-446.
[155] *Islamic Times Magazine?*, vol. i, Islamabad, 1990, pp. 9-13.
[156] Kochan, *ibid.*, pp. 168-196.

or museums while their leaders were arrested. Similarly, Jewish synagogues were closed down and leaders arrested and accused of spying. In 1988, there were no Hebrew schools in the Soviet Union and only one orthodox rabbi serving over 2 million people.[157] The situation with Islam was not dissimilar. In 1924, all Sharia courts were denounced. Between 1928 and 1941, mosques were reduced from 26,000 to 1,000, then further reduced to 350 in 1980, and there were two Koranic schools, with a total enrolment of eight students. Religious activities were carried out in secrecy and their leaders, some of whom still remembered the past freedom of worship, became prominent actors in what became known across Eastern Europe as 'the underground movement'.

Beyond these lay the system of bureaucracy which was introduced. The system encouraged mediocrity and sycophancy. Progression to the top was based on expletive consideration as ideological pronunciations rather than productivity and results were promoted. The middle class, most of whom found themselves out of the party elite circles, developed dispassionate and cynical attitudes towards the system. The alienation of the middle class, the most vital group in production, had an adverse effect in determining the pace of economic development and thereby breeding social pressure for change.

It is against this backdrop that we must view with suspicion the Soviet Union's emergence in the post-World

---

[157] Moscow Summit Publication of USIS, Moscow, 1989, p. 4.

War II period to take up the position of defender of nationalist struggles in Asia and Africa and social revolution in Latin America. It was an irony that back home all attempts at nationalist expressions were suppressed and choked violently. In fact, the world was fed with a different image, as in 1971 when the then Soviet leader Leonid Breznev said:

> *The Soviet people had come into existence a new human community, sharing territory, state economic system, culture, the goal of building communism and a common language—Russian.*

At the occasion of the fiftieth anniversary of the revolution in 1977, Breznev again described unity in the Soviet Union as having 'no equal in history'.[158] However, considerable evidence did exist at the time to show that the process of struggle and the quest for national identity and self-determination had been going on in the Soviet Union from the very beginning.[159] Over the years, this

---

[158] Andropov Yuri, *Speeches at 50th Anniversary of Formation of the Soviet Union.* Moscow: Novosti Press, 1985, p. 60.

[159] In the late 1960s, as response to russification, petition samizats, public demonstrations started to be made. L. Hajda, 'The Nationalist Problems in the Soviet Union', in *Current History*, October 1988, p. 327. The nationalist dissent which came later had therefore been building up since the time of Josef Stalin, but had to operate in covert till the time of Leonid Breznev.

created ethnic tensions, distrust, and subterranean factious pressure. Although the world was presented with the fiction of a friendship of people it was clear to close observers that any crevasse in the system would make room for a volcanic outburst of these molten forces.

The Falling Apart of the State

A man dressed in a pre-revolutionary military costume burns a Soviet Union flag during a rally in Moscow following a coup attempt led by a hardliner communist that eventually failed. 23 August 1991

Mikhail Gorbachev emerged in 1985 as General Secretary of the Communist Party Central Committee and Soviet leader with a strong determination to 'give communism a human face' by bringing about political and economic reforms. He introduced the twin concepts of *glasnost*—openness and *perestroika*—economic reform.

While these two objectives eventually brought about change, as they were by themselves very positive, the course of events that followed showed that Gorbachev did not fully apprehend that beyond anything at the time the principal centrifugal force in the state was the threat of subnationalism and disintegration. He made no reference to the nationality problem until the 27th Party Congress in 1987, when he cautioned in passing about the need for restraints in pursuing nationalist objectives. Gorbachev's caution only came after some events in Alma Alta in 1986 involving riots borne out of ethnicity.[160]

Similar riots had occurred there in the 1977/80 period over the burial of a Kazakh soldier killed in Afghanistan in a non-Muslim cemetery. All over Central Asia, nationalist sentiments against the system began to rekindle following various Islamic remarks from Moscow in the wake of the 1986 riots. In the Baltic republics, regular pro-nationalist demonstrations and cultural activities occurred between 1987 and 1988. In Lithuania, for instance, the appointment

---

[160] In the course of economic transformation, an inept and corrupt Communist Party boss—D. Kuneve, in the Central Asia Republic of Kazahstan, was replaced with a dynamic Russian. Although Russians form a sizeable percentage of the population, the event led to wide-scale riots and containment by the Soviet troops.

of its national Bishop Vincent Sladkev as a cardinal in 1988 by Pope John Paul II fuelled the upsurge of nationalist feeling around the Church. Nationalism in Lithuania was under the vanguard of a mass organisation—*Sajudis*, which was initially formed for the purpose of promoting *perestroika*. By the time elections were held in early 1990, several non-Communist political groups participated, leading to the emergence of pro-democratic and nationalist governments, which declared independence on March 11, 1990.

Similar developments in Estonia led to the formation of two nationalist groups—Estonia People Front and Estonian Citizens Committee, which won the elections conducted in March 1990. In Latvia, the National Front, which emerged as the most prominent pro-democracy political organisation, also won the local election in early 1990 and began to embark on a transition programme to end Soviet rule. Similar events began to occur all over the country.

In the Slavic republics, especially Ukraine, a union of writers and intellectuals concentrated their focus on the development of their language, literature, and revival of religion. In fact, the activities coincided with the celebration of the millennium of Christianity in the Kiev Rus, while the Ukrainian Popular Movement was also formed, calling for greater political and economic autonomy. Similar populist organisations also emerged in Moldova and Belorussia.

The outcome of elections conducted in early 1990 in the Slavic republics reflected the change of political opinion. (Several pro-democracy officials were returned, but the strong presence of the Communist Party was also reflected.) The nationalist situation in Transcaucasia was most profound due to what is believed as their high cultural consciousness and advancement. They were also demographically less pluralistic and self-administering. In Armenia, for instance, the All Armenia Movement sprang up with a militant arm—the Armenian National Army. The outburst of such a nationalist feeling heralded the mass uprising that took place in Armenia in 1988 over a contentious autonomous region (Karabakh) occupied by the Armenians, but placed under the Azerbaijan Republic in the course of the Stalinist reforms. The interethnic feuds and pogroms that ensued led to mass demonstrations from both sides and the large-scale presence of refugees.

In the wave of strong anti-Russian and separatist emotions, across the country, Russians also reacted by calling for democracy and economic autonomy which became common in Moscow and Leningrad. We must not forget that actual economic activities were concentrated around the Russian Federation, but at this time, there were about 600,000 Russian refugees fleeing from other republics. In the spring of 1990, elections took place in the Russian Federation, and the reformist-minded groups led by Boris Yeltsin, Gavril Popov, and Anatoly Sobchak subsequently took over the Federation. Soon after the election, Yeltsin announced the sovereignty of Russia.

President Boris Yeltsin waves to a crowd
in August 1991 in Moscow

President Bill Clinton and Russian President at the Kremlin

In May 1990, leaders of such popular movements from Estonia, Ukraine, Belorussia, Azerbaijan, Armenia, Georgia, and Uzbekistan formed the Union of Democratic Forces. These bodies came up with agendas for restructuring the various republics and organised demonstrations on a mass scale. These included the Armenia riots in 1988, Georgia in April 1989, Uzbekistan in May 1989, Kazakhistan in June 1989, and Moscow and Leningrad, 1990. The initial response of Gorbachev and the party to the upsurge in the nationalist movement was perfunctory. Gorbachev confirmed the existence of such activities at the 28th Party Congress in 1990 when he said:

> *Comrades, inter-ethnic relations have deteriorated in the period under review (since 1989) and especially lately. We did not grasp the significance of this promptly enough and failed to see the dangers in good time. You may recall that the 27th congress whose decisions are being reviewed, examined the matter as though it had long been settled . . . there are historical and religious reasons. And of course we are now having to pay for past crimes committed against entire nations . . . we failed to see the development in time. All of us let us honestly admit though that everything was all right on this score, everything was solved and we mostly proposed toasts of people's friendship.*[161]

---

[161] Gorbachev, op. cit.

This historic speech by Gorbachev made in response to internal criticisms does not only give the historic and immediate causes of the problem but also gives an indication to the action in 1988 and 1989. He was more emphatic by adding in the same speech that 'suddenly we become aware of the problem but we did not react at once. Neither did we make a correct assessment at once'. The government's initial reaction was to condemn these activities, crack down on them militarily, in some cases leading to lots of casualties. It is reported that in the Baku (Azerbaijan) riot of January 1990 as much as about 3,500 people were killed. Gorbachev also acknowledged 'bloodshed and considerable loss of life on ethnic grounds . . . with thousands of people being compelled to abandon their homes and wander about the country'. So as late as January 1991, Soviet troops and tanks were sent to Lithuania. Lithuania was also subjected to a period of economic blockade.

Demonstrators march on the Kremlin in January 1991
calling for the resignation of Mikhail Gorbachev over
the crackdown against Lithuanian authorities after
the declaration independence in March 1990.

The non-representative action was to embark on a
programme of building a real union of sovereign states
through the use of party apparatus. The party body for
nationalities prepared a draft platform which was discussed
at the party congress in 1989. The Council of the Supreme
Soviet was commissioned to prepare a new treaty of the
Union. In December 1990, the Congress of Deputies
approved the draft and passed it to the Congresses of the
various republics to study and react before being finally
ratified by the Supreme Soviet.

What emerged at the end was that the Confederation of
Independent States was a very loose political association that

only focused on cooperation in a general nature—a kind of move towards regional integration. But the attempt to solve the nationality problem within the context of the party did not seem to have been very helpful in creating confidence. For instance, a leader of the Ukraine Nationalist Movement remarked at the time that the outcome would still be the same old house with a repaired facade. As Shireen Hunter has argued, the problem was more fundamental as all these republics began to view their incorporation in the union as a coercive colonial act and that needed to be fought as vigorously as a nationalist movement in Asia and Africa.[162]

Gorbachev's inability to clearly grasp the state of affairs and act early has been compared with the manner in which the Russian Prime Minister Sergei Witte handled the 1905 Father Gasping Riots, which built up to the 1917 Bolshevik Revolution.[163] It was only later that Witte acknowledged in his memoirs that there was no Russia; what existed was a conglomeration of different people kept together by the power of the bayonet.

So Gorbachev's attempt to suppress the revolts by a show of might and by half-measured reforms, often supervised by the same redundant and despised old traditionalists, was

---

[162] S. Hunter, 'Nationalist Movement in Soviet Asia', in *Current History*, October 1990.

[163] Simes, *ibid.*, pp. 105-106.

the wrong treatment in the circumstances.[164] However, he seemed to have had virtually no other alternatives, if the old hard-liners who constituted the majority of the state and party apparatus and the military hierarchy were to be taken along.

Researchers attribute the revival of intense ethnic nationalism in the Soviet Union to a number of reasons—political, social, economic, and external influences. It has been argued that since World War II, the Soviet Union achieved rapid social modernisation leading to the emergence of an urban middle class. The effect of such an improvement in educational and socioeconomic levels had positive values on national integration, but also fermented the germination of ethnic awareness and cultural renaissance.[165] It also created the related paradox of social development and political consciousness towards democracy. However, the system that operated was not congenial for any form of self assertiveness.

---

[164] It said that men make history, and definitely Gorbachev is one of them. His appearance in the scene has given world history a quantum leap into the future. Despite what has been termed his lack of vision in handling the nationalist problem, the domestic environment in which he operated must be taken into cognizance. He could not have done better.

[165] Burg, Steven, War or Peace?: Nationalism, Democracy and American Foreign Policy in Post-Communist Europe, New York: New York University Press, 1996, pp. 349-560.

The introduction of *glasnost,* therefore, uncapped the Pandora box which Gorbachev never envisaged and was not able to cap thereafter.[166] The effusive manner in which the Soviet people reacted to the openness underscored the pressure that had built up within the system for over seventy years.

Related to this was the aftermath of *perestroika.* Economic reforms from the centrally planned Soviet system to a free market system require a mid-term period of gestation, but the structural changes introduced were at great social cost. The consciousness of the Soviet people was not up for this, so they were confronted with a complete slowdown in the economy leading to inflation, housing shortages, and unemployment, all creating room for social upheavals. The presence of refugees at the scene led to further stresses and escalations of the tension.

Two forms of influence existed on the international scene. There was intense political pressure from the Western powers for more reform which was not immediately backed up by an inflow of funds to alleviate the social pressure of change. The other form of influence had elements of political undertones, but was based on the need for more cultural and religious openness, especially from the Vatican, Armenians in exile, the world Jewish congress, the organisation of Islamic states, and other religious bodies.

---

[166] M. Gorbachev, Speech at 28th Congress of Communist Party Central Committee Meeting. Moscow: Novosti Press, 1990, p. 67.

At the birth of the Soviet Union in 1917, the leaders of the Bolshevik had more than the normal ambitions of statesmen as they wanted to build a dynamic and prosperous society completely devoid of oppression and exploitation of man by another. But in their search for establishing a society where the common heritage is used for the benefit of all, all the values of the old system, including religion, were regarded as taboo.

However, as George Orwell tried to show several years back in his classic novel *Animal Farm,* such a system was only practicable in theory and bound to be short-lived. This is because one thing which the human spirit cherishes is freedom, especially the liberty to associate with others and with his Creator and the liberty to work and be rewarded for it.

Part III

Anecdotes for the Legacy of Crisis

Chapter Twelve

Globalisation versus National Integration

A gainst the backdrop of what we have seen, the dominant theme for several decades across the world is the search for solutions to the avalanche of problems of coexistence that confront human societies. Although the basic concern in society is often regarded by many to be the inexorable conflict between individual interest and collective will, increasingly this has been reduced to the micro level, and the more protracted combat between the aspirations of composite units against each other at a higher level is taking the centre stage of political discourse.

Let us begin with the syllogism of those who tend to see the solution in greater integration between nations. It is commonly suggested nowadays that the unending problems of state formation have been overtaken by the successful trend of interstate integration, regional integration, and the overall spate of globalisation which not only nowadays dominates international relations but is also having direct impact on the lives of ordinary people. This line of argument prescribes that a more rewarding political agenda for the third millennium would be in reducing the effect if not the total elimination of national political boundaries *in lieu* of a more coalesced interstate political arrangement.

Based on this line of thought, the suggestion presents itself that at a time when the entire world is becoming a 'human village' it would seem obsolete to invest academic rigour or political debates on how to strengthen nation-states.

The Meaning of Globalisation

Before delving in to consider the discussions on this, let us pause to ponder on what globalisation is all about. As we have seen in the rest of this work, and maybe due to the dynamism of the phenomenon, hard and fast definitions are rare, but a number of omnibuses and generally appropriate characterisations which seem to enjoy widespread acceptance exist. Some leading scholars prefer to refer to the whole process as that of *integration* or *globalism* while others such as the former president of the *Law and Society Association,* Professor Susan Silbey, categorise the current trend as *post-modern colonialism.*[167]

Regarding the actual characterisation of the phenomenon, few other prominent researchers on the subject call it the 'emergence of a global community', and leading German think tank the *World Society Research Group,* in a recent article, defined the trend as involving the 'institutionalization of trans-border relations and the diffusion of actors'.[168]

While attempting to suggest newly evolving meanings and drawing dividing lines between the several new terminologies, such as international community and international society, they continue by further expounding that the process entails a gradual and maybe radical osmosis

---

[167] Susan Silbey, 'Presidential Address of Law and Society Association', in *Law and Society Review,* vol. 31, no. 2, 1997, pp. 207-336.

[168] See in vols. 53/54 of the *Law and State Review,* the articles called 'Globalization in Action Faced With the International Challenge of the Global Society and the Future of the Individual at the Dawn of the 21st Century' by Professor Charles Bokonga Ekanga Botombele of the University of Antwerp and another piece called 'In Search of World Society' by the World Research Group at Institut fur Politikwissenschaft der Technischen Hoschschule Darmstadt.

from state centricism to world society. In other words, there is a diffusing of state independence in action and a focusing of transnational social relations and an overlapping of different actor levels in various fields.[169]

The truth is that the above view of the German School has originated from the tradition of Weberian ecliptism of seeing the ongoing process of globalisation as inextricable from the complex inter-relationship between couple of concepts. These are *Vergemeinschaftung* or community formation where the emphasis is coming together and sharing of the feeling of solidarity and *Vergesellschaftung* or society formation, which stresses on interdependence and interaction of actors and the social forces they represent. Our understanding of these views is that the ultimate result of such mutual superimposition is the non-contradictory, indeed natural progression of society from local, regional, and national foci towards a global society.[170]

However, trying to understand this phenomenon of globalisation so imminent in the air at the beginning of this third millennium in a rewarding manner would take

---

[169] For more on this see R. W. Cox, 'Social Forces, States and World Order: Beyond International Relations Theory', in *Millennium*, vol. 10, 1981. A more recent work by same author called 'Global Restructuring: Making Sense of the Changing International Political Economy', in Richard Stubbs and R. D. Geoffrey Underhill (eds.), *Political Economy and the Changing Order*, Toronto, 1994.
[170] See World Research Group, *ibid.*

us to maybe a boring odyssey which perhaps goes back to a book in English literature by Daniel Defoe called *Robinson Crusoe,* which has for a long time enjoyed much literary appreciation. Besides the very sharp and effective way in which the many exciting adventures on the strange island were presented, what has made that piece particularly outstanding is its instructive nature. Obviously inspired by the reminiscences of the Scottish seafarer Alexander Selkirk who got marooned on a faraway South American island, the story conveys the plot of human interdependency. It shows that no one can live in total solitude and would sooner or later need others. This is what has also been manifested in the course of human history in the relations between various human communities, states, and nations. Even where human societies try to live in economic, social, or political self-sufficiency, they discover before long that there is a need to be in touch with other human groups. Accordingly, whenever each group has maintained its political and cultural self-sufficiency, they have always found a need to properly interact with others for economic maximisation, depending on their capacities.

The benefit has always been mutual, especially from an economic sense as the dictates of geography have conferred on the different groups varying acquirements and endowments, which are often enough for them. But these could also be to the benefit of others and at the same time impose on them diverse scarcities that could be easily met by others.[171]

It is against this backdrop of individual and societal interdependence and cooperation that human society has in all generations persisted. The nation-state itself, which later rose up under the banner of avowed national 'civism' and protectionism, still found this interstate symbiosis an essential condition for its very survival. This, according to former U.S. President Jimmy Carter, is why issues affecting the peace, women, children, or even 'the earth, our home' in faraway places such as Cambodia and Somalia are of such paramount importance to American children back in the comfort of their homes in, say, Washington.[172]

The traditional linkages and interaction between human societies were dictated by the limits and confines of geography, communication, and technology. However, as the years passed by, the twentieth and twenty-first centuries have recorded a greater shifting towards a closer world across national and continental frontiers. This has not only been made possible by the obvious mastery which man seems to be gaining over the barriers of location and communication placed by nature but also by the changing circumstances of

---

[171] For more on this, it may be useful to read the article called 'The Interdependence of States and the Theory of Interstate Relations', Andreas Osiander in *Laws and State Review*, vols. 53/54, pp. 42-67.

[172] For more on this, reference could be made to Jimmy Carter, *Talking Peace: A Vision for the Next Generation.* New York: Puffin Books, 1995.

political and social evolution. Today, advances in computer, communication, and telecommunication have made the world a global village.

First Session of the League of Nations
in Salle de Reforme in Geneva

At the beginning of the twentieth century, the traumatism and panic over war forced men to begin to mix in the form of a standing 'concert' to avoid its reoccurrence and work towards more global political cooperation and dialogue. The Covenant of the League of Nations was primarily political, to create a permanent forum for dialogue and conference diplomacy. When this did not work out as desired, the further shock of war brought men together in San Francisco in 1945 to declare in the chapeau to the

United Nations Charter to 'practice tolerance and live together in peace with one another as good neighbours'. On the other hand, having seen the atrocities of war, the UNO had a bigger mandate to also promote economic, social, and cultural cooperation. Today, the UN has agencies with mandates over virtually every subject.

Sadly at the global level, four decades of what became the 'Cold War', i.e. between 1945 and 1990, could not assure the satisfactory fulfilment of the lofty ideals of the United Nations, and the frequent use of the veto power between the two superpowers only succeeded in relegating the body's relevance. Multilateralism for that period became synonymous with zero-sum ends.[173]

The Fruits of Integration

It was only the Western Europeans that introduced the objective of enhanced global confederacy a kind of *civitas civitatum*—at least in their backyard. Although German Scholar Tilmam Evers takes the bringing of concert

---

[173] See Nick Birnback, 'Making and Keeping the Peace', in *Global Agenda*. New York: University Press of America, 1994, pp. 1-7. Also see Ingvar Carlsson and Shridath Ramphal, *Our Global Neighbourhood*. London: Oxford University Press, 1995.

diplomacy in Europe back to the *Diet of Worms* of 1495,[174] the present union, however, took roots from a simple body which begun in 1958 as a European Coal and Steel Company (ECSC) union and thereon adding a European Atomic Energy Community (EURATOM) in 1962. The actual European Economic Community was born in 1967 and went to become a full union in 1992 at the Maastricht Treaty. Today the twenty-seven-member European Union, as it is called, is a full-fledged confederate political entity or supranational statehood with its own legal system, monetary system, immigration policies, labour laws, parliament, and all the attributes and paraphernalia of a state. Strictly speaking, the European Community has even more of the characteristics of statehood than do several political states. They do not only have a geographically fixed land mass and population, but at the level of the Community, there exists the capacity to maintain law and order. By setting best community standards in virtually all aspects of human existence and also sharing wealth commonly to ensure the maintenance of irreducible norms, the EU has constituted itself into an ombudsman and peer manager.

The relative success of integration in Europe and the huge benefits, especially in terms of the 'spread or distributive effect' which the collective efforts brought to

---

[174] Tilmam Evers, 'Supranational Statehood. The Case of the European Union: Civitas Civitatum or Monstrum?', in *Law and State Review*, vol. 51, 1995.

all, have therefore spurred many other regions to begin to fuse in unison. Take Latin America, for example; apart from the fact that such bilateral integration efforts between Colombia and Venezuela have recorded such resounding success at least at the economic level, the Andean Pact is gradually emerging as one of the most successful integration efforts among developing countries. The relations between Colombia and Venezuela have arisen out of the common history. Until 1831, along with Ecuador they belonged to one country called Gran Colombia under the great liberator, Simon Bolivar. In the 1990s, especially under the presidency of Carlos Andres Perez in Venezuela (1989-1993), the two countries brought their economies much closer together. By 2012, their bilateral trade had reached over $3.28 billion per annum and each country had emerged as the other's main trading partner. This rebuffs conventional economic theory, which has tended to assert that developing countries which had similar export products could not be each other's strong trading partners.

Then there is the Mercosur in the southern cone, the Central American Economic Union, the CARICOM in the seaward Caribbean islands, and the group of three comprising Mexico, Venezuela, and Colombia. At the end of 2005, the Andean Pact which was founded in 1969 brought together the five countries—Bolivia, Colombia, Ecuador, Peru, Venezuela, and Panama, which had an estimated GDP of $745.3 billion. In 2011, its GDP PPP was also estimated at $902.86 billion with the exclusion of

Venezuela. Considering the size of the economies, this is a very high figure. The Andean pact also has a parliament, a very effective development fund, a bank, and all the other trappings of an economic union. An Association of Caribbean States has been formed and the North American Free Trade Agreement (NAFTA) has already taken off between Canada, Mexico, and the United States with aims of expanding southwards. The plans, especially after the Miami Summit of the Americas and other summits, most particularly the one of San Antonio in 2012, pointed towards the creation of one regional market. Trade within the Mercosur (i.e. among Argentina, Brazil, Paraguay, and Uruguay) grew from $10 billion in 1991 to $88 billion in 2010.

Older bodies such as ALADI and the SELA now see their roles to be working towards a common hemispheric market by the beginning years of the twenty-first century. What even seems more interesting is the mesh of associations and the more complicated integration designs and webs between these various bodies and between individual countries.

In other regions such as South-east Asia, the overall impact of these events has been to spur interest in the expansion of the ten-member Association of South East Asian Countries—ASEAN (Indonesia, Malaysia, Singapore, Cambodia, Brunei, Laos, Vietnam, Myanmar, Philippines, and Thailand), the twenty-one-member group of Asia Pacific Economic Cooperation (APEC), and other similar bodies across the world. The trend in, say, South Asia has been the same as the 603 million people ASEAN with a combined nominal GDP of $2 trillion continues to spread its wings wider to bring in as many countries in the largest region together. Today, intra-ASEAN trade reached 25 per cent in 2012 valued at over $520 billion per annum and targets 35 per cent despite the trend of economic slowdown.

Besides the mammoth economic gains, it has also been suggested that with the end of bipolarity several states both old and new have found that having their destinies solely in their hands has even become burdensome. They need the support and help of others. The Joint Chairman of the Commission on Global Governance concludes:

> *They (states) must secure their future through commitment to common responsibilities and shared future. The need to work together guided the visionary men and women who drew up the Charter of the United Nations. (But) what is new today is that the interdependence of nations is wider and deeper. What is also new is the role of people and shift of focus from states to people. An aspect of this change is the growth of international civil society.*[175]

So against this eloquent background, the question could be asked if we still need to bother about national integration

---

[175] Carlsson and Ramphal, *ibid.*

and state formation, especially in Africa where several states for years remained on the escarpment of collapse. The answer is yes, as in the arena of this introspection comes the realisation that states representing the peoples of the world are the actual building blocks for the much valuable priority of erecting the structure of a 'global neighbourhood'.

As even the Commission on Global Governance which makes a forceful argument for a 'global civil society' and a humanistic focus of international relations acknowledges, 'sovereignty—the principle that a state has supreme authority over all matters that fall within its territorial domain is the cornerstone of the modern interstate system'. After analysing in detail the importance of this, the report says in a later paragraph that 'existing norms regarding sovereign equality, territorial independence and non-intervention need to be strengthened'.[176]

It is otiose to make light of the move towards globalisation and its overwhelming dynamism, nor in any way overstretch the importance of states at a time when the global mood seems more otherwise disposed. However, the universalists-globalists would need to appreciate that the imperativeness of the ideal of a well-ordered community of states, sharing their economic and political lots, would need a foundation of well-ordered societies at the micro level. Hence, the task of formulating and actualising thoughts on state formation as we have attempted to do here,

---

[176] Carlsson and Ramphal, *ibid.*, pp. 68-72.

in a sense, goes beyond a mere *modus vivendi* for internal peace and national harmony to actually prescribing the quintessential framework and ethical code for international communitarianism.

This is why Peter Rinderle, a leading theorist on the New World Order, argued that there exists 'a qualified analogy between persons and states' and that an orderly composed community of states would have to draw its strength and conservancy from the nourishment of seemingly microscopic 'civil-legal conditions' which define the physical existence of the maze of human social unions.[177]

As this relates to the African case, instead of directing all efforts at how the national economies and the massed regional resources could be concentrated for collective benefit, much energy, scarce resources, and time are being expended to seeking solutions to political conflicts. For instance, under the leadership of Nigeria, the Economic Community of West African States (ECOWAS) spent the better part of the 1990s trying to find the solution to the civil war in Liberia, and immediately peace came in sight there, problems then started in neighbouring Sierra Leone, Cote d'Voire, Guinea, and now Mali. In Central Africa, just as the political predicaments of Rwanda and Burundi seemed to have been resolved, civil war came in former Zaire and thereon civil crisis in Congo Brazzaville and Central

---

[177] Petet Rinderle, 'The Idea of a Well-Ordered Community of States', in *Law and State Review*, vol. 52, 1995, pp. 8-35.

African Republic. These political crises have created further distractions from the economic challenges that need to be addressed for social development.

Going more to the south-east, neither the South African Development Community (SADC) nor the East and Central African Economic Cooperation Association could really be optimal in their efforts without putting out the flame of civil conflict in Mozambique, Angola, the Democratic Republic of Congo, Rwanda, Burundi, and Zimbabwe, just as the countries in the East and Horn of Africa could not be able to embark on such lofty programmes with wars and refugee problems pouring out of Sudan, Ethiopia, Eritrea, and Somalia.

Over and above the disruption to meaningful economic programmes, at the level of both the individual and surrounding states, the figure on how much is being spent is staggering, and the pace of regional integration becomes thwarted by already mutually disintegrated component parts. In a well-condensed work entitled *The Relationship between Political and Economic Reform in Africa,* Henry Bienen and Jeffrey Herbst have shown that the pace of economic development continues to be thwarted by the spate of political instability and that hopes for change remain slim as long as the crisis is the defining ingredient of African politics.[178]

---

[178] Henry Bienen and Jeffrey Herbst, 'The Relationship between Political and Economic Reform in Africa', in *Comparative Politics*, October 1996, pp. 23-29.

So while globalisation, regional integration, and other forms of multilateralism offer great prospect for engendering economic and social well-being and by extension political place, the nation-state will remain its building block. The search for peaceful and harmonious existence at the sub-regional, regional, and perhaps the global level cannot therefore be pursued at the expense of enthroning peace and integration at the local level. Virile and stable states must therefore be put in place in order to attain global peace and order.

Chapter Thirteen

Integration by Consensus, Power Sharing, and Communication

O ne of the most critical factors which shows up in discussions on state formation and remains very active today is that of creating a proper political ambience for the purpose of ensuring proper sense. of belonging to all constituent parts. The alternative to political peace is conflict, which simply means the pursuit of political goals by the use of some form of force—civil wars, revolutions, invasions, and coups.[179] But as we have seen with the now extinct Soviet Union or is now being pursued in parts of the Arab world, such an alternative has only led to the further withering away of the state. It therefore behoves the architects and managers of various multinational polities to devise ways and means of ensuring the existence of some form of consensus opinion or unanimity.

On Governance by Consensus

Such a position has been held true since the genesis of Lockean thought, when the legitimacy of a political sovereign was thought to hinge around its ability to create a consensual accord among the centre and the component parts, as well as between the ruler and the ruled. At the beginning of the American state, virtually each of the founding fathers had his own ideas on how this could be achieved. While Alexander Hamilton, the leader of the Federal Party, argued for a powerful national government with strong executive power (urban industrialism), his rival, Thomas Jefferson, a democrat, preferred a laissez-faire style of agrarianism, incorporating largely independent states. In between them stood others such as James Madison, who

---

[179] For a yet more detailed definition of this, see Jack Plano and Milton Greenberg, *The American Political Dictionary*. New York: Holt, Reinhart & Winston, 1985, p. 6.

while agreeing on the need for a strong centre insisted on it being checked through a regime of checks and balances to ensure that the interests of the units were not impinged on.[180] It was based on this that such leaders as the South Carolina political activist John Calhoun (1782-1850) expounded the doctrine of *Concurrent Majority* which insisted on the need for democratic decisions to be taken only with the concurrence of all the major segments of the society.

It is in the middle of the search for this consensual framework that the American state went through civil war, and now out of the mesh of these and other related ideas, it has been able to build a largely strong society. This process of building up a consensual foundation involves a number of political actions. Several authors like Professor Ruth Lapidoth have suggested that the best way of instilling peace and order in such societies is by working out appropriate modalities for granting various forms of autonomy and self-governance to component parts, since the issue of margins of self-determination and cultural homogeneity remains some of the critical factors in the fuelling of civil crisis.[181]

If properly worked out, she and others of this persuasion suggest that such forms of autonomy for each unit would be done without detaching from the other units, and this could

---

[180] See nos. 10 and 50 of the Federalist Papers.
[181] Lapidoth, *ibid.*

drastically reduce the tension which comes with the quest for self-assertiveness.[182]

Many others as well, represented by the ideas of the United States Institute of Peace researcher Timothy Sisk, advocate that well-conceived formulas for sharing power to various groups may be the way out, since the most vexed question remains that of access to the corridors of decision-making.[183] This, he posits, could be by some form of zoning of key political positions and proportional representation in the scheme of things. Both of these positions hold true, because in the first place uptightness and unease normally emerge in such political setups, due to the inherent craving for identity and a hold on power. As a matter of fact, any plural society that tries to ignore these realities of power diffusion and need for measures of autonomy in the building of a stable democracy is bound in the long run to fail like the former Soviet Union and Sudan, which recently went through a splintering process after atrocious decades of civil war.

---

[182] Several good books are available on the subject. Some of these include: Larry Diamond and Marc F. Platter (eds.), *Nationalism, Ethnic Conflict and Democracy*. Baltimore: John Hopkins University Press, 1995; Donald Horowitz, *Ethnic Groups in Conflict*. Berkeley: University of California Press; Joseph Montville (ed.), *Conflict and Peacemaking in Multi-ethnic Societies*. Lexington Books; Timothy D. Sisk, *Power Sharing and Mediation in Ethnic Conflicts*. Washington: United States Institute for Peace, 1996.

[183] Timothy D. Sisk, *Power Riming and International Mediation in Ethnic Conflicts*. Washington: United States Institute for Peace, 1996, p. 67.

Power Sharing

Let us for a minute say a word about power sharing arrangements. In some cases, clientelist types of political associations have been built up between various groups while in many other cases forms of coalition or cohabitation alliances (France) or collective leaderships (the defunct Soviet Union) are from time to time made to ensure political peace.

In modern times, a terminology, *Consociationalism,* was developed to describe these forms of political attitudes which, while respecting the concept of *majoritarianism* in politics, seek alternative ways of mutual survival in societies deeply criss-crossed by racial, religious, linguistic, or similar divisions. This was seen in both Austria and the Netherlands after World War II, in Lebanon, Australia, and in South Africa where the Mandela Government had to integrate the former minority government during the nuptial stages of their political dialogue, and eventually the governance of the new republic.[184]

In Nigeria, a very ethnically and religiously plural gigantic nation power sharing often referred to as respect for the 'Federal Character Principle' is entrenched in law. It is defined by Ladipo Adamolekun as 'to ensure that

---

[184] For more on the definition of Consociationalism, see *Oxford Illustrated Dictionary*, vol. vii. Oxford: Oxford University Press, 1994, p. 67.

appointments to public service institutions fairly reflect the linguistic, ethnic, religious and geographical diversity of the country'. Application of the principle in the Federal Civil Service and the military has amounted to a confused balancing of the merit principle and quota system, based essentially on state of origin. Irrespective of the imperfect outcome in some cases, it emphasises sharing of power; fair and equitable representation of Federal Character Commission exists by law to ensure compliance with this principle.

In what it describes as 'neighbourhood ethics', the eminent authors of *The Report of the Commission on Global Governance* suggested the imperativeness of such power sharing arrangements in a largely democratising world.[185] Similarly, while making a caution on the increasing use of the principle of the right of self-determination for the purpose of political fragmentation, the former United Nations Secretary General Boutros Boutros-Ghali in his *Agenda for Peace* insisted on the need for sovereign governments to continuously ensure proper political participation of the component units.[186]

Former United States Senator Daniel Moynihan who was one of the leading authorities on the subject, while not opposing the inalienable right of self-determination

---

[185] Our Global Neighbourhood: The Report of the Commission on Global Governance, Oxford Press, USA, 1995.
[186] Boutros Boutros-Ghali, *An Agenda for Peace*. New York: UN Publications, 1992, paras 17-19.

of various groups, called for more efforts at globalising some form of *Madisonianism* that would involve well-cut compromises, devolution, and ad hoc accommodation between various groups for the sake of mutual existence.[187]

But one thing that has emerged from the entire length of this study is that the process of nation building and internal integration, in the modern state, has not been limited to one set of approach or through prescribed sets of rules for all countries. Rather, this has taken a variety and multiplicity of forms, changing and adapting themselves to distinctive national pluralistic circumstances.

Accordingly as we have seen, Canada, India, Switzerland, and Israel have in differing ways all tried to create a sense of belonging and participation among various segments of the society, not only through political means of power sharing and levels of autonomy but also through social and economic factors. For instance, whereas the more developed countries have laid great stress on the development of a strong social welfare economy to ensure optimum well-being of all citizens, the less economically strong India has focused on an effective labour-based green revolution to feed its teeming population and in the past consciously ensured that the main political parties are trans-ethnic and trans-religious. Even the BJP, which has a strong sectionist tilt, after its electoral victory, decided to pick Atal Bihari Vajpayee, a moderate figure, as Prime Minister in order to

---

[187] Moyniham, *ibid.*

mollify fears of other religious groups. He held the office of Prime Minister as leader of the Bharatiya Janata Party (BJP) in 1996, 1998-1999, and 1999-2004. Vajpayee led India through a period of unprecedented economic growth and achieved the restoration of diplomatic ties with Pakistan.

For the Venezuelan state, the year 1998 was determined as significant due to the fact that it presented an opportunity for one or two generations of political scientists to look back and see how they had attempted to build a stable democratic state. But considering the fact that Venezuela was the first country in Latin America to enter this prestigious 'democratic club', that year in a way marked the *cuadragesimo aniversario* of political progressivism in the entire Latin America.

In comparing the transition from what Guillermo O'Donnell called bureaucratic-authoritarianism to democracy between Europe and Latin America, Professor Nikolaus Werz lately asserted that in the former case this involved revolution, but in the case of the latter, it was relatively peaceful.[188] Hence, in the move by France, Russia, Germany, Italy, Portugal, Spain, and even Greece towards civil liberalisation, there was a time when a virtual breakdown of the *ancien regime* occurred and was often followed by some form of violent revolution, but in the case of Venezuela and the rest of Latin America, the ruling

---

[188] Nikolaus Werz, 'Democracy and Forms of Government in South America', in *Law and State Review*, 1997, pp. 100-125.

elite worked out some forms of 'integrative techniques and informal alliances'—*estado de compromiso* among themselves, averting such large-scale type of change.[189]

Integration by Compromises: The Latin American Experience

In retrospect, 1958 was significant in that after nearly one and a half centuries of rocky Venezuelan political tides, in that year, when the last military strong man, General Marco Perez Jimenez, was ousted and the nation installed its first truly democratic government, it was against a mood for national reconciliation and compromise. Having won the general elections in 1958 under the dynamic and much urbane leader Romulo Betancourt, the leaders of the victorious centre-left Accion Democratica Party invited their counterparts in the centre-right Social Christian Party (COPEI) and other political leaders to an agreement with them in a 1962 deal termed 'Pacto de Punto Fijo'. This was essentially a national reconciliation 'covenant' under which they agreed to adopt moderate political attitudes towards

[189] Werz, *ibid.*

each other to ensure the perpetuity of democratic values and thereby avail the country an era of political peace.[190]

While some political historians are still divided as to the effects of this deal as it relates to the sustenance of ethical values of democracy in the Venezuelan state, some others such as Carlos Romero would yet question what constitutes that national consensus per se.[191] There is no doubt that *Pacto de Punto Fijo* has afforded the country much of the *stability* which it had experienced till the emergence of Hugo Chavez on the scene. That is why the country could easily stamp out left-wing guerrilla factionalism which continued to rock virtually all other neighbouring countries in various degrees. It was the spillover of the Punto Fijo spirit after thirty years that also helped to repel two abortive attempts in 1992 by a restless military led by Colonel Hugo Chavez, attempting to return to power through violent means.

It is perhaps as a result of the passion for the effectiveness of the Punto Fijo deal that an animated Oxford scholar

---

[190] A few good books in English exists, tracing the course of transition from authoritarianism to democracy in the case of Venezuela. It may be interesting for instance to read Glen L. Kolb, *Democracy and Dictatorship in Venezuela.* Connecticut: Connecticut College, 1974; Romulo Betancourt, *Venezuela: Oil and Politics.* Boston: Houghton Mifflin, 1978; Guillermo Moron, *A History of Venezuela.* London: George Allen & Unwin, 1964.

[191] The views of Carlos Romero over this thorny issue of defining 'consensus' could be found in his various contributions in the Carcas—*El Nacional* newspaper.

Professor Luis Castro Leiva called for the re-enactment of a new national deal under which leading political groups addressed a number of issues to present a common consensual platform in the 1998 presidential election.[192]

Communication as a Tool for Cooperation

Related to the earlier option of working out various forms of national deals is the idea of adopting or rather cultivating an appropriate communicative ambience among various groups. In most social science faculties, the importance attached to disciplines that relate to communication is assuming a central place. On a further consideration, the importance of changing the existential ambience through appropriate rules of language makes it more meaningful when one considers that language, as represented by words, has always been a strong instrument for either construction or destruction of relationships between either individuals or whole societies.

This is why the Bible categorically warns that 'death and life are in the power of the tongue'.[193] Without going into the epistemological problems of whether there does exist a philosophy of language, it is appropriate to underline

---

[192] The speech by Professor Leiva was made at the valedictory speech before the Venezuelan National Congress to mark the 40th Anniversary of Democracy, 23 January 1998.

[193] See the Book of Proverbs 18: 21.

that language has always been a priceless asset in the phenomenological analysis of a people's way of life.[194]

Dale Cannon posits that it is well accepted by linguists and social anthropologists that the ends which the ethos of a given society serves to protect and the language so used mutually reinforce each other. He asserts further:

> It is said that the structure of language—being the principal medium in which the culture ethos comes to express—both moulds and is moulded by the characteristic traits of culture and its patterns of thinking . . . the words a speaker utters, are nothing less than his means of taking up a position in the world of meaning which he has come to know and appreciate through becoming a speaking member of the community which share the world.
>
> The linguistic resource available to the speaker are seen to be his means of entry into communication or communion with the community and its world of meaning; they usher him into his own distinctive modality of dwelling in the world.[195]

---

[194] Dale Cannon, 'Dwelling in the World through Language', in *International Philosophical Quarterly*, March 1972, p. 28. Also for further reading see, Rebate Christensen, 'On the Problematic of a Philosophy of Language', in *IPQ*, March 1976, p. 33.

[195] Cannon, *ibid*. A yet more detailed reading could be found in William J. Gavin, 'William James on Language', in *IPQ*, March 1976.

Quite often, problems of political nature, arising out of conflict of interests among integral units, appear confusing or seem intractable. In situations as we have in most African states, it would appear plausible to draw an analogy with 'the dilemma of a prisoner' with whom the judicial authorities negotiate or arrange to own up to his guilt as a way of pinning down other more inured persons charged along him. In confessing guilt, the befuddled incarcerated may stand the chance of getting a lighter sanction, but then he may sink alone should other accomplices prove more obdurate and have alibis that set them free. Moreover, the prisoner's dilemma is further increased by the fact that it may serve the collective interest of the compatriots in crime to maintain group taciturnity and in so doing all come out free or all sink together.

In all, a non-cautious approach by a 'speaking' prisoner can lead both himself and all his other associates into more problems; his way out therefore may be nearer through what Professor Julia de Barragan calls *El lenguaje de la cooperation*. This calls for an injunction on the importance of not losing sight of the objective of getting targeted results.

Extended to global multi-ethnic states, the hypothesis on appropriate communicative skills raises a call on the need for corporate existence of the various nation-states, especially at a time when most of the world is coming closer as we saw earlier. In other words, it is essential for the various national leaders and other civic institutions of mass appeal, such as the press or religious institutions, to realise, appreciate, and believe in the resourcefulness of coexisting in their present state structure and peaceably in the shared world.

A conscious policy therefore has to be devised to instil the fact that the singularity of action of individual groups and extremism of position also on their part would sooner or later only sour the happiness of common existence, as the end result, as we have already, are crisis, suffering, and ultimately violence, conflicts, and wars in which there are no winners but only losers.

The natural corollary of this is that the language of the cooperation model emphasises the importance of adopting a communication skill that works on the need for accentuating the areas of complementarities rather than on the divergences. For example, among Christianity, Islam, and civil canon, there are many areas of agreements—the sanctity of human life, peaceful existence, love for humanity and self, respect for environment and nature. This calls for the development of appropriate *reglas del lenguaje* or 'rules of language' which would be directed at fortifying cooperation and peaceful coexistence.

Chapter Fourteen

The Law as an Integrator

Another important point that seems to have been strongly emphasised by South American researchers is the role of law in the society.[196] While it is essential that all efforts be made to put in place a conducive cooperative atmosphere, the role which the laws

---

[196] This kind of idea permeates the various thoughts of some of the Caracas scholars such as Luis Castro Leiva, Eva Gueron, Carlos Romero, and Graceila Soriano de Garcia-Pelayo. But again for the sake of brevity, let us concentrate on the ideas of Barragan.

of the land could actually play in the integrative process has also been emphasised.

Barren's Law Dictionary simply refers to the terminology 'law' as 'those pronouncement and rules which a competent legislative authority have instituted to guide an individual's action in society'.[197] The 123 North Western Report brings this point out more crisply when it says that law is:

> *The aggregate of those rules and principles of conduct promulgated by the legislative authority or established by local custom. Our laws are derived from a combination of the divine or moral law, the laws of nature and human experience as has been evolved by human experience. Human laws must therefore continually change as human experience shall prove the necessity of new ones to meet new evils which have taken upon themselves new forms, or as the public conscience shall change, thus viewing matters from different moral view points.*[198]

The definition and relevance of the terminology would appear to vary with usage, but in a much simplistic sense, its end should be said to be the pursuit of 'peace, order and common good'.[199] In the words of the Christian jurist

---

[197] Steven H. Gifis, *The Law Dictionary*. New York: Barron's, 1995, p. 269.

[198] Gifis, op. cit.

[199] Mortimer, *Introduction to the Great Books*, vol. i. Chicago: University of Chicago Press, 1991, p. 751.

Thomas of Aquinas, 'Nothing else than an ordinance of reason for the common good, made by him who has care for the common good, made by him who care for the community.' That is why the progenitors of the Western legal tradition derived the maxim: *ibi societas ibi jus*. In a publication in which they tried to unite the different conceptions of various legal traditions, such as Judeo-Christian, Chinese, African, Islamic, or Hindu, the International Association of Legal Sciences concluded that law was not a mere makeshift, but an ideal; not just a set of rules, but a body of remedies; and finally not just a collection of rules, but a method for resolving conflicts.[200] So in the law-making process, factors such as established custom and moral injunctions provided the raw material for making decisions. Similarly, the corpus of natural law, which we have already touched on, automatically forms the other ingredient of the substratum of the law of the land. The difference between natural law and law of the land as Hegel noted is that whereas the former is something discovered by the examining nature, the latter is 'posited' and originated by men—positive in content. One is immutable and indeterminable; the other is transient and amenable to change.

---

[200] Rene David (ed.), 'The Legal Systems of the Word: Their Comparison and Unification', in *International Encyclopaedia of Comparative Law*, vol. 11, 1.

The task of putting in place a juridical order is actually far more than the *original position* or state of nature as given by John Rawls. If it was merely a case of men voluntarily surrendering their independence to a collective will and thereby submitting piously to its dictates, the problem would have been easily solved. If that were the case, mere adherence of lawmakers to the natural law and a combination of some moral principles would have provided an answer to all of society's needs.

On the contrary, the national state system, especially in Africa and Asia, has become more known for political and cultural heterogeneity as it emerged from the already existing political units each with diverse juridical systems. As Barragan asserts, each cultural unit no matter how small it is has an in-built juridical system, so this state of affairs in various ways raises special problems and in the words of Professor Punzo suggests the need to 'develop new resources of human consciousness'.

The Valorative Function of Law

It is against this background that several scholars put forward that if law has to form the foundation of society by providing a regulation for social relations it has to possess a strong social purpose.[201] The essence of a republican state

---

[201] Julia Barragan, *Como se Hacen Las Leyes*. Caracas: Tecnica Planeta, 1994, pp. 14, 32-43.

is the ethical ground on which it is built. This could be in three main ways: First and foremost, law must be able to resolve conflicts which arise between individuals and groups without losing sight of the objective of not destroying the social relations.[202] This is imperative, especially in political groups as in Africa where wide cultural variations exist.

In the second place, laws of the land could serve the social process of transmitting valorative messages.[203] It has been mentioned already that where cultural diversities exist, a mesh of norms and values, both at the group and individual levels, occurs. In their social functions, the laws have to focus on transmitting the common rather than individual values that will sustain the community. Likewise, the actual implementation of such well-conceived laws should transmit messages as to the degree by which it views certain violations. For instance, sanctions that carry the death penalty or life imprisonment transmit a clear message as to society's disapproval of certain acts. This was why in the search for peace in the Middle East, both Israeli and Jordanian judicial authorities have in times past taken very strong exceptions to attempts at stirring up religious animosity in an already tense political atmosphere by defamatory religious activities directed at each other.

This presents food for thought for most post colonial states where the laws are still those inherited from their

---

[202] Barragan, *ibid.*, 1994, p. 26.
[203] Barragan, *ibid.*, 1994, pp. 45-78.

masters. The existing laws in such countries may be carrying across valorative messages that would be more relevant to England, France, and Spain or Portugal of the 1920s and have nothing close to the present-day needs of Gambia, Senegal, Peru, or Angola. Whatever the price, post-colonial nations would have to weigh the opportunity cost of having in place laws that do not transmit any valorative message or, worse still, the wrong messages vis-à-vis the search for national integration.

The Valorative Benefit of the Law

The last social consideration, which in some sense seems to sum up the other two, is the fundamental function of the law as integrator of all symbolic differences. These could be ethnic or cultural as in the case of most of Africa or merely symbolic on social issues in some of the older democracies. This calls for the need to have an open and analytical mind towards understanding other points of view and forms of human expressions.[204] The lawmaker should be prudent in not rushing to impose one system of values on others for the sake of just arriving at homogeneity. This was the case with the defunct Soviet Union, where *Sovietisation* became synonymous with *Russianisation*.

---

[204] Barragan, op. cit.

The nearest resemblance to the experience of the Soviet Union is that of Sudan. The contrast was however that the Arabs adopted laws that were more focused on cultural integration. Having acquired independence in 1956, Sudan was inhabited by the Muslim Arabs of Nubian descent in the north and the animist and Christian Nilotes in the south, who were the blacks. This rich ethnic diversity was supposed to serve as a tool for the enrichment and promotion of cultural harmony, but successive leaders could not harness these potentials to promote national integration.

But rather, the cultural and religious values and laws of the north were imposed over other parts of the country. The southern part of Sudan resisted the continuous Islamisation of the country and fought for their cultural identity. John Garang de Mabior, Joseph Oduho, Salva Kiir, Samuel Abujohn Khabas, and others formed the Sudanese Liberation Army/Movement (SPLM) and fought a long war for the liberation of South Sudan. This fight was one of the most atrocious and came at a time when the Sahara part of the country was affected by drought. It was one of the most poignant disasters. However, it did not diminish the aspiration of the people in fighting for their liberation.

The territory of South Sudan and Darfur also became the home to oil wealth in the country, and it created more determination for the fight for autonomy. The war lasted between 1983 and 2005 after the signing of Comprehensive Peace Agreement (CPA) in January 2005, bringing the civil war to an end. The peace agreement also gave the people of South Sudan the right to self-determination.

In January 2011, the southern part of Sudan explored the clause in the peace agreement of 2005 on the right to self-determination. A referendum that was carried out had an overwhelming support for secession of South Sudan. The victory of the referendum gave birth to the newest nation in Africa—South Sudan, on July 9, 2011. This has therefore put a stop to the long fought war between the north and south, although occasional tensions over oil well arises from time to time.

The issue of law guiding the distribution of land in the Southern African countries of Namibia, South Africa, and Zimbabwe is a major factor that has to be considered towards the attainment of independence. Land legislation was consciously embedded in the constitution of these countries to create harmony and promote national integration between the white settlers and the black majority. For example, the Native Land Act of South Africa of 1913 was put in place to prevent the encroachment of blacks into white area. This law also created land reserves for the blacks and also prevented the sale of white territories to the blacks, thereby giving about 80 per cent of land to the whites. The constitution of these countries on independence, therefore, also made provision for the redistribution of land through a policy known as the 'wiling buyer—willing seller' approach. This approach was meant to make any forceful takeover of white-owned land by the government or bands of individuals illegal.

However, many have seen this approach to not work in the proposed land reform programme aimed at redistributing land to the black majority. The South Africa government's planned attempt at diverting land to black majority in the past was unsuccessful due to the laws in place. The people have therefore called on the government to speed up the land reform policy with the assertion that the economic future of the country depends on it.

The government of Namibia made land reform a priority in the constitution that was enacted in 1990 after its independence. It, however, made allowances for the seizure of land with compensation when it is of collective interest of the nation. Despite this land reform policy enacted in the 1990 constitution, the government still observed the 'willing seller—willing buyer' approach.

The scenario in Zimbabwe is completely different as the government of Robert Mugabe jettisoned the 'willing seller—willing buyer' approach and adopted a radical measure known as the 'fast track' process through land invasions to implement the redistribution of white-owned farmlands. The forceful acquisition of lands came with an intense legal battle in the law courts of Zimbabwe. Victims of this forceful acquisition got some reprieve in the courts but were unable to bring into effect such court orders to enable them to reclaim their land. In September 2005, the parliament carried out a constitutional amendment which was signed into law, depriving the original landowners that lost their land through the 'fast track' process of the right to challenge the decision of the government in the law courts.

A lot of reaction and criticism came from the international community, mainly from the Western world, spearheaded by the United Kingdom and the United States over the 'fast track' land reform process of President Robert Mugabe's government. It also came with myriads of economic sanctions and blockades that adversely affected the economy of Zimbabwe, which resulted in widespread hunger and high inflationary rates.

From the point of view of national integration, the case of Zimbabwe was not a best practice relative to the experience of South Africa and Namibia.

In such cases, the risk of internal agitation and eventual disintegration is imminent, even if delayed for a few years. So a better approach, just like the case of language of cooperation, should be for lawmakers to strive towards identifying and extrapolating areas of intergroup identicalness, the same used as 'necklaces' for the much coveted integration.

'The Law as Builder of Community'

The other option is on the premise that human societies have a social setting, and the juridical order put in place to regulate human actions must respect the need for its existence as a community. To better illustrate this, Barragan whom we have already quoted uses the analogy of a village festivity—*La Aldea era una Fiesta*—where, without compulsion, everybody celebrates its patron saint's day, both by making available their best talents in the preparations and by contributing at the hour of celebration the choicest wine.[205]

As a matter of fact, in the preparations towards the festival, the common target was never individual benefits or loss in terms of contributions of kind. The young men and women accepted joyfully the task of physical preparations while the adult men had the role of supplying the wine, the partaking of which was critical for the purpose of the spirit of communal coexistence. *La Aldea* (the village) was conceived as belonging to all, and everybody's interest was knitted together into every other person's interest.

But somewhere along the line, some individuals for the sake of personal aggrandisement began to give second-class wine, thereby diluting not just the physical taste of the wine but also in so doing bringing a serious metaphysical change in the more important spiritual ambience which had held the people together. Therefore, attempts were made at imposing sanctions on those responsible for bringing about this breakdown in communal love and fellowship.

---

[205] Julia Barragan, *The Village was in Festivity: The Normative Power of Self-Exception*, Monograph, 1995.

One of the main theses in the *La Aldea* motif is the inability for society's diverse and mounting problems to be effectively resolved by a regime of sanctions. Sanctions were placed in the village, which by analogy bears a lot of resemblance to the traditional political and social setting, against those who contributed negatively towards the common good. But it was soon to be discovered that the sanctions were addressing only the symptom of the defiant conduct, i.e. bringing bad wine into the common pool, and was quite unable to tackle the root cause of the problem— why do some choose to act contemptuously? Barragan therefore suggests a new approach that will help mend the broken wall in society. She advocates the need for a kind of recourse to more human centred approaches to the problems of social relations.

A simple example may be enough. In an informal research recently conducted in a Nigerian university, names of those who broke traffic lights within the campus or jumped queues in the cafeteria were published weekly in an internal magazine. Within a few weeks, the social sanction imposed on those whose names were published helped to sanitise both the problems in the university. As we saw in Barragan's *La Aldea*, the attempt to solve the problem of auto-exception by coercive means was futile as the umpires along the lines would be always corrupt and men on each occasion found ways of circumventing new laws without being detected. One could not disagree that the best thing in the circumstances is to make them feel the social effect of their action. If those who indulge in auto-exception are not praised as being smart and offered safe nesting havens, but rather smeared as 'outcasts', especially in social terms, they would perhaps conduct themselves in ways so odious to the commonwealth.

In this simile of *La Aldea,* we therefore encounter a scenario of the immediate circumstances which culminate in the pursuit of individual interests or some other self-centred group advantage. The other is the allowing of 'self-importance' exceptions to the rule. In the aspiration towards returning the *Aldea into fiesta,* Professor Barragan emphasised on the need to work towards returning into a social community. She demonstrated that measures which insist on control would only provide temporary assistance, but those which try to re-establish the lost societal brotherhood would endure more durably. One thing which appears obvious from the above is that men tend to conduct themselves better where the expected penalty for their acts of auto-exception is less physical and is rather more mental. We shall return to this in the next chapter while considering the putative role of traditional values in national integration.

This would necessitate the tillage of correctional measures in society that would be more directed at rebuilding the community rather than castigating the offenders. This may again be the spirit in what the South African Truth and Reconciliation Commission was all about. It tried to undertake the daunting task of bringing healing to past wounds not by punitive sanctions, but by helping to create a more conducive atmosphere for mutual existence between the black and white segments of the society.

Still in Africa, this experiment was again applied by two Nigerian Presidents—Musa Yar adua (1951-2010) and Dr Goodluck Jonathan. At the height of the resource and environment-based conflict in the early to late 2000s and religious fundamentalist 'Boko Haram' conflict, they adopted dialogue, amnesty, and rehabilitation. The Niger Delta peace experience seemed to have achieved a meaningful result. The engagement of the religious extremist in the north and the extension of olive branch itself, though too early to assess, is already producing meaningful results.

Chapter Fifteen

Paradigms for Conflict Management

While conflicts could be avoided or their occurrence reduced significantly either through cultivation of an enabled cooperative environment or by law-making, it cannot be denied that their likely occurrences are inevitable. Therefore, all of man's recorded attempts at directing his social existence into something close to the peaceful ideal have been short-lived, unfulfilled, and as elusive as a journey to twilight would seem.

Accordingly, more than any other preoccupation including the pursuit of material existence, man has made his highest investments in the search for peace and resolution of the myriad conflicts that marked the course of human history. This is understandable as peace forms the substance upon which society can thrive.

But then most conflicts could be pre-empted and prevented or handled before they exploded into large conflagrations; one of these or a combination of various forms of peaceful resolution of conflicts could be resorted to.

Social contract philosophers posit that it is the subsistence of force in the state of nature—man's natural habitat that in the first place compelled him to enter into the *general will,* thereby forming a human society of the state. On their part, sociologists have always recognised armed conflicts, among political units, which by the way represents the highest expression of application of force, as a social institution developed by custom and accepted by law.[206]

It is for this reason that Clausewitz merely referred to war as 'nothing but the continuation of political relations by other means'. The preoccupation of statesmen and academics over the years has only been how to regulate, control, and conduct conflicts and not necessarily how to abolish them. But during the nineteenth century, serious thoughts began to emerge on debarring and outlawing the resort to force in conflict resolution.

Rather than continue the centuries-old tradition of codifying laws that would define the 'art of war' in the

---

[206] *Encyclopaedia Britannica,* vol. xxviiii, p. 628.

words of Sun Tzu, thoughts shifted on how to make peace and settle disputes peaceably.[207] Therefore, specific law-making conventions were sparse, until the period between 1899 and 1907, following The Hague Conventions of Pacific Settlement of International Disputes. This was followed by the Covenant of the League of Nations that was drawn up in 1919 and eventually the Charter of the United Nations was drawn up in San Francisco in 1945.[208]

First Session of the United Nations in Flushing Meadow Park, New York, 23 October, 1946

---

[207] Even before then, in line with customary practice, international law had developed various means towards peace making.

[208] Starke, *ibid.*, p. 463.

Besides these, several other more specific conventions dealing with conflict resolution at both global and regional levels have been developed. For instance, the International Court of Justice had been engaged in extensive work on judicial settlement of disputes and regional arrangements, such as the 1948 Inter-American Treaty on Pacific Settlement, are also in place. On the African continent, the Organisation of African Unity (OAU), now African Union (AU)obviously due to the prevalence of member countries tending towards destabilisation, has developed one of the most effective bodies for peaceful resolution of conflicts.

In all these conventions, world political leaders and lawmakers have opted for the amicable settlement of disputes rather than the centuries-old approach of force. Article 33 of the United Nations Charter crisply summarises this thus:

> *The parties to any dispute, the continuance of which is likely to endanger the maintenance of international peace and security, shall, first of all, seek a solution by negotiation, enquiry, mediation, conciliation, arbitration, judicial settlement, resort to regional agencies or arrangements or other peaceful means of their choice.*

Although the above concern of the United Nations is the overall maintenance of international peace, it realises from experience that threats to international peace would arise if splinters of political problems even at national level could degenerate to engulf a sizeable portion of humanity. It therefore prescribed a rather elaborate list of approaches towards peace-making and ended up allowing the blank check 'or other means of their own choice'. In chapter seven, the Charter, however, puts in place laws that could allow the collective will of humanity towards peace to adopt against parties in conflicts coercive means of compliance with prescribed measures towards peace.

The architects of the UN Charter were not oblivious to the fact that the list of means towards peace making is in no way exhaustive. Furthermore, there is no compartmentalisation among the options. For instance, whereas *arbitration* and *judicial settlement* are considered more formal, others such as *negotiation, good office, mediation, conciliation*, and *inquiry* are all informal and similar in content and procedure.

So both in definition and actual practice there are overlaps; hence, in most cases peace makers adopt a combination of several of these strategies. This is why some scholars, such as Professor Starke, rightly note, for instance, that negotiation cannot take place without the involvement of good offices and mediation.[209] In the same manner, enquiry or fact finding while on the one hand only focuses on ascertaining objectively the issues at stake, on the other hand only paves the way for some other means of settlement, namely, negotiation, mediation, and good offices. Looking at

---

[209] See Starke, *ibid.*, p. 487.

mediation and good offices, the tool which they both apply is negotiation which involves simply 'using persuasion and bargaining to achieve desired aims'.[210]

Again just like mediation, good offices involve a third party 'go-between'. This is the nature of the overlap, interplay, and mutual usefulness that exist among the various options. So, although these different approaches have their distinguishing characteristics, when it comes to minute details, they are largely the same and are all directed at arriving at peace or preventing conflict by non-coercive means.

Primacy of Mediation and Shuttle Diplomacy

Short of applying some of the more elaborate peace processes, an effective use could be made specifically of *mediation.* It would be necessary to isolate this procedure and lay some stress on it. Possibly due to its informal and fluid nature, this procedure is regarded as one of the oldest forms of pacific settlement of disputes known to man. Popes and kings acting in the capacity of neutrality had always come in to broker peace in case of conflict between allies. Maybe that is why unlike most other jargons in the social sciences, the definition of mediation as a political concept is

---

[210] J. Leo Cefkin, *The Background to Current World Problems.* New York: David Mckay, 1967, pp. 82-84.

quite simple. Professor Cefkin renders it as a friendly offer of potentially attractive proposals towards resolving a given conflict by an impartial third party.[211]

Another author considers mediation to be 'the practice under which, in a conflict the services of a third party are utilised to reduce the differences or to seek a solution'.[212] Yet Amos Lakos provides a very simple, although much embracing definition:

> *A form of peaceful settlement procedure by which a third party is used by disputants in finding a solution to the dispute or to decrease the level of conflict. The aim of the mediator is to reduce or solve the conflict. The function of the mediator is to provide open communication channels, to change the images of the disputants themselves about each other, and to provide additional ideas to enhance commonalty of interest.*[213]

The party tendering that mediation may be a state, a juridical person, or an individual. Although unlike arbitration, no prior agreement exists with regards the acceptability of the proposals towards a solution, and the entire process remains informal, nevertheless, mediators

---

[211] Cefkin, op. cit.

[212] *Encylopaedia Britannica*, vol. viii, p. 999.

[213] This is found in the introductory note to the section on Medication in Amos Lakos, *International Negotiations: A Bibliography*. New York, 1989, p. 99.

actively work towards peace. Unlike good offices, he goes beyond suggesting viable options for settlement to present them and work out ways and means towards an acceptable compromise.

Some hold the opinion that the lack of procedural elaboration remains a major limitation to the usability of mediation as a form of conflict resolution; that is why Starke argues that this approach would likely end up servicing other more formal procedures that would labour more on the facts and the procedures. However, going back through history, it has achieved some good results by itself and not as an ancillary to other efforts. It is important to add that such efforts include among others, the 1825 British intervention in the settlement of issues between Portugal and Brazil; and Pope Leo XII intervention between Germany and Spain over the Carolina waters in 1885. More recently, the Soviet Union in 1965 successfully was the go-between for India and Pakistan, including arranging a meeting in Tashkent. Similarly, the United States, Norway, and Spain have been most active in the search for peace in the Middle East. Portugal, on its part, had been very active in the brokering of peace among various warring parties in Angola and Mozambique, its former colonies in Africa. Other countries such as Nigeria and Venezuela have in their specific regions taken advantage of their petrodollar to take on mediatory roles in internal political crisis in many of their neighbouring countries.

The United Nations as an institution has in its over six decades of existence relied enormously on the use of mediators for various disputes while many regional bodies have followed this cue in appointing mediators to resolve conflicts that emerged in their respective vicinity. These include Palestine, Kashmir, and Essequiburio. Dag Hammarskjold, the second Secretary General of the United Nations, paid the high price for peace with his own life in search for solutions to the Congo crisis in 1961.

As mediation continues to gain currency as a favoured schema for conflict resolution, one trend which has become pronounced is the increasing role assumed by individuals in this regard. No doubt the contributions of Dag Hammarskjold and the subsequent secretary generals of the United Nations, as well as those of their personal envoys in bringing about peace in various parts of the world, have been profound and easily cited.

The same could also be said of 'shuttle diplomacy' which came to prominence during the tenure of Henry Kissinger as U.S. Secretary of State and Chester Crocker as Assistant Secretary of State. Other examples are the personal diplomacy followed by successions of religious leaders such as popes and bishops. For instance, Pope John Paul II mediated the Beagle Channel dispute successfully between the two 'Catholic nations' of Argentina and Chile. In the rest of Latin America, Catholic bishops including Miguel Obando Bravo of Nicaragua, Gregorio Rosa Chavez of El Salvador, and Samuel Ruiz of Mexico have been very active in helping to bring about peace in various hotbeds of tension in the rather embattled continent. Church mediation has also been known in other areas including East Timor, where Catholic Bishop Carlos Felipe Ximenes Belo led in the search for peace. While mediation at the level of the United Nations, governments, and the Church could easily be classified as institutional, personal diplomacy by prominent individuals has increasingly recorded huge successes. In the past, academics such as John Burton and Herbert Kelman facilitated talks among Cyprian, Israeli, Palestinian, and British leaders. During the Cuban Missile Crisis of 1962, the role of journalists John Scali in bridging the communication gap between the United States and the then Soviet Union was enormous. The same was done by the educator Brian Wedge in the Dominican Republic after the 1965 United States invasion. Former U.S. President Jimmy Carter recorded huge successes in Somalia, Haiti, Central America, etc.[214]

Preventive Diplomacy

It is indeed closely related to this, or on reinforcing this, that we find the opinion of the former United Nations Secretary General Dr Boutros Boutros-Ghali relevant. He had professed in his famous *Agenda for Peace* what was

---

[214] See Carter, *ibid.*

called 'preventive diplomacy', whereby the peace-making process could foresee and intervene through the process of confidence-building measures to avert crisis. This cannot be more applicable anywhere in the world than Africa and Asia as most of these crises are easier and less expensive to manage before they escalate. The emphasis of such preventive diplomacy as it relates to Africa would be to create sufficient internal capacity for confidence building and prompt crisis resolution capacity.

This is very effective in India where such bodies as *Lok Adalat* are involved in peace making and in the diffusion of personal and group tensions as they try to come up. Already in several African countries such bodies as the *Ombudsman, Public Complaints Commission, Justices of Peace*, and the like are in existence. However, there is yet a need for more research on specific confidence-building measures that would be useful, adaptable, and applicable to individual sociopolitical needs of the various countries on the further use that could be made of traditional and religious institutions. However, this can only be achieved through concerted international collaboration and financial support by way of both financial aid and technical support in the organisation of seminars, workshops, and other confidence-building programmes.

Chapter Sixteen

The Citizen as Foundation for Sustainable Integration

In suggesting options for better national integration in the modern state, the need exists for further reflection on the place of the individual in the social community. This is important because society is made up of different individuals and it only subsists for their benefit. So an important need exists for a better understanding of the debt and gains which these intricate relations offer.

It is argued by some that the underlying problem seems to be how efficacious basic rules of law may be established in order to furnish a labyrinth for the equitable allotment of benefits, duties, and obligations of the collectivity, vis-à-vis the individual.

In a historical context, the average individual has little problems with 'benefits' that accrue to him from the common will. As Machiavelli rightly points out, this is because the interests of the individual are best met by being spared from tyranny and the basic assurances that the necessities of life are at his disposal. So he states that 'one who becomes a Prince through the favour of the people ought to keep them friendly, and this he can easily do seeing that they only ask not to be oppressed'.[215] This is obvious because tyranny would be more inclined towards increasing the duties and obligations which individuals are expected to take on in the 'interest' of the common good. Rather, the basal concern through all generations has been to what extent could 'duties' and 'obligations' be ascribed to a person.

As we saw earlier in chapters three and four, the individual out of either compulsion by the forces of natural existence or mere instinct voluntarily submits his sovereignty to that of the group. Like any other type of linear relationship, the nexus binding man and his society together therefore produces benefits and duties both ways. Accordingly, the individual, for instance, expects the

---

[215] Nicolo Machavelli, *The Prince*, chapter ix, reprinted by the University of Chicago Press, 1991.

corresponding reward of having his interests protected by corporate sovereignty. Rousseau had reasoned that man voluntarily gives up his natural rights to the commonwealth with the hope that it will in turn help maximise his relative gains in terms of enjoyment of life. This gives birth to rights for both sides and could be compared with the symbiosis that exists between the two hands in agreeing to wash each other for the mutual purpose of remaining clean. The gesture is reciprocal.

In the words of Prof. Jon Elster, Norwegian political and social theorist, some basic problems come to light on how to allocate the blessings arising from the common existence, which are short, and how to share the 'necessary burdens', which seem to be in multiples.[216] The polemics consequently begin as to where to draw the line between the duties of the commonalty and those of the individuals. Another problem is to what extent the society as a corporate entity and those who make it up could impose duties and obligations for each other and what obligations are there to compel the individual towards compliance to duties assigned or expected by the group. Hence, the underlying question is: What does the society expect of the individuals towards its self-survival and what does it have in stock for the individual to make him an integral part of the social commonwealth?

---

[216] Jon Elster, *The Cement of Society: A Survey of Social Order.* Cambridge: Cambridge University Press, 1989.

No doubt there exists a kind of filial ligature between man and his 'fatherland' or 'nativeland', as some others would call it. Hence, Simon Bolivar once said with regards to his highest hopes and ambitions in life that it centres around finding relevance and fulfilment only in liberation of his land (*'mi unico amor siempre ha sido el de la patria mi unica ambicion su libertad'*).

The relationship between the individual and his society has been defined and described in varying ways: member, citizen, national, etc. At the level of what is called 'community' were the bonds of relationship between the people, and at the more corporeal level, it could be said that the individual is a 'member', but at the large and, of course, more punctilious level of the modern state, the individual is described as a 'citizen'. Irrespective of which terminology is preferred in describing the individual and the diverse renderings as we shall see, what is important is that the compact of citizenship becomes glued from the time that an individual is born or becomes naturalised into a place of stay.

Who is a citizen?

Generations of thinkers have argued that the bond of citizenship begins when the union of men comes under juridical laws which Rousseau puts thus:

> *Each of us puts his person and all his power in the*
> *common under the supreme direction of the general will,*
> *and in our corporate capacity, we receive each member*
> *as an indivisible part of the whole.*[217]

However, others such as Hegel disagree with this notion, arguing that the decision of citizenship is not with the individual, but is imposed on him at birth. A person is born into a state, and from then onwards he becomes in a sense shackled with that as:

> *it is false to maintain that the foundation of the state*
> *is something at the option of all its members. It is nearer*
> *the thought to say that it is absolutely necessary for every*
> *individual to be a citizen.*[218]

Still, J.S. Mill and Simon Bolivar among others see the conception of citizenship as having a strong correlation with the existence of a democratic government and the mental disposition of the individual towards the service of the common good.

From a purely legal and more contemporary point of view, Steve Gifis defines the terminology as 'a member of a nation political community, one who owes allegiance to and

---

[217] Rousseau, *The Social Contract*, book 1, chapters 6-8, reprinted by the University of Chicago.

[218] Hans Hegel, *The Philosophy of Right*, para. 47, reprinted by the University of Chicago.

may claim protection from its government'.[219] On their part, the writers of the *Encyclopaedia Britannica* brought out the elements encompassed in the above definition better, when they added that it is a:

> relationship between an individual and a state, defined by law of that state, with corresponding duties and rights in that state. Citizenship is derived from the historical relationship between the individual and his city. Citizenship implies the status of freedom with accompanying responsibilities.[220]

Some other authors like Hugh Seton-Watson seem to define citizenship in terms of its coterminous relationship with the twin concept of 'nationality'. He asserts that nationality which has the rather academic and impersonal meaning of belonging to 'nation' overlaps with the concept *of staatsangehorigkeit*—the citizen of the state.[221]

But Okwudo, with specific reference to the ethnic intermix in Africa, brings down this further by defining nationality as the concept of belonging to a group who are held together by a 'common language, culture or history. For example, the Yoruba, Hausa-Fulani, and Ibo people of Nigeria, or the Ashanti and Ewe people of Ghana'. However,

---

[219] Gifis, *ibid.*, p. 72.
[220] *Encyclopaedia Britannica*, vol. iii, p. 332.
[221] Seton-Watson, *ibid.*, p. 4.

he asserts that with the rise of the nation-state system and the submersion of these nationalities into the bigger state, a new concept arose, that of citizenship: 'which persons are full members of a particular state. The right of citizenship is granted by the state and citizens enjoy this as long as the state grants or allows it'.

The Price of Citizenship

Having been accepted as a member of a social setting or an organised society, the individual's greatest commitment towards the general lot is often referred to as 'duty'.

Though simple and much frequently applied, the terminology 'duty' conjures up much division as it relates to definition and the application, and when applied to *man's relationships to his social* environment, it becomes even more complicated.

Barron's Law Dictionary, in different inferences, defines the concept as 'obligatory conduct owed by a person to another'.[222] Definitely, such obligatory conduct towards one another was created in the process of giving up the absolute sovereignty of our individual independence in the light of social existence. For instance, recognising the right of others to basic existence and pursuing the essential necessities of life. In a more legal context, Barron's adds that the laws

---

[222] Gifis, *ibid.*, p. 151.

could create duties and require that they be 'done of forlorn by a determinate person' and could be imposed by specific contracts entered into between individuals in the course of existing together.[223]

This definition, however, is better explained by the Webster Dictionary definition as: 'which a person is bound by any natural, moral or legal obligation to do or perform; the obligation to do something'.[224]

The above definitions, more than introducing us to the diversity of definition, help delineate some salient issues. These include the fact that the laws, cited as evidence of nature, morality, or the land, impose direct duties on individuals. In response to a question that was posed regarding the 'duty' to keep one's word, John Locke brings this out in the trinity of man's obligation towards morality and the land:

> If a Christian be asked he will give as reason: Because God who has power of eternal life and death, requires it of us. But if a Hobbyist be asked why? He will answer: Because the public requires it, and the Leviathan will punish you if you do not. And if one of the philosophers had been asked, he would have answered: Because it was dishonesty, below the dignity

---

[223] Gifis, *ibid.*, p. 273.
[224] Perhaps of all the thinkers mentioned above, the one that illustrated this umbilical cord connecting the citizen to the state in the clearest manner is Rousseau.

of man, and opposite to virtue, the highest perfection of human nature, to do otherwise.[225]

Let us look at the more contemporary thoughts of John Rawls who these days is easily credited as one of the few philosophers who has tried to explain the contradictions of the gapping polarities and receding confluence of human society.

With an altruistic poise in explaining society, Rawls has dared to prescribe, as it were, a recipe that forms an amalgam of liberalism and socialism. This is why Professor John Harsanyi refers to Rawlsianism as 'the most important contemporary non-utilitarian moral theory' to which Rawls himself acknowledges in the opening part of the classic—*A Theory of Justice*—that the study departs from the classical utilitarian approach and moves towards the social contract philosophy.[226]

So with a basically Kantian approach, Rawls emphasises the fundamental connection between social justice and such virtues as equity, fairness, and the existence of civic duties. It is for this reason that he says that 'a society is well ordered when it is not only designed to advance the good of its members but when it is also effectively regulated by a

---

[225] Mortimer, *ibid.*, p. 282.

[226] John Harsanyi, 'Modelos teoriticos del juego y la decision en la etica utilitarian', in *Etica y Politica*, 1993, p. 34.

public conception of justice'.[227] Although the work of Rawls has often been called the 'new social contract philosophy', what seems to set his work apart from the Enlightenment philosophers is the deep preoccupation with justice much unknown to them at that time.[228]

Founded on these, Rawls traces the principles of justice to some form of contract entered into by the ancestors of humanity at the dawn of history. In this primeval stage, which he calls the 'original position', it is assumed that those involved are wholly altruistic and ignorant to their own political or social conditions. Accordingly, they are completely unaware of their own personal interests in a scenario which he calls the 'veil of ignorance'. John Harsanyi describes the position thus: 'Assumption is that each participant in the original position will choose among alternative conceptions of justice on the basis of highly irrational "maxim principle" which requires everybody to act in such a way as if he were absolutely sure that whatever he did, the worst possible action of his would be obtained'.

While prescribing the foundation of a durable system of justice as depending on fairness, Rawls alludes to the fact that it creates some obligations for the individual. Simply, the principle on which these obligations arise is stated as:

---

[227] John Rawls, *A Theory of Justice*. London: Oxford University Press, 1971, p. 5.
[228] D.F. Sheltens, The Social Contract Philosophers, in the History of Ideas, 1977 p. 327.

Obligation to do his part by the rules of an institution whenever he has voluntarily accepted the benefits of the scheme or has taken advantage of the opportunities it offers to advance his interests, provided that this institution is just or fair.[229]

These are in addition to his 'natural duties', as opposed to obligations which are created by the institution of juridical order and apply to all without choice. While he alludes to the enjoyment of benefits in the case of obligation, natural duties arise naturally from the existing arrangement. Thus, he gives the example of natural duty of not being cruel to other people or that of mutual self-help.

Moreover, these natural or moral duties help define more clearly the existing institutional ties and the interpersonal relationships. It is for this reason that he advocates that natural duties have to be performed in 'good faith'. So basically the individual owes duties to society that must be performed.

The Gains of Citizenships

Some other contributors to this subject see the emphasis of the state as not what it gets from the *citizen* but what it

---

[229] Rawls, *A Theory of Justice.* London: Oxford University Press, 1971, p. 343.

gives. *Citizenship* of the republic is meant for the individual's happiness and protection. As Bolivar said in another of his letters to Francisco de Paula Santander in 1820, '*Ciertamente el oro y la plata son objectos preciosos, pero la existencia de la republica y la vida de los cindadanos son mas preciosos aum.*'[230]

The organised society was therefore expected to extend to the citizen's absolute protection. In other words, the unquestionable importance of silver and gold is nothing in comparison to the welfare of the citizen. As one of the most prolific thinkers on this subject, Bolivar asserted that the well-being of the citizen is as important as the very existence of the republic itself. We can see the importance of this when it is considered that the Trojan War was itself fought just for the purpose of protecting the rights of a Greek citizen, Menalus, whose wife, Helen, was carried away by the Trojans to Paris.

The state has the duty of not only providing for the citizens in a manner that will serve the full attainment of his God-given talents and delectation but also protect him in times of need. If we were to dissect Rawlsian thoughts further to look at them in more detail, it would be realised that he underlines the need for the state to ensure that the citizen receives social justice where necessary and that his rights as a human being are properly defended. For Rawls,

---

[230] Certainly, gold and silver are precious objects, but the existence of the republic and the life of its citizens are much more precious. Martinez, 1995, p. 44.

what creates the duties and obligations for performance on the part of the citizenry is the composure of the system of social justice which is put in place.

Paul had in various inferences been one of the most forceful exponents of the celestiality of the citizenship of proselytes. However, on his arrests and subsequent trial, Paul, at a critical time, exercised his rights of also being not only a Jew of 'heavenly calling' but also a Roman citizen after he had been subjected to torture and the denial of due legal processes.[231] But by the time he invoked his prerogative of *Pax Romana*, the following is recorded:

> *And as they bound him thongs, Paul said unto the centurion that stood by, is it lawful for you to scourge a man that is Roman and not condemned. When the centurion heard that, he went and told the chief captain saying: Take heed what thou doest: for this man is a Roman . . . Then straightaway they departed from him which should have examined him: and the chief captain also was afraid after he knew that he was a Roman.*[232]

Unlike Jesus Christ, whose simple Jewish citizenship could not take him to Caesar in Imperial Rome and had to die, Paul was taken on the long and tortuous journey to Rome at public cost, where he was ultimately set free. Paul

---

[231] This could be found in the Acts 22-28.
[232] Acts 22: 25-28.

therefore continued living in Rome to carry on his normal life. So as could be seen in the above example, the right of citizenship carried with it protection, immunity, social justice, and a right of abode within the territory.

The concept of the basic rights of the individual has in various countries been entrenched in national constitutions as Bills of Rights, and at the international level, standards have been prescribed by such codification as the Universal Declaration of Human Rights and the Inter-American Convention on Human Rights. This is why although Rawls has in a detailed form prescribed the importance of 'duty and obligation', he also gives two exceptions under which laws may be disobeyed—civil disobedience and conscientious refusal.

While limiting the causal consideration of civil disobedience to three similar domestic situations, he extends that of conscientious refusal to the external scene. It is imperative for governments to note that internally the purpose of civil disobedience is to call public attention to the need for a sense of justice. So civil disobedience must therefore be allowed. Besides, it also serves to alert all, both within the country and the rest of the world, to the violation to the covenant of the accord.

Another benefit and cardinal right of citizenship, which has persistently been highlighted from Thucycides to Mill and Plato to Bolivar, is the right of being adequately educated enough to properly appreciate political processes, which has been regarded as a cardinal right of citizenship. With the advancement of the concepts of Representative

Government and the obsolescence of ascribed social stratification, which existed in many societies, the centuries-old debate about franchise and suffrage also seem to have become accepted as indispensable ingredients of citizenship.

The Religious Obligation of State Building

A proper understanding of where the individual fits into society as dictated by various religious beliefs is important in examining the integrative process. Secularism and civic humanism seem to hold sway in contemporary times, especially in the Western world. It is however true that a large percentage of the world population in the less developed countries are more likely to be swayed in their behaviour by what they perceive as a religious injunction than what they see as a civic obligation. So it would serve our purpose of searching for national integration to see the areas of mutual overlap between political philosophy which we just saw and those of religious injunction and, in so doing, use one to strengthen and better explain the other.

Let us turn to the Scriptures. For the sake of brevity, let us use the Holy Bible as an example, more so as it details very clear rights and obligation of citizenship. But what seems to give particular value to biblical teachings is the profundity, as it relates not only to man's relationship with God but also the direct connection to the very social and political foundation of human society.

In fact, in the Ten Commandments, believed by Christians and the Israeli nation to be the basis of the modern Western codification of law, only three of the elements relate to man's relationship with God and the rest relate directly to duties assigned to the individual within the community. In all other places where the Bible had touched on man's relationship with God, it always added the aspect of an interpersonal relationship. The service unto God was seen as incomplete where duties to the state and towards other individual have not been discharged.

Therefore, duty towards the common good is seen as part of the divine plan of worship. As a matter of fact, the Hebrew word *sadiq* from which the word righteousness is derived has a judicial connotation meaning literally 'innocent'.[233] For a ruler, this means the duty to install a good government and execute good judgement, and for the people, this means treating one's neighbours well. As Metzger asserts, 'In Rabbinic literature, righteousness is often specified to mean generosity in general.'[234] In the much famed 'Lord's Prayer', Christians are instructed to go back to 'pay your debt' before expecting prayers to be answered, thereby further underlining this point.

Duty as seen in the Bible therefore has two levels: God's responsibility towards his people on the one hand and the

---

[233] Metzger, Introduction to the Apocrypha (New York: Oxford University Press, 1957) p. 655.

[234] Metzger, *ibid.*, p. 655.

people's commitment towards God to carry out their duties towards Him and towards fellow men on the other. As Christian theologians, such as John Calvin and Aquinas, have tried to show, violation of the natural or moral laws carries the same weight of sin as violation of the positive divine laws, such as the Ten Commandments and others enacted in Leviticus.

So among other things, the citizen is obligated to work towards the achievement of civil governance by paying taxes and giving other services, such as military service, and in showing respect and subjection and praying for the constituted authority. Above all, they are also expected to pursue the course of peace with all other members of society, as much as it is possible. In Matthew, Chapter 22, Jesus gave the perfect example by paying his taxes. Rather than using the divine powers that he had—which he had copiously used to help others—to stop the tax collectors from seeking his due, he preferred to convert the guts of a fish into money in order to respect the law.

Similarly, at the Garden of Gethsemane, when one of the twelve disciples cut off the ears of one of the captured Roman soldiers, he preferred to follow the law by placing the ear back.[235] In the same way, it is recorded in the Bible that Jesus Christ obeyed the law up to death and only preferred to rise back on the third day, apparently since Rome had not yet enacted a law against resurrecting from death.

---

[235] The twelve in some way also invariably acted as the Lord's bodyguards.

As a matter of fact, the further prescription of regulations related to the expectations of citizenship go a long way to include detailed critical interpretations on the overall moral behaviour, since that is the only way to make the ultimate promotion to the City of God at death. These include such obligations as love and abstinence from things that are likely to bring civil strife either with individuals or indirect infringement of the laws of the land.

So Christians are instructed to shine as a light in their societies and act as the 'salt of the earth'—in other words, the preservative of moral rectitude. Hence, the unfettered service to the community is seen as intrinsic to the very object of worship and faith in God. In the New Testament, while the Christian as a sojourner or pilgrim on the earth is expected to forebear the corrupting influence of the *cosmos*, it remains his fundamental duty to work towards the preservation of peace in human society. It is also in this vein that the Book of Ecclesiastes, which is actually the memoirs of King Solomon, remains one of the most profound in its analysis of the contradiction in human society. It states:

Let us hear the conclusion of the whole matter: Fear God and keep his commandments: for this is the whole duty of man.[236]

---

[236] Ecclesiastics 12: 13. The truth is that this book was written in Palestine about the year 1000 BC.

A look at the writings on culture and jurisprudence of Islam contained basically in the *Shari'ah* shows that similar duties and obligations created between the citizen and the society insist on full and uncompromised compliance on both sides. Being different from Christian theology, which insists on human inward compliance, the *Shari'ah*, through a system of rituals, details minute aspects of man's obligation towards the state and fellow people and vice versa. It covers both ethical and legal standards for the community and hence classifies some acts as *mandub*—praiseworthy and capable of bringing divine favour, while others as *makruh*—blameworthy.

What is important is that, in whatever case, it imposes on the citizen the need to conform to a constituted authority and obey the laws of the organised society. However, in a Lockean or Rawlsian manner, it makes exemptions for defiance if the system is ungodly.

Conclusion

Quest for the Common Good

In an article called 'Communal Conflicts and Global Security', a leading expert on conflict management, Professor Ted Robert Gurr, stated that in recent times although progress towards the objective of a more pluralistic world system has emerged, however, we have also seen an increase in cross communal, cross social, and indeed ethnopolitical grievances.[237] According to this researcher:

---

[237] Ted Robert Gurr, 'Communal Conflicts and Global Security', in *Current History*, May 1995, pp. 212-217.

every form of ethnopolitical conflict, increased sharply from the 1950s through the early 1990s. Non-violent political action by communal groups more than doubled between 1950 and 1990, and both violent protests and rebellion quadrupled.[238]

In the period after the year 2000, rather than abate, the situation has exacerbated to include religious-inspired conflicts of this extremely violent predilection. The threat of religious nationalism which tries to legitimise its relevance within the framework of secular nationalism, cultural identity, and democratic modernism continues to rise.[239] Some other students and observers of political trends have started to caution that even the claims of increased global political pluralism and liberalism are being threatened by the rise of illiberal democracies, producing deluded democracies and thereby the possibility of political conflict.

So across the world, many dictators either attempted or succeeded in concocting fictitious democratic processes around themselves to legitimise their hold on power while others simply rejected due electoral processes to perpetuate

---

[238] Gurr, *ibid.*

[239] Mark Juergenmeyer, 'Religious Nationalism: A Global Threat', in *Current History,* vol. 95, no. 604, November 1996, pp. 372-376. Actually the authors suggest the need for political and social reforms to make room for such pressures which are likely to be on the rise.

their stay.[240] So, in the recent past in cases such as Peru, duly elected democratic institutions were simply dismissed, while in Nigeria, the winner of Presidential election in 1993 was thrown into jail and died while in incarceration.

In what the *Economist* magazine calls the rise of despotic democrats, in several countries (including Indonesia, Zambia, Zimbabwe, and Kenya), duly elected advocates of democracy on assuming power have found themselves clamping down on any form of opposition and sticking to power almost indefinitely.

No region is free of these challenges to collective existence. For instance, it may be argued that since 1976 there has been no successful military coup in Latin America and the region has had a good track record of very low non-ethnic political violence. But this region has seen an upsurge of ideological—and social-related conflicts. In particular, there has been a phenomenal rise in Native Indian ultraism not only in Mexico but also in Ecuador, Peru, and all over Central America. Moreover, it must not be forgotten, as Professor Jorge Dominguez points out, that the Hispanic American democracy is still threatened by *fracasomania*.[241]

---

[240] For more details on this, see Fareed Zakaria, 'The Rise of Illiberal Democracies', in *Foreign Affairs*, vol. 76, no. 6, December 1997, pp. 22-43 as well as another article called 'Democracy Without Illusions', by Thomas Carothers, in *Foreign Affairs,* vol. 76, no. 1, January 1997, pp. 85-99.

[241] Jorge Domingyez, 'Latin America's Crisis of Representation', in *Foreign Affairs*, vol. 76, January 1997, pp. 100-114.

It is easily recalled that when Professor Luis Castro Leiva was asked by the Venezuelan Congress to give a valedictory speech to celebrate the forty years of the country's democracy, he also alluded to the fact that democracy in the region, going by the experiences of Colombia, Argentina, Peru, and of his homeland, was still shaky.[242] No wonder, 'Commander' Hugo Chavez came to practice his own brand of people-based democracy.

In the views of these two scholars, this trend is no doubt considerably influenced by the strong interplay of the forces of poverty, low productivity, and multiplicity of ineffectual civic institutions.[243] It is true that some plural societies such as Switzerland, India, Israel, and Canada have achieved large margins of success, but even then, with waves of human migrations, such as the arrival of more people from some of the eastern regions, there is yet more need to develop and fine-tune new paradigms for better integration, as no one set of options gives all-round success.

As we saw in the case of Canada, though having achieved remarkable successes at the socioeconomic level, the country was fraught with ingrained political concern. As a matter of fact, the Canadian Supreme Court not too long ago had to confront the task of deciding the legality of *Québecan* unilateral separatism. Towards the east, the

---

[242] Speech by Professor Luis Castro Leiva before the Special Session of the Venezuela Congress, 23 January 1997.

[243] Moises Naim, 'Latin America: The Morning After', in *Foreign Affairs*, vol. 74, no. 8, July 1995, pp. 45-68.

electoral process in India, including the re-emergence of Mrs Sonia Gandhi in the 1990s to continue the family legacy of dynamic leadership under the Congress Party of old, did not seem to have given the country any surety of peace; rather the resurgence of religious—and socioeconomic-related sectarianism and violence has kept that country highly strung with uneasiness. The success of the strongly pro-Hindu Bharatiya Janata Party (BJP) in the March 1988 general elections did not only underscore this point but also left an atmosphere of looming tension down the road. But besides these few examples, the political destiny of many countries across the world remains ominous and some still point towards the path of collapse as was the case with the former Soviet Union.

Similarly, we have seen an insistence on the imposition of Western models on single party and socialist democracies of former Eastern Europe, China, Cuba, and North Korea. While it remains to be seen how such change to Western political idealisation would engender common well-being on the long run, although we have seen rather inchoate economic well-being in China, the immediate impact on the societies which have yielded to such change are violence, confusion, and total disorder. In Yugoslavia and the former Soviet Union, this has led not only to the dismemberment of the political structures but also orchestrated a spiral of civil wars. In Russia, China, as well as the Czech and Polish republics, it has led to high crime rates and other social vices, and after many years, the appalling gap between the 'haves' and the 'have-nots' has become even wider.

While not holding an explanation for political repression, Fidel Castro could not have been more correct in observing during the visit of Pope John Paul II (1920-2005) that the Cuban society, where literacy rate, life expectancy, and overall social security remain the best in Latin America under a 'dictatorship, is the most humane society in the region'. Pope John Paul II visited Cuba in February 1998. In his keynote welcome address at the Havana Airport, Fidel Castro again raised his much known argumentation that although the Western models allow the right for more political openness in terms of expression and association, the very structure of the society still denies the poor the ability to take advantage of these ideals. Yet the poor in such a political setting still suffer economic and social deprivation. He therefore prefers a political order where the limitation of 'political freedom' would help the lower social echelons to have more just access to social well-being.

Since foreign models always find it difficult to work in new political settings, the fundamental question therefore is: how best can the society be organised to meet the standard of fulfilling the common good? In other words, how can diverse groups live in peace and build strong nation-states, which will engender economic well-being and social justice to all?

Again, the question of how such an understanding of the duties and obligations imposed by the various belief systems could contribute towards the integrative process in Africa particularly, and elsewhere, would remain an area of interest for further investigation by the social sciences. As part of the task of building strong states and uniting the various forms of religious expression, the need would exist for some form of ecumenical understanding for the inculcation of such values in the individual proselytes. In other words, beyond the imperative of identifying the areas of overlap, say, between Christian teaching and Islam and the positive values which they could contribute towards society, there exists a singular need to emphasise the role of the individual.

The responsibility therefore falls on religious leaders who by virtue of their vocation have privileged access both to those who run the state apparatus and those who simply follow, to point out and insist on adherence to those common areas in the main religions as it relates to duty and obligation. Another notion that readily comes to mind is the need to re-examine the pedagogical curriculum as it relates to what is called 'religious education', towards focusing more on tutoring this aspect of the role of the individual towards society and vice versa as outlined in the various creeds. For instance, the available school curriculum for West Africa shows that much of the emphasis as it relates to Christian religious study is the history of the Jews and a historic rendering of the life of the early Christian movement. While this is good and important, there is a need for the change of a focal point to a more correlative working with the efforts of religious instruction as it relates to civic responsibility, both of the state and the individual.

Bibliography

Allswith, E., *The National Question in Soviet Central Asia* (New York: Praegis, 1974)

Anthony, Michael, *The Golden Quest: The Four Voyages of Christopher Columbus* (London: Macmillan Caribbean, 1992)

Aquinas, Thomas, *Summa Theologica*, Parts 1 and 2

Aristotle, *The Republic* (reprinted, Chicago: University of Chicago Press, 1991)

Atiner, Shiner, *Islamic Peoples of Soviet Union* (London: Kegan Paul Press, 1989)

Barragan, Julia, *Etica y Politica en la Decision Public* (Caracas Ediciones Sepratas, 1993)

Barragan, Julia, *Como se Hacen Las Leyes* (Caracas: Tecnica Planeta, 1994)

Barragan, Julia, *The Village was in Festivity: The Normative Power of Self Exception* (Monograph, 1995)

Bendix, *Kings or People: Power and the Mandate to Rule* (Berkley: University of California Press, 1978)

Bennett, William, *The Devaluing of America* (New York: Summit Book, 1992)

Bertensons, H. (ed.), *Documents of the Christian Church* (London: Oxford University Press, 1964)

Betancourt, Romulo, *Venezuela: Oil and Politics* (Boston: Houghton Mifflin, 1978)

Bienen, Henry and Herbst, Jeffrey, 'The Relationship between Political and Economic Reform in Africa', in *Comparative Politics* vol. 29, no. 1 (October 1996)

Birch, Anthony H., *The British System of Government* (London: Allen and Unwin, 1986)

Birnback, Nick, 'Making and Keeping the Peace', in *Global Agenda* (New York: University Press of America, 1994)

Bissel, William, *Making India Work*, Penguin Books, India, 2009

Bodenheimer, Susanne J., *The Ideology of Development: The American Paradigm for Latin American Studies* (Beverly Hills: 1971)

Bokonga Ekanga Botombele, Charles, 'Globalization in Action Faced With the International Challenge of the

Global Society and the Future of the Individual at the Dawn of the 21st Century' University of Antwerp, vols. 53/54 of the *Law and State Review*

Boutros-Ghali, Boutros, *An Agenda for Peace* (New York: UN Publications, 1992)

Buchanan, James, *The Limits of Liberty: Between Anarchy and Leviathan* (Chicago: University of Chicago Press, 1975)

Cannon, Dale, 'Dwelling in the World Through Language', *International Philosophical Quarterly* (March 1972)

Cardoso Fernando Henrique and Faletto Enzo, *Dependencia y Desarrollo en America Latina* (Mexico City: 1969)

Carlsson, Ingvar and Ramphal, Shridath, *Our Global Neighbourhood* (London: Oxford University Press, 1995)

Carothers, Thomas, 'Democracy Without Illusions', in *Foreign Affairs*, vol. 76, no. 1 (January 1997)

Carpenter, *Alejo Guerra del Tiempo* (Madrid, 1993)

Carter, Jimmy, *Talking Peace: A Vision for the Next Generation* (New York: Puffin Books, 1995)

Cefkin, J. Leo, *The Background to Current World Problems* (New York: David Mckay, 1967)

Christensen, Rebate, 'On the Problematic of a Philosophy of Language', in *IPQ* (March 1976)

Cockcroft, J. & Johnson, D. *Dependence and Underdevelopment: Latin America's Political Economy* (New York: Anchor Books, 1972)

Codding, George A., *The Federal Government of Switzerland* (Boston: Houghton Miffling, 1961)

Cox, R. W., 'Social Forces, States and World Order: Beyond International Relations Theory', in *Millennium*, vol. 10 (1981)

Cox, R. W., 'Global Restructuring: Making Sense of the Changing International Political Economy', in Richard Stubbs and R. D. Geoffrey Underhill (eds.), *Political Economy and the Changing Order* (Toronto: McClelland & Steward 1994)

Daniels, Norman, *Reading Rawls* (Stanford: Stanford University Press, 1989)

Darwin, Charles, *Origin of Species* (Chicago: Great Books, 1859, reprinted 1993)

David, Rene (ed.), 'The Legal Systems of the Word: Their Comparison and Unification', in *International Encyclopaedia of Comparative Law*, vol. 11 (1983)

Davies, H. A., *Outlines of World History* (London: Oxford University Press, 1959)

Diamond, Larry and Platter, Marc F. (eds.), *Nationalism, Ethnic Conflict and Democracy* (Baltimore: John Hopkins University Press, 1995)

Dietman, Alfonso, 'El Personalismo Negroafircano y Su paradigna Latinoamericano', *Politae Bulletin* (Caracas: UCV, 1976)

Domingyez, Jorge, 'Latin America's Crisis of Representation', in *Foreign Affairs*, vol. 76 (January 1997)

Elliot, Florence, *A Dictionary of Politics* (Middlesex: Penguin, 1969)

Elliot, Florence, *A Dictionary of Political Science* (London: Penguin, 1969)

Elsenhaus, Hartmut, 'Dependencia, Underdevelopment and the Third World', in *Law and State Review*, vol. 36 (1987)

Encyclopaedia Britannica, 1768 (edn.), vol. xv, 1993 (edn.), Encyclopaedia Britannica, Inc.

Encyclopaedia Britannica, Macropedia, vol. xxviii. Encyclopaedia Britannica, Inc. (1974)

Encyclopaedia of Social Sciences, vol. xi-xii (London: Macmillan, 1957)

Enloe, Cynthia H., *Ethnic Conflict and Political Development* (Boston: Little, Brown, 1973)

Evers, Tilmam, 'Supranational Statehood. The Case of the European Union: Civitas Civitatum or Monstrum?', in *Law and State Review*, vol. 51 (1995)

Fanon, Frantz, *Peau Noire, Masque Blanc* (Paris: Editions du Seuil, 1952)

Fisher, Roger and William, Ury, *Getting to Yes* (New York: Penguin Books, 1993)

Forsey, Eugene, *F. I. Sistema Politico de Canada* (Serie de Consulta No. 3, Ottawa, 1991)

Frankel, Max, *Partnership in Federalism* (Bern: Peter Lang, 1977)

Gabriel, Mark A., *Islam and Terrorism* (Lake Mary: Frontline Publishers, 2002)

Gage, Thomas, *The English-America: A New Survey of West Indies* (London, 1648)

Garcia-Pelayo, Graciela Soriano, 'Notion of Dischronic Development: A New Paradigm for Understanding the Past and Present of Latin America', *International Studies Association* (Acapulco, 1993)

Garcia-Pelayo, Manuel, *Idea de La Politica* (Caracas: Colecion Cuademos, 1967)

Gavin, William J., 'William James on Language', in *IPQ* (March 1976)

Gifis, Steven H., *The Law Dictionary* (New York: Barron's, 1995)

Gorbachev, Mikhail, Speech at 28th Congress of Communist Party Central Committee Meeting (Moscow: Novosti Press, 1990)

Green, V. H. H., *Renaissance and Reformation* (London: Edward Arnold,1964)

Gunder Frank, Andre, *Capitalism and Underdevelopment in Latin America: Historical Case Studies of Chile and Brazil* (New York: 1967)

Gurr, Ted Robert, 'Communal Conflicts and Global Security', in *Current History* (May 1995)

Hailey, Lord, *Native Administration and Political Development in British Tropical Africa 1940-42* (HMSO, 1951)

Hajda, L., 'The Nationalist Problems in the Soviet Union', in *Current History* (October 1988)

Haneef, Suzanne, *What Everyone Should Know about Islam and Muslims* (Lahore: Kazi Publications, 1979)

Harsanyi, John, 'Modelos teoriticos del juego y la decision en la etica utilitarian', in *Etica y Politica* (1993)

Hawking, Stephen, *A Brief History of Time: From the Big Bang to Black Holes* (London: Bantam Books, 1988)

Hegel, Hans, *The Philosophy of History* (reprinted, Chicago: University of Chicago Press, 1991)

Hegel, Hans, *Elements of the Philosophy of Right*, para. 47 (Cambridge: Cambridge University Press, 1991)

Hellwege, John, 'Underdevelopment, Dependencia and Modernization Theory', in *Law and State Review*, vol. 17 (1978)

Hill, R. and Peter, Frank, *The Soviet Communist Party* (London: Allen & Unwin, 1986)

Hill, Stuart and Rothchild, Donald, 'The Contagion of Political Conflict in Africa and the World', in the *Journal of Conflict Resolution*, vol. 30, no. 4 (December 1986)

Hobbes, Thomas, *Leviathan*, part 1 (reprinted, Chicago: University of Chicago Press, 1991)

Holifield, E. Brooks, *Era of Persuasion* (Boston: Twayne Books, 1989)

Horowitz, Donald, *Ethnic Groups in Conflict* (Berkeley: University of California Press, 1985)

Igali, Boladei, 'Nationalism in the Soviet Union', in *Pakistan Journal of International Affairs* (1991)

India Yearbook 1995 (New Delhi: Government of India)

Jacobs, Samuel, *House of Commons Debates* (30 March 1997), quoted in McArthur, p. 177

Juergenmeyer, Mark, 'Religious Nationalism: A Global Threat', in *Current History*, vol. 95, no. 604 (November 1996)

Kant, Immanuel, *Postulate on Public Rights* (reprinted, Chicago: University of Chicago Press, 1991)

Kantorowicz, Ernst H., *The King's Two Bodies* (Princeton: Princeton University Press, 1957)

Kaplan, Robert, *Daedalus* (Spring 1995)

Kaufman, Robert R., Chernotsky, Harry I, & Geller, Daniel, or directly in James N. Roseau (ed.), *Linkage Politics: Essays on the Convergence of National and International Systems* (New York: 1969)

Kaufman, Robert R., Chernptsky, Harry I., and Geller, Daniel, 'A Preliminary Test of the Theory of Dependency', *Comparative Politics*, vol. 7, no. 3 (April 1975)

Kochan, L., *The Jews in Soviet Russia State since 1917* (London: Oxford University Press, 1978)

Kolb, Glen L., *Democracy and Dictatorship in Venezuela, 1945-1959*, (Connecticut: Archon Books, 1974)

Kummerly, *Switzerland* (Bern: Publication of the Ministry of Foreign Affairs, 1992)

Lakos, Amos, *International Negotiations: A Bibliography* (New York, 1989)

Lane, D., *Politics and Aid Society in the Soviet Union* (London: Martin Robertson, 1978)

Lapidoth, Ruth, *Autonomy: Flexible Solutions to Ethnic Conflicts* (Washington: United States Institute for Peace, 1996)

Las Casas, Bartholomew de, *Histaria de las Indias* (Madrid, 1559, later printed in Madrid in 1875)

Lashin, A., *Socialism and State* (Moscow: Progress, 1978)

Levi-Strauss, Claude, *Structural Anthropology* (Basic Books, 1974)

Lively, Jack and Lively, Adam, *Democracy in Britain: A Reader* (Oxford: Blackwell, 1991)

Locke, John, *Spirit of the Law*, book 11 (reprinted, Chicago: University of Chicago Press, 1989)

Machavelli, Nicolo, *The Prince*, chapter ix (reprinted, Chicago: University of Chicago Press, 1991)

Mackie, J. L., *Ethics* (London: Puffin Books, 1977)

Mboya, Tom, *Freedom and After* (London: Andre Deutsch, 1963)

McArthur, Tom, *Oxford Companion to the English Language* (London: Oxford University Press, 1992)

Meekinson, J. Peter (ed.), *Canadian Federalism: Myth or Reality* (London: Methuen, 1968)

Merquior, J. G., *Liberalism: Old and New* (Boston: Twayne Books, 1991)

Mijares, Augusto, *The Liberator* (Caracas: Ediciones de La Presidencia de la Republica, 1991)

Miranda, Francisco, *Travels in America* (1784)

Momogliano, Arnold, 'Time in Ancient Historiography', in *International Review of Social History* (1975)

Montgomery, John Warwick, *The Shaping of America* (Minneapolis: Bethany Fellowship, 1976)

Montville, Joseph (ed.), *Conflict and Peacemaking in Multi-ethnic Societies* (Lexington Books, 1990)

Moron, Guillermo, *A History of Venezuela* (London: George Allen & Unwin, 1964)

Mortimer, *Introduction to the Great Books*, vol. i (Chicago: University of Chicago Press, 1991)

Moscow Summit Publication of USIS (Moscow, 1989)

Moyniham, Daniel Patrick, *Pandemonium Ethnicity in International Politics* (Oxford: Oxford University Press, 1993)

Muller Rojas, Alberto, 'Militares y politica exterior de Venezuela', in Romero, Carlos (ed.), *Reforms y Politica Exterior en Venezuela* (Caracas: Editorial Nueva Sociedad, 1992)

Myrdal, Gunner, *Challenge to Affluence* (London, 1963)

Naim, Moises, 'Latin America: The Morning After', in *Foreign Affairs*, vol. 74, no. 8 (July 1995)

Nozick, Robert, *Anarchy, State and Utopia* (New Jersey: Basic Books, 1977)

Nyerere, Julius, *The African and Democracy* in *Africa Speaks*, James Duffy and Robert Manners (eds.) (Princeton: D. Van Nostrand, 1961)

Olson, Richard, *The Emergence of the Social Sciences* (Boston: Twayne Books, 1993)

Orwell, George, *Animal Farm* (Harcourt Brace Jovanovich, 1984)

Osiander, Andreas, 'The Interdependence of States and the Theory of Interstate Relations', in *Laws and State Review*, vols. 53/54, 1996

Ostrom, Vincent, *The Political Theory of a Compound Republic* (Nebraska: University of Nebraska Press, 1987)

Oxford Advanced Learners Dictionary (Oxford: Oxford University Press, 1995)

Oxford Illustrated Dictionary, vol. vii (Oxford: Oxford University Press, 1994)

Perlmutter, Amos, *Military and Politics in Israel* (London: Frank Cass, 1977)

Plano, Jack and Greenberg, Milton, *The American Political Dictionary* (New York: Holt, Reinhart & Winston, 1985)

Pocock, J. G. A., 'The Florentine Moment', 'Between Gog and Magog', in *Journal of the History of Ideas*, vol. 48, no. 2 (1987)

Putnam, Robert D., *Making Democracy Work: Civic Traditions in Modern Italy* (Princeton: Princeton University Press, 1993)

Quaison-Saekey, Alex, *Africa Unbound* (London: Andre Deutsch, 1963)

Rawls, John, *A Theory of Justice* (Cambridge: Harvard University of Press, 1991)

Rawls, John, *A Theory of Justice* (London: Oxford University Press, 1971)

Reshetar, J. R., *The Soviet Union: Government and Politics in the Soviet Union* (New York: Harper Publications, 1978)

Rinderle, Petet, 'The Idea of a Well-Ordered Community of States', in *Law and State Review*, vol. 52 (1995)

Romero, Carlos, 'La Complejidad Organizational en el sector exterior de Venezuela', in Carlos Romero (ed.),

Reforms y Politica Exterior en Venezuela (Caracas: Editorial Nueva Sociedad, 1992)

Rousseau, Jean-Jacques, *The Social Contract*, book 1, chapters 6-8 (reprinted, Chicago: University of Chicago Press, 1986)

Scheltens, D. F., 'The Social Contract Philosophers', in *Journal of the History of Ideas* vol. 2, no. 38(UCLA: 1977)

Senghor, L. S., 'What is Negritude?' Speech at Oxford University, reprinted in Mutiso and Rohio (1985)

Senghor, Leopold, *On African Socialism* (Paris: Praeger, 1964)

Seton-Watson, Hugh, *Nations and States: An Enquiry into the Origins of Nations and the Politics of Nationalism* (London: Methuen, 1977)

Shakespeare, William, *Julius Caesar in Complete Work of William Shakespeare* (Oxford: Oxford University Press, 1990)

Shaykh Uthman, Dan Fodio, *Handbook of Islam* (Suffolk: Diwan Press, reprinted, 1985)

Shevtsov, A., *The State and Nations in the USSR* (Moscow: Progress Publishers, 1992)

Silbey, Susan, 'Presidential Address of Law and Society Association', in *Law and Society Review*, vol. 31, no. 2 (1997)

Simeon, Richard and Ian, Robinson, *State, Society and the Development of the Canadian Federalism* (Toronto: University of Toronto Press, 1990)

Simes, D., *Gorbachev's Time of Troubles in Foreign Policy* (Spring 1991)

Sisk, Timothy D., *Power Riming and International Mediation in Ethnic Conflicts* (Washington: United States Institute for Peace, 1996)

Sisk, Timothy D., *Power Sharing and Mediation in Ethnic Conflicts* (Washington: United States Institute for Peace, 1996)

Skinner, Robert, *Machiavelli and Republicanism* (London: Oxford University Press, 1992)

Smiley, Donald, 'Cleavages and the Canadian System', in Bolaji Akinyemi, Dele Cole, and Walter Ofonagoro (eds.), *Readings in Federalism* (Lagos: NIIA, 1979)

Smith, Abdullahi, 'The Early States of the Central Sudan', in F. H. Ade Ajayi and Micheal Crowder (eds.), *History of West Africa*, vol. 1 (Columbia Press, 1971)

Smith, M. C., *The Plural Society in the West Indies* (Los Angeles: University of California Press, 1965)

Socrates, *The Republic* (reprinted, Chicago: University of Chicago Press, 1991)

Starke, *General Principles of International Law* (New York: Butterworth, 1967)

Sturm, Fred, 'Dependence and Ibero-American Philosophy', in *Journal of History of Ideas* (1980)

Sunkel, Osvaldo, 'National Development Policy and External Dependence in Latin America', in Yale H. Ferguson (ed.), *Contemporary Inter-American Relations* (Englewood Cliffs: 1972)

Tocquevile, Alexis, *Democracy in America* (reprinted, Chicago: University of Chicago Press, 1991)

Ury, William, *Getting Past No: Negotiating Your Way from Confrontatin to Cooperation* (New York: Bantam Books, 1993)

Van Doren, Charles, *A History of Knowledge* (New York: Ballantine Books, 1991)

Vioiti da Costa, Emilia, *Crowns of Glory, Tears of Blood: Demerara Slave Rebellion of 1823* (London: Oxford University Press, 1994)

Walker, D. J. R., *Columbus and the Golden World of the Arawaks* (Kingston: Ian Randle Publishers Limited, 1992)

Webster Dictionary

Werz, Nikolaus, 'Democracy and Forms of Government in South America', in *Law and State Review* (1997)

Williams, Eric, *Documents of West Indian History* (Port of Spain: PNM, 1963)

Williams, Eric, *Documents on West Indian History* (Port of Spain: PNM, 1965)

Williams, Eric, *Capitalism and Slavery* (New York: Schocken Books, 1969)

Wolff, Robert, *Understanding Rawls* (Princeton: Princeton University Press, 1990)

Yongchen, Wang, *Green Action in China* (Beijing: Foreign Language Press, 2006)

Young, Crawford, *The Politics of Cultural Pluralism* (Madison: University of Wisconsin, 1981)

Yuri, Andropov, *Speeches at 50th Anniversary of Formation of the Soviet Union* (Moscow: Novosti Press, 1985)

Zakaria, Fareed, 'The Rise of Illiberal Democracies', in *Foreign Affairs*, vol. 76, no. 6 (December 1997)

Zhang, Guoqing, *Food, Population and Employment in China* (Beijing: Foreign Language Press, 2006)

INDEX

Caracas, Venezuela, 93, 319
Caribbean islands, 298
Carter, Jimmy, 294, 342
Cartier, Jacques, 161
Castile, Spain, 135
Catalans, 142
Catholic cantons, 153
Catholic Counter-Reformation, 153
Catholic nations, 341
Cefkin (professor), 339
Central Africa, 302
Central African Economic Cooperation Association, 302–3
Central African Republic, 302
Central American Economic Union, 298
Central Europe, 8, 141
central government, 89, 91, 155, 167, 197, 200
centrist ambition, 89
Chandigarh, India, 193
Chang Kai–shek, 211
charismatic leader, 24
Charlemagne, 106
Charles I (king), 114–15

Chavez, Gregorio Rosa, 341
Chavez, Hugo, 86, 314
Chief Governor, 50
Chile, 135, 341
China, 4–6, 181, 183, 194, 206, 208–11, 213–15, 217–18, 226, 240, 259–60
Christendom, 153
Christian conviction, 40
Christian faith, 38, 41, 185
Christian God, 39
Christian groups, 95
Christian Nilotes, 325
Christian Platonists, 38
Christian political dogma, 106
Christian religion, 229
Christian scholars, 58
Christian theologicians, 38, 45, 361
Christian theologies, 35, 61, 363
Christian thinkers, 39
Christian thought, 37–38, 61, 211
Christian traditionalist, 40
Christomimeles, 107

Eskimos, 161, 171
Estonia, 277, 280
Estonian Citizens Committee, 277
Estonia People Front, 277
Etats Generaux, 108
Eternal Glory, 46
Ethiopia, 230, 238–39, 303
Ethiopian Jews, 95, 231
ethnicism, 10
Etruscans, 222
Europe, 7, 38, 51, 58, 83, 97, 103, 106–9, 111, 119–22, 130–31, 134–36, 139, 141–46, 149, 152–55, 162, 184, 221–22, 225–26, 258, 260, 266, 272, 284, 297, 312
European, 21, 58, 106, 116, 119–20, 134, 137, 144, 152, 162, 185, 241, 264, 269, 272
European Coal and Steel Community (ECSC), 144
European Coal and Steel Company (ECSC), 297

European countries, 130, 143–44
European Economic Community (EEC), 144, 297
European Institute of Technology, 146
European Jews, 230
European Union, 91, 145, 297
evangelism and proselytising, 95

F

Falashas, 230
farce, 28
Far East Asia, 97
Father Gasping Riots, 283
Federal Character Commission, 310
Federal Character Principle, 309
federal civil service, 175, 310
Federalism, 81, 89–90, 93, 97, 125, 172, 199
Federalist-minded people, 97
Federalist victory, 89

114, 122, 124, 224–25, 227–28, 231, 233, 352, 359–62

Golden Temple, 194

Gorbachev, Mikhail, 258, 268–69, 275, 282

Graeco-Romanic scholarship, 38

Gran Colombia, 298

Great Depression, 166

Greek, 10, 30, 44, 76, 83–84, 88, 127, 222, 224, 231, 356

Greek mythology, 103

Greek philosophy, 40, 210

Greek sophists, 21

Green Revolution, 194, 204, 311

gross domestic product (GDP), 131, 145, 179, 209, 226, 229

gubernare, 70

Guinea, 302

Gulf of Saint Lawrence, 161

Gupta Empire, 184

Gypsies, 261

H

Habsburg, 97, 141, 152–53

Hadith, 53, 105, 240

Hague Conventions of Pacific Settlement of International Disputes, 335

Haiti, 133, 342

Hamat Gader, Israel, 229

Hamilton, Alexander, 27, 78–79, 125, 306

Hamilton Temple-Blackwood, Frederick. *See* Lord Dufferin

Han group, 218

Hausa-Fulani, 350

Heavenly City, 47

Hebrew, 230, 232, 273, 360

Hegel, George Wilhelm Friedrich, 69

Hegel, Hans, 28–29, 32, 321, 349

Hegelian, 28

Hellenic cultures, 84

Hellenistic, 52

Helsinki Final Act, 271

Helvetia, 151

Khobar Towers, 249
Kiev Rus, 277
Kiir, Salva, 325
Kinda tribe, 239
Kindi, al-, 55
King Cotton, 130
Kingdom of heaven, 106
Kissinger, Henry, 233, 341
Knesset, 231
Koran, 53, 56, 105, 240–41
Koranic schools, 273
Korea, 69, 209, 226
kubernan, 70
Kuomintang Party, 211
Kurds, 223, 261
Kuwait, 245, 247, 252, 254

L

Lakos, Amos, 339
land legislation, 326
Landy, Bernard, 178
Lapidoth, Ruth, 11, 178, 307
Lashkar-e-Taiba, 196, 249
Latin American, 92, 96, 169, 313
Latin heritage, 151
Latvia, 277

Law and Society Association, 291
lawmakers, 24, 50, 125, 322, 324, 328, 336
Laws of Nature, 124
Lebanon, 246, 309
Leiva, Luis Castro, 85, 96, 133, 315, 319
Lenin, Vladimir, 258, 262, 265, 267, 272
Leningrad, Russia, 278, 280
Leviathan, 33, 352
liberation of South Sudan, 325
Liberia, 302
libidinous obsessions, 103
Libya, 95–96, 252, 255
Liebermann, Joseph, 233
lieutenant governor, 176
Lincoln, Abraham, 77, 127, 129, 133, 210
Lithuania, 261, 276–77, 281
Locke, John, 18, 25–26, 69, 116, 352
Lok Adalat, 201, 343
Lok Sabha, 200
London, England, 18, 163, 169–70, 249

Smith, Adam, 31

Sobchak, Anatoly, 278

social and political organisation, 11

social animals, 29

Social Christian Party, 313

social contract and theology, 13

social contract philosophers, 16, 21, 24, 116, 334

social defiance, 29

Socialism, 263

social justice, 26, 126, 353, 356–58

social sciences, 3, 338

social theory, 38

society, 4, 11–12, 20–21, 24–25, 27–28, 31, 35, 47, 50, 53, 55–56, 63, 75, 77, 87, 92, 102, 105, 119–20, 122, 127, 136–37, 139, 145, 213–14, 231–32, 261, 286, 289, 292, 307, 309, 311, 315–16, 319–20, 322, 330–32, 334, 345–48, 353, 355, 359, 361–63

socioeconomic, 22–23, 236, 284

Solomon, 104, 197, 362

Solomon's temple, 224

Somalia, 8, 148, 249, 251, 294, 303, 342

Sorbonne, France, 136

South Africa, 309, 326–28

South African Development Community (SADC), 303

South African Truth and Reconciliation Commission, 331

South America, 120, 133, 135, 312

South American island, 293

South Asia, 183–84, 189, 240, 300

South Carolina, 307

South-east Asia, 240, 249, 299

southern cone, 298

South Korea, 69

South Sudan, 325–26

Sovietisation, 269, 324

Soviet Union, 5, 32, 97–98, 214, 217, 246–48,

T

Zoological Centre of Tel
   Aviv-Ramat Gan, 229
Zuckerberg, Mark, 233
Zwingli, Ulrich, 153